Investing with the Best

Russell Taylor left Oxford with a degree in Politics, Philosophy and Economics and worked initially as an economist and investment analyst for merchant bankers Kleinwort Benson. He then became the City editor of the *Observer* and also wrote and presented BBC TV's first ever financial series, 'Money Matters'. Returning to the City, as a director of Hambros Bank, he developed their unit trust business, and left them to set up the Italian International Bank. In recent years he has concentrated on family investments, and he returned to full-time writing two years ago with the *Sunday Times* 'Money Managers' series. He is married with one son and divides his time between London and Suffolk.

Investing with the Best

Russell Taylor

PAPERMAC

For Norah

First published 1989 by
PAPERMAC
a division of Macmillan Publishers Limited
4 Little Essex Street, London WC2R 3LF
and Basingstoke

Associated companies in Auckland, Delhi, Dublin,
Gaborone, Hamburg, Harare, Hong Kong,
Johannesburg, Kuala Lumpur, Lagos, Manzini,
Melbourne, Mexico City, Nairobi, New York,
Singapore and Tokyo

British Library Cataloguing in Publication Data
Taylor, Russell
   Investing with the best.
   1. Investment – Manuals
   I. Title
   332.6'78

   ISBN 0-333-48363-4

Designed by Chris Warner

Typeset by Rowland Phototypesetting Limited
Bury St Edmunds, Suffolk
Printed in Great Britain by
Cox and Wyman Limited, Reading, Berks.

Contents

- The basics of control: portfolio strategy, investment theme, cash management accounts, and administrative control
- Cash is the most aggressive investment
- Bonds are for certain income and portfolio stability
- Convertibles are the designer security for the private investor
- Shares are for growth of income, but not all shares are the same

- Case study: how retired teacher Len J needs to define a post-Crash portfolio strategy for his £50,000, and why his portfolio is not properly diversified despite several unit trust holdings
- Investment performance and Modern Portfolio Theory – or do investors ever get what they pay for?
- Portfolio diversification – the difference between control and elimination of company risk
- Case study: how two private client stockbrokers would manage Len J's portfolio
- Technical analysis, or how charts are supposed to foretell the future
- Kiss; or Keep it Simple, Stupid – the private investor's way to investment success

- Domestic or overseas investment, and the doubling up of risk
- Case study: how investing in investment trusts reduced the risk and increased the reward for the Quicklie family
- The best and cheapest choice – investment and unit trusts, and insurance bonds
- The new 'separated value' investment trusts, and the kick of such 'investment cocktails'
- Unit Trust Portfolio Management Services – the standard of value and service

Acknowledgements

This book developed out of a series of articles for the *Sunday Times* on how investment managers construct and run portfolios for their clients, what they charge, and how they justify their fees. Except for the courage of some investment managers – more refused my offer than accepted it – this book would not exist. Though not all portfolios are used as illustrations in this book, I would like to thank the following who were prepared to allow the readers of the *Sunday Times* to judge their competence at running a portfolio during the 1987 'bull market' frenzy:

Stockbrokers: Bryan Johnston, Bell Lawrie Ltd; Roddy Macleod, Gerrard Vivian Gray Ltd; Martin Riley, Henderson Crosthwaite Ltd; George Stoddard, Parsons & Co, now Parsons Penney Ltd; Murdo Tolmie, Penney Easton Ltd, now Parsons Penney Ltd; Joe Mara, Shearson Lehman Brothers Ltd; Edwin Lillie, Wood Mackenzie Private Client Department, now Robert White & Co Ltd.

Fund Managers and Investment Advisers: Bilmes Financial Management Ltd; Fidelity Personal Portfolio Management Service; Foreign & Colonial Investment Management Ltd; Royal Trust Asset Managers Ltd; Thornton Management Ltd.

Particular thanks are due to Brian Connell, manager of the personal financial planning department of the London office of accountants Grant Thornton. He had the unenviable task, often performed at weekends, of monitoring the movements of twelve large portfolios, and producing regular valuations to show not only the investment skill of those managers, but also the costs of their management.

My gratitude is also due to those of my readers who allowed me to use their personal investment circumstances as illustrations of the principles of investment; apologies are perhaps owed to those investment managers who, not aware of the ulterior motive behind these requests, answered my readers' queries and so appear in this book.

Much of the historical and theoretical material in this book is the work of market analysts employed by the major research brokers. Their firms are acknowledged in the tables and graphs, and my thanks for the use of this information goes both to their firms and to themselves. Though the facts are theirs, the conclusions drawn from them are my own; this needs to be said as by no means all analysts, and very few investment salesmen, will agree with my opinions on how private individuals should manage their affairs.

A final debt is owed to Richard Lambert of the *Financial Times*; though I do not know him personally, it was his article on Joseph de la Vega that strengthened my belief that in security markets it truly is '*plus ça change, plus c'est la même chose*'.

Introduction

We're basically selling hope, and hope's been real good to us.

Investment salesman quoted by an American financial writer, but expressing the credo of investment advisers the world over.

Last year Mrs Philippa B learned that her husband had cancer. Fortunately, with a successful business and some months to prepare, he was able to leave her and their two young children well provided financially. But not long after his death came the October stock market crash. Philippa had no relatives with any knowledge of financial matters, nor professional advisers, so she was on her own. Naturally, she arranged to see her bank. Shortly thereafter she wrote to me in some distress at the *Sunday Times*.

B to Taylor – December 1987

I am writing to you in the hope that you will be able to give me some financial advice . . . I have a sum of money coming to me from the sale of my husband's share of his business. I am very frightened and worried about how to invest this money . . . I have had an interview with a Barclays Bank financial adviser but I became very confused and worried about the risks involved and their scale of charges . . .

Taylor to B – December 1987

Though frightening things are happening on the stock exchange, there is no need for you to be worried. At the moment your money is safe in building societies. Indeed, investment is not a matter to be carried out quickly, but only after thorough planning. Also, people in the investment world use 'risk' rather more specifically than the rest of us, and you need to understand this if you are to manage your money, and control your adviser. It does not mean 'loss' as you and I take it to mean, but making a smaller 'return' than might have been achieved with an alternative investment.

See that the building society money is placed in their highest interest-bearing accounts. This means that you will have to give them at least three months' warning if you want to withdraw any money. This does not matter as it will take longer than this to plan your investment policy.

The key thing you need to do is to decide how much you and the children need to live on: work out the figures either on a weekly or monthly basis, then check them on a yearly calculation to make sure you included everything; be over-generous with estimates.

This income figure is important. It establishes what your investment objectives are for your money. With that we can establish the type of investment policy you need, and the best sort of adviser for you. Then your letter to me, plus your required income, can become the briefing letter for your financial adviser.

Above all, don't worry. Cash is the best investment to have at the moment, and you have it. Time is on your side in terms of investment, and you have that too. So don't be rushed into doing anything quickly.

B to Taylor – January 1988

My husband used to give me £900 a month housekeeping, but he also paid for the cost of the car and holidays. I can make do with less than this, and probably £600 would cover our basic needs. Fortunately the car was new last year, so it won't cost too much to run.

I can't go back to my former Civil Service job because of the hours – I think it is important for the children that I am around when they come home from school – so I am taking a secretarial course. This should enable me to earn more than the £2000 a year I get from my book-keeping job. However, I am not much enjoying the course, and would prefer to start a business from home if possible. Several friends have asked me to help with the decorating of their homes, and this is something I should like to develop.

Taylor to B – January 1988

The more income you need from your investments now, the less you can expect it to increase in the future. But you need it to increase, partly to maintain its value against inflation, and partly to support the children as they get older. As you say, you need to invest, and not leave the money on deposit.

Once your husband's share of the business is paid, you will have £112,500 of investment capital. Say you aim for a yield before tax of 7 per cent. This means an annual income of £7875. Yield is important to understand. It is what you get to spend from your investments at the price you must pay for them. Simply put, you multiply the 112,500 by 7 and divide by 100 to get 7875.

This is a reasonable yield with the present state of the stock market, and you should expect your income to go up by about 5 per cent a year. This is the result of the companies you have invested in paying out higher dividends on their shares.

In addition, your widow's pension and the annuity is a further £3026 or a total 'unearned' income of £10,901. Your single person and child allowance is £3795 so you have a taxable income of £7106. Tax at 27 per cent is £1919 – it may be only 25 per cent after the next budget – so you will have £8982 to support yourself and the children.

This is £748.50 per month compared to the £900 you have been used to. It's more than you said you needed, and ought to cover all the basic needs of the family. This should give you the freedom to develop your interior design work from home. Now look at your budget again. Decide whether you can make do on this, assuming you don't take a job but develop your own business instead. This agreed figure, together with safety of capital and growth of income, then becomes your investment objective. Then any earnings from your business can be for savings, presents, and holidays.

B to Taylor – February 1988

I have written to the Stock Exchange, and also to the Association of Investment Trust Companies, and both have now sent me their list of stockbrokers. But there are so many of them, and none near me. How do I know which will be interested in my business, and which are good?

Taylor to B – February 1988

Distance is not a problem, since you are looking for an adviser who will handle your money on a discretionary basis. That means, once your policy has been agreed, he will get on with it, and tell you what he has done after he has done it. After you have appointed him – or her – you can communicate by letter and telephone.

Everything else is a real worry. Unfortunately, there is no 'Which' Good Stockbroker Guide, and so you have to do the work yourself. There are some basic rules.

● *Most major London stockbrokers, whatever they say, are not interested in private client business. They only want to buy and sell for the 'institutions' – life assurance companies, pension funds and the like. It would help the ordinary investor if the Stock Exchange classified the list they send out between research based institutional brokers, and those who specialise in private clients.*

● *The costs of provincial – or country town based – stockbrokers are much less than those of their London competitors. The efficient amongst these can cover their costs with serious clients who have as little as £10,000 to invest, and many now run managed portfolios of shares of £2500 under the government Personal Equity Plan initiative. You are an attractive client with £100,000.*

● *Stockbrokers are businesses like any other. Some are good, some bad but the way they handle your first approach will give you an idea of how well they are likely to look after your money. Stage one is to develop your original letter to me into an investment brief. I will suggest a list of private client specialists, and you decide from those replies who you think is keenest to help you.*

Philippa wrote to me because I was writing a weekly series in the *Sunday Times* which actually showed how professional advisers set out to look after the financial affairs of four typical, though mythical, clients. I had two reasons for wanting to write this series, and the *Sunday Times* was equally keen to show its readers that investment was more than the financial equivalent of a day out at the races.

By 1986 many professional and private investors seemed to have forgotten both the lessons of 1972–75 when share prices lost over 70 per cent of their value, and the basic principles of portfolio management. Instead, abetted by the privatisation programme, inexperienced investors were regularly sold on the idea that the stock market provided everyone with a 'free lunch'. The problem was not making money, but selecting the trust or fund that would make the most in the shortest time. History has shown that this approach, time after time, leads to disaster and tears.

Investment management is neither free nor cheap, though some of it is so cleverly packaged that we can be forgiven for assuming that it is. So the series was also designed to show, not only what investment services cost, but what we get for what we pay.

'There are lies, damned lies, and statistics,' said Mark Twain, and he must have been talking about his investment adviser at the time. Investment performance is difficult to compare because stockbrokers and investment managers rarely disclose details of what they have achieved for clients. Unit trust and life assurance managers, on the contrary, always proclaim the superior performance of their fund, but with figures and comparisons chosen to flatter their own ability.

Share prices throughout the world fell further, faster than they had ever done before in October 1987. All of us 'lost' money in those frantic few weeks but how much did we lose, and did we lose 'real' money or just 'book' money? This book is about the 'how' and the 'why' of actual returns achieved during this period for the *Sunday Times'* 'clients' by different types of investment manager.

It is also written around the real experiences of investors who wrote to me for advice and help after they had found that their 'advisers', so full of money-making ideas before October, were now reluctant to come to the telephone. No one should have lost real money in the Crash. Those of us who did so were badly advised and ignorant of the basic skills of portfolio investment.

Financial markets are not the cool, rational gatherings of popular imagination, with heartless financiers calculating how to squeeze an extra penny of profit from a deal. On the contrary, they are the scenes of savage fights between reason and emotion. As we all know from our own experience, love drives out reason. On stock markets the world over, greed and fear rout common sense every single day of the year.

No book ever written can promise to make anyone rich – that still needs luck, skill and diligence – but this one should stop us getting suddenly poor through stock market investment. It is not about how to buy shares, nor how to calculate a dividend yield. Plenty of books exist that do this, and some of the better ones are listed in the notes.

A Stock Exchange survey disclosed that there are 1.6 million of us who own four or more shares in portfolios valued at over £50,000, and another 2.4 million who hold two or three shares. Though the survey did not ask, many of these must also be amongst the 1.75 million of us owning some 5 million unit trust accounts so these smaller portfolios probably average £10,000 or so.

A few of these 4 million already know how to make the stock market work for them. The majority, and the other 5 million with only one or two shares, make money for the financial markets. The government makes no secret of its desire that we should become direct investors, and not continue to 'opt out' through unit trusts, life assurance policies, and employee pension schemes.

To do that is to become a serious investor. This book is for those of us who want to become so, regardless of the amount of capital we presently have. It is about a systematic approach to investment which will allow us to control our emotions, and so give the market averages a chance to make us rich.

They will do that, if we give them half a chance, for these are the savings markets of the twentieth century. They have been the best and safest home for our savings since 1920 despite Communist revolution, Wall Street Crash, Great Depression, Second World War, confiscatory taxation and hyperinflation.

On the basis of average stock market performance since 1920, and assuming there was no personal tax, investors simply using their common sense ought to double their money in real terms – that is after adjusting for the increase caused by rising prices – every twelve years or so. Few of us succeed and, no doubt, such exemplars as do sensibly keep quiet about it.

Why are we all not richer? Why does our unit trust manager, or stockbroker, so frequently fail to make us as much money as others seem to make, let alone make us really rich? And if the stock market is such a splendid place for our savings, why does folklore tell us that it is a place of financial disasters?

The first section of this book is about the history of stock markets, and why they behave in the peculiar way that they do. Until we understand that whatever happens on the stock market, has happened before, and will happen again we cannot prepare ourselves for the sheer physical excitement of buying and owning shares. It is that surge of adrenalin which is so injurious to our financial health.

Investment is also a game, more stimulating than chess, more exciting than backing the horses, and more certain than the pools. Properly played, it is also a game with no losers, and that is not something that can be said about the others. There are relative losers, of course, so the second part of the book is about the theory of how to play in such a way that we don't lose in absolute terms, but still do relatively better than our friends.

All investment has risk, even depositing money in a building society, and this is an important first lesson. Investment is not only about shares. It is also about cash, about currencies and about bonds, which are the IOUs of companies and, rather more importantly, governments. All four are essential elements in the design of an 'investment portfolio' that will meet our financial objectives, ensure our income needs and survive market panics. The book is also about the purpose of investment, the different types of investment we can choose, and how we offset the risks of one with those of another to achieve the investor's objective. This is the greatest possible return with the least possible risk.

Not all of us will have the time to be a serious investor, but knowing the theoretical standards allows us to judge proposals made to us. The third part of the book is about how to find investment advisers, what they are likely to cost, and how we must decide whether they are competent or not. This is also for those with the energy and interest to be their own investment manager and how 'investor psychology' can be exploited so that we have a chance to outperform the market.

The book is written in the belief that, as private investors, we are predominantly concerned with keeping what we've got, while still trying to make more. We want to know how heavily the odds are stacked against us, and whether there is any way of evening them up. We want to know what the survival rules are, and how to apply them. Finally I believe we want to have fun doing this, and not spend every waking hour worrying about it.

It is also written in the spirit of a *Financial Times* story concerning two hikers in the Rocky Mountains, who disturbed a grizzly she-bear with her cub. As one desperately looked around for a tree big enough to give him safety, the other dropped his rucksack and began to put on his running shoes.

> 'Why do that?' said the first. 'Surely you know that no one can escape an enraged bear over a short distance?'
>
> 'Certainly,' replied the other, 'but I'm not aiming to outrun the bear – only you.'

'Know yourself' was the essential advice of the Delphic Oracle; this maxim could only be replied to by the enquirer. 'Know your objective' is the necessary first step that we, as potential investors, must take. There are many further answers we will need before we should start investing but, of course, asking the right question is often the most important part of getting the right answer. This is the purpose of this book.

Chapter One

Eventful years

When Charlie last saw Jack, Jack was setting up a business with Jimmy, another acquaintance. Charlie asked how things were going.

'Oh, excellent, excellent,' said Jack, 'though I can't tell you how Jimmy is, because I've not seen him for a year or two.'

'But how can that be, if the business is doing so well, and the two of you are partners?'

'That's exactly it,' replied Jack. 'You see, when we started out, I had the experience and Jimmy had the money. Now I've got the money, and Jimmy has the experience.'

Twenty years ago stock market affairs would have been a matter of indifference to most of us. This is no longer so. Forty years of peace have made us rich again. That Victorian staple of melodrama – the family legacy – now affects us all; how to invest legacies significantly larger than any cash 'lump sum' we have ever before owned is a problem that will face many of us.

Morgan Grenfell is one of London's merchant banks with, as an investment manager, a particular interest in how rich we might become. Their expectations are that half of the middle-aged households in Britain will inherit property valued at three times their average annual income.

Already, nearly £5 billion a year goes into the savings and investment markets as the pioneers of the nineteen-fifties 'property owning democracy' die, leaving to their children unwanted homes. By the end of the century, this figure is expected to be £9 billion a year. The management of such fortunes is perceived as one of the great business opportunities of the next decade.

We, the potential owners of such wealth, need to understand the principles of investing for otherwise, like Jimmy, we will gain our experience the hard way. Ever since the publication of Professor J K Galbraith's book* on the Wall Street Crash of 1929, it has become a truism to say that the investment world is dominated by two emotions only – those of fear and greed. Investors, both professional and amateur, seem uniquely prone to crowd hysteria: investment is not an activity in which Kipling's dictum

> if you can meet with triumph and disaster
> and treat those two imposters just the same

is at all easy to follow. However, only by developing methods of protecting ourselves from market emotions will we be sure that our stock market investments turn out as well as our parents' property purchases.

Investment success: skill or luck

By 1987, most investment managers had enjoyed more than ten years of a rising share market, with a fast accelerating rising – or 'bull' – market from 1982 onwards. £1000 invested in Micropal Statistics Index of UK General Unit Trusts in 1976, and with income reinvested, had become £8476 by September 1988 despite the Crash in October. £1000 invested in 1982 had grown to £3572. Not surprisingly most investors were, by the beginning of 1987, ascribing their success to skill rather than the luck of a rising market.

Investors everywhere were encouraged to believe that investment was all about 'performance', or achieving capital gains. Dividend income was spurned, the result of a world in which such income was heavily taxed first by inflation, which destroyed the value of much of what was earned, and then by a government which taxed anything that might be left. A whole generation of investors knew that investment skill was all about growth in capital values.

---

* *The Great Crash*, J K Galbraith, Penguin, London 1957.

Figure 1: The investment success of unit trusts depends as much on the success of the market as on their management skills.

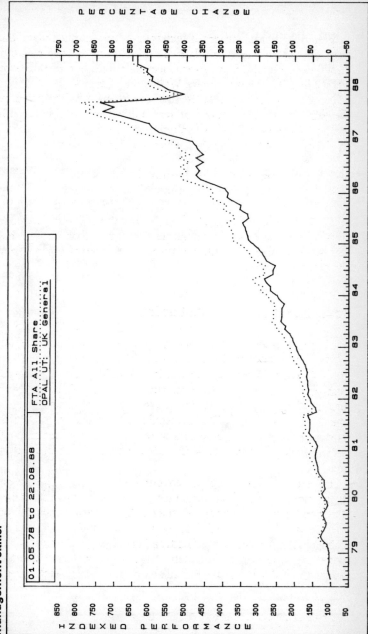

Source: *Micropal*

Windfalls and pitfalls

On the whole this suited the investment houses, of which by far the most important to us are the life assurance companies and the unit trust management groups. 'Service' is difficult to sell, but a 'product' is both easier and more profitable. Investment 'products', with their tremendous quotient of hype and hope, are ideal for an enthusiastic, commission-hungry, and naive salesforce.

Investors were hungry for windfalls, and no more concerned about the realities of investment, and the source of those wonderful 'capital gains' than their adviser-lately insurance salesman but now self-promoted financial expert. The years went by, and memories faded of the pitfalls of stock-exchange investment. Then came October 1987, and a sudden remembrance of all those folk memories of South Sea Bubbles, Victorian railway disasters and the 1929 crash and Great Depression. Private investors, encouraged into stock market investment for the wrong reasons, are now rushing out for equally wrong ones.

Investment gains and income growth

Investment is about establishing an objective, deciding on a strategy, and then being patient. Any investment strategy needs time to mature and, even if prices move faster than a decade ago, investment still takes three to five years to pay off. It is not for the impatient because, surprising though it may seem, capital gains are all about income. These figures from the London Business School and Hoare Govett show that, without the compounding effect of the annual dividend payments, shares did very little better than a building society deposit:

The value of alternative investments 1955–1987

£100 invested in	before inflation	after inflation
Shares with dividends	£9460	£980
Shares without dividends	£1560	£160
Deposit with interest	£1380	£140

The purpose of investment is the purchase of a stream of future income. The advantage of shares as investments is that these are the only quoted investments that promise to increase that income. This is because only shares entitle us to 'share' in the profits of an enterprise; that is because by buying a share, we participate in the risk capital – or equity – of that business. If the company does badly, we are the first to be hurt either by the reduction or total disappearance of our dividend income, or even the loss of our capital as a result of bankruptcy.

That danger is known as company risk amongst investment professionals, and is much less of a hazard than it was. This is because of the importance of institutional investors within the share markets. A generation ago these – the life assurance companies and pension funds – were forced to favour the equity markets over fixed income investments because of the effect of rising prices on the value of their funds.

This 'cult of the equity' in turn developed a research business that serviced these investors with advice on which stock markets, industries and companies seemed the most attractive to buy. All this analysis has made it difficult for crooked company promoters, and has helped to democratise knowledge of company affairs. What it has not done is to change the nature of stock markets, and 'market risk' is as great a risk today as it was for the first modern investors nearly four hundred years ago.

Market risk and portfolio management skills

Market risk simply means that every so often the stock market does what it did in October 1987. This does not invalidate investment in shares as these figures from another London research broker show:

Security	Total return 1973–87	Equal to annual rate
Shares	+ 715%	+ 15.0%
Gilts	+ 502%	+ 12.7%
Deposit	+ 449%	+ 12.0%
Retail Price Index	+ 360%	+ 10.7%

Source: Phillips & Drew

Figure 2: The growth of the market since 1975 was not without problems.

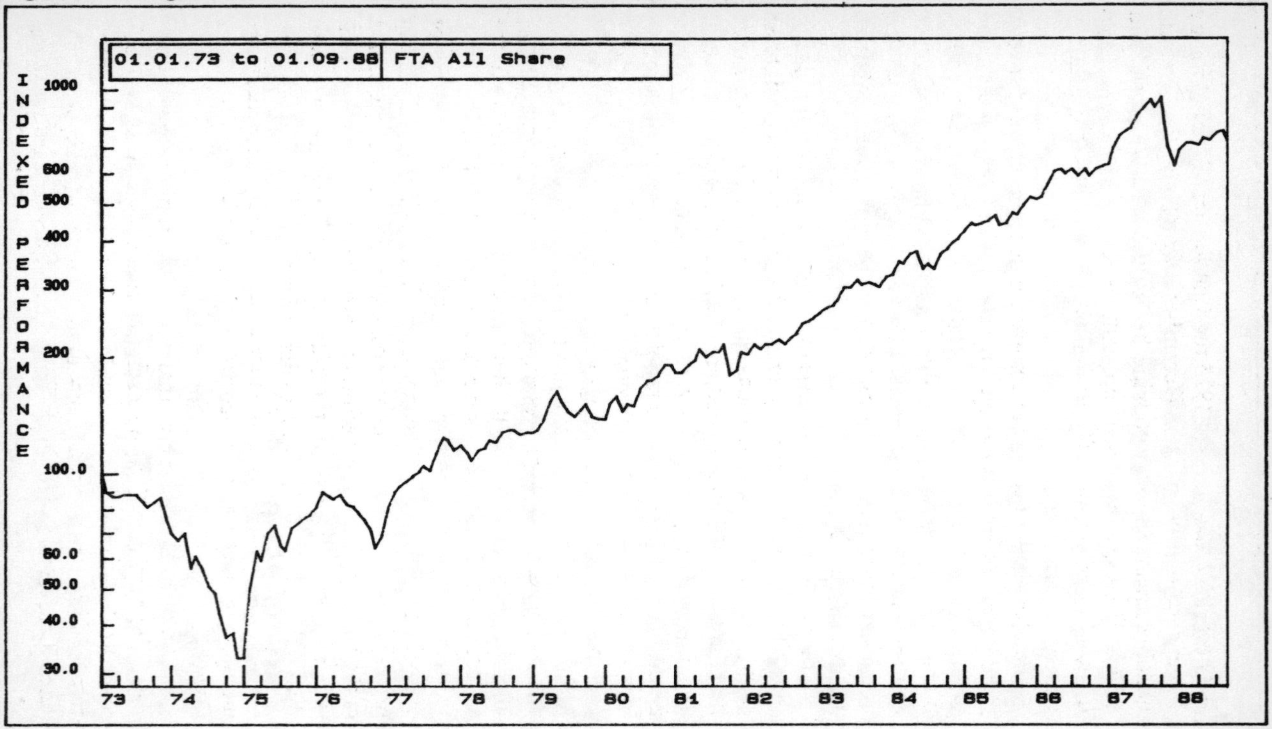

01.01.73 to 01.09.88 | FTA All Share

Source: Micropal

Between 1972 and January 1975 the London share market fell by 70 per cent in value, while in December 1987 it hit bottom after the October crash. Investors buying before the 1972–74 crash, and selling after the '87 crash, are still better off than those who invested in government bonds – gilts – or deposited their money with a building society.

'Total return' is the way of comparing different types of investment, or different portfolios; it is the sum of the change in the value of the capital from one year to another, and the income earned during that year. The capital value of a deposit does not change, of course; the interest rate changes. Thus it is only the interest earned that makes up the return on the deposit. Capital values of shares and bonds do change.

This is why the skill that investors must acquire, or buy, is not the ability to pick 'winners', such as the top-performing unit trust of the year or the share that has risen most in value. That needs luck, not skill. What is needed are the skills of portfolio structure and management, the ability to develop a 'team' of different investments, each of which supports and complements the other, in a combination that meets our investment objectives but also protects our capital when things go wrong.

These skills are important in view of all-too-frequent market crashes. The Micropal figures quoted earlier, and the memory of most investors, suggest that share prices rose steadily after the collapse of the London stock market between 1972–74.

Memories lie. The very savage 'bear' – or falling – market of 1972–74 took place in an economic environment of rapidly rising prices, high taxation, and 'ungovernable' Britain. It was the period of the Heath government's efforts to introduce trades union legislation, the coal strike, and the three-day week. Share prices fell more than they had in 1929, down to only a third of their value of May 1972. Nearly all of Britain's finance companies and 'secondary', or minor, banks had to be saved from bankruptcy by the Bank of England.

These were also the years that the Organisation of Petroleum Exporting Countries (OPEC) exercised its strength, first by quadrupling oil prices within a year and fifteen-fold before the end of the decade. This was the prime cause of the ruinous inflation of the late nineteen-seventies. The New York market also fell badly, Hong

Kong collapsed to only a tenth of earlier 'highs' while the Japanese government was forced to rescue the major Tokyo investment houses from bankruptcy. Understandably, after that investment trauma, nothing else seemed quite so awful.

But market behaviour does not change. The London market fell again in 1976, 1979, and 1981.

In fact, the 1981 collapse looks very similar to that of 1987, being both very sharp and sudden. The shock of 1987 was that share prices throughout the world fell simultaneously whereas always before, even though world stock markets do generally behave in a similar fashion, the falls occurred after considerable time lags.

October 87: welcome to a truly global market

The universality of the 1987 crash reflects the significant changes in the investment world that have occurred over the last decade. Though markets have always been global, in that investors have taken their lead from the sentiment of the world's major financial centre, and most of us are convinced for at least some of the time that the grass is greener on the other side of the hill, previously markets have been divided by time and custom, and market regulations have insulated the security markets from the money markets.

Satellites and improved telecommunications now give instant access to markets anywhere in the world. The development of new investment 'instruments' spanning money, foreign exchange, bond and share markets created a financial market place that has never before existed. Together these changes brought to term a real 'global market'; parturition during the second week of October 1987 was painful and frightening.

For, though the technical capacity of markets has changed with easier communications, the human reality of markets is still the same as it was when news was carried by horse and sailing ship. Wildly volatile prices are the essence of financial markets because they are the mirror of our emotions. By understanding how our emotions betray our reason in financial affairs, we will also learn to invest profitably and safely.

Figure 3(i): Sharp and sudden falls are a feature of stock markets.

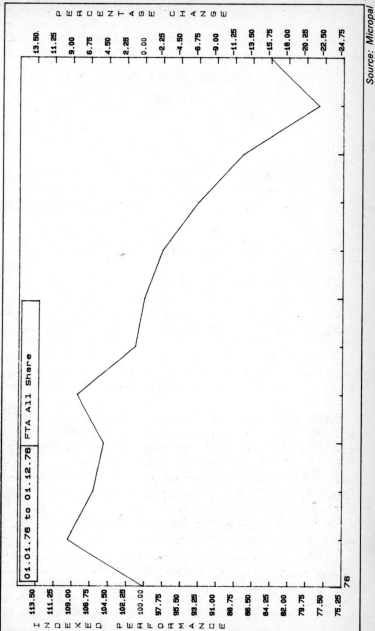

01.01.76 to 01.12.76 FTA All Share

Source: Micropal

Figure 3(ii)

02.04.79 to 03.12.79

OPAL UT: UK General
FTA All Share ....

INDEX
107.50
106.25
105.00
103.75
102.50
101.25
100.00
98.75
97.50
96.25
95.00
93.75
92.50
91.25
90.00
88.75
87.50

PERCENTAGE CHANGE
7.50
6.25
5.00
3.75
2.50
1.25
0.00
-1.25
-2.50
-3.75
-5.00
-6.25
-7.50
-8.75
-10.00
-11.25
-12.50

Source: Micropal

Figure 3(iii)

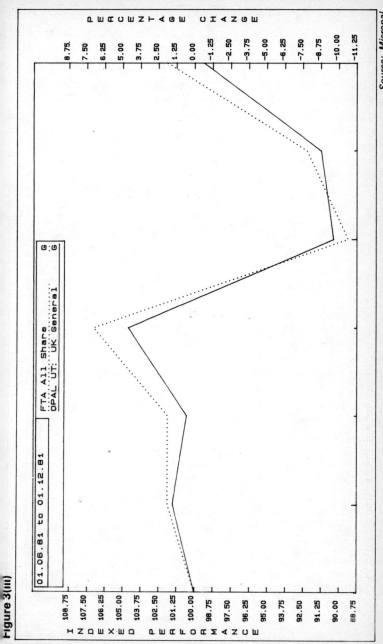

Source: Micropal

The need for advice

Any serious investor needs help, partly because information is the foundation stone of investment success, and we cannot afford that on our own, and partly because it is sensible to refine our investment ideas with a market professional. Whatever the publicity handouts, nearly all institutional funds are managed through hierarchical committee structures. There is a purpose in that, and one that we should bear in mind. Investment generates excitement, and excitement breeds ideas, but not all are wise and some are foolhardy in the extreme. Justifying ideas helps to improve decisions.

However, two years after 'Big Bang', or the transformation of the London Stock Exchange into the International Stock Exchange, the promised cheaper and more efficient share dealing seems as far off as ever. Stockbroking partnerships, as a consequence of Big Bang, were converted into subsidiary companies of banks, insurance companies and 'financial services' conglomerates. Far from commissions getting smaller, they have increased, and a lot of stockbrokers now say they no longer want our custom.

A second important lesson for investors is to develop a healthily sceptical attitude to everything about the investment markets. The major London research brokers do not want our business, but then it is many years since they did. Whatever may be the state of stockbroking costs, there are still two or three hundred stockbroking firms that are more than happy to take on clients with £10,000 to invest.

Many of them, and some banks too, will manage share portfolios of less than £3000 under the Personal Equity Scheme. Offsetting tax savings against management costs, such schemes as those of Lloyds Bank and Bank of Scotland, or stockbrokers Albert E Sharp of Birmingham, Rensburg of Liverpool, and Williams de Broe of London cost us virtually nothing compared to investing through a unit trust, or dealing on standard terms through a stockbroker.

Investment management charges and fees are complex, and often made deliberately more so. The gap between the cheapest and most expensive is a factor of 4 and we need to familiarise ourselves with the cost table in the notes to this chapter. Those of us who simply want a professionally managed share portfolio, for as little as possible, are best advised to use the savings schemes of the investment trust groups. This is by far the cheapest and safest way to invest in the stock market, and has the lowest annual management fee – 0.5 per cent.

The next best way for those of us who want a more personal service is to use a stockbroker. This can be either on a discretionary basis, if we lack the time or interest, or through an advisory account if we want to manage our own portfolio. For once, cheapest is best, though finding a good stockbroker, as will be seen later, does take some effort on our part.

We can, and do, pay considerably more for investment management than for stockbroking services though normally what we are buying so expensively is fund management, and not portfolio management. The difference between these two becomes clearer from the experience of some of the case studies. However, the extra fees do not buy better investment services, only glossier packages, higher marketing costs, and bigger sales commissions.

Unit trust and stockbroking costs are almost certainly going up and, if we are to pay charges, we owe it to ourselves to pay for the best. The key test of investment management performance is who best satisfies our objectives. Since we won't know the answer until it is too late to remedy the situation, we need to learn how to recognise and choose good managers. To do that we have to understand some of the history and workings of the investment world.

The need for caution

The Financial Services Act replaces the Prevention of Frauds Act, and creates a new self-regulatory system of investor protection. Each major sector of the investment market now has a self regulatory organisation (SRO) – see Figure 4 – which is responsible for authorising, monitoring and disciplining the individual firms that operate under the aegis, and within the rule books, of the SRO. SRO-authorised firms then operate within recognised stock exchanges, such as the one in London.

The SROs are for investment fund managers – IMRO; life assurance and unit trust companies – LAUTRO; stockbrokers –

Figure 4: The New Regulatory Structure.

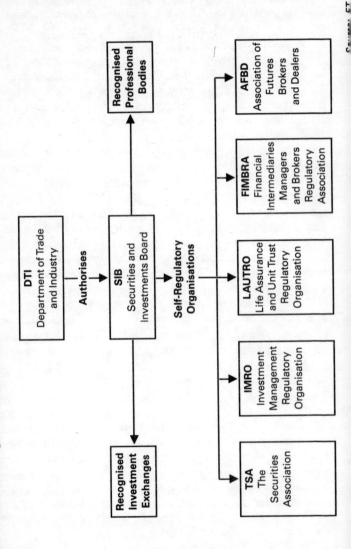

Source: FT

DTI Department of Trade and Industry

Authorises →

SIB Securities and Investments Board

Recognised Professional Bodies

Recognised Investment Exchanges

Self-Regulatory Organisations

TSA The Securities Association

IMRO Investment Management Regulatory Organisation

LAUTRO Life Assurance and Unit Trust Regulatory Organisation

FIMBRA Financial Intermediaries Managers and Brokers Regulatory Association

AFBD Association of Futures Brokers and Dealers

TSA; investment and insurance brokers – FIMBRA. Options and futures traders make up the fifth SRO or AFBD. Each of the five SROs comes under the Securities and Investment Board (SIB) and their separate rule books need to comply with SIB's overall standards. Lawyers and accountants acting as investment advisers must be authorised by their respective professional bodies, the Law Society and the Institute of Chartered Accountants.

Needless to say, there is much overlapping of SRO membership, and considerable uncertainty as to what the rules actually mean. This is partly the result of the complexity of the financial markets, and partly that regulations of this type are so new, that all the rules are new as well. It is also true that the rules have gone so far beyond the original intention of protection for the private individual, that their very complexity makes them impossible for us – and indeed for many practitioners – to understand.

As the banks and building societies abandoned the regular savings market in the nineteen-sixties and nineteen-seventies because of its perceived unprofitability, the life assurance companies developed alternative products for this important market. Unable to sell savings schemes through their sales networks, unless authorised as licensed dealers, these were dressed up as life assurance contracts. This had the added advantage of giving some tax relief on the investment.

Many of these new investment/assurance products were very successful. As inflation made fixed interest savings particularly dangerous, more and more firms joined the game, and also developed the sale of unit trusts. The success is shown in the figures. Some 24 million of us hold about 80 million life policies and, though many of these are for 'protection', commission structures ensure that many are 'investment' products. The numbers of us who invest in equity markets through life assurance companies dwarf the 4 million of us who directly own shares in two or more companies, or the 1¾ million of us who share some 5 million unit trust accounts. The relative success may have something to do with incentives. Morgan Grenfell calculate that the expenses and commissions of the life assurance companies belonging to the Association of British Insurers amounted in 1986 to some 24 per cent of that year's premium income. This figure can be compared with an equivalent 6 to 7 per cent for the unit trust industry.

There were problems with the Prevention of Frauds Act, under which these investment firms should have been licensed. Possibly the greatest weakness of all was the unwillingness of the Department of Trade and Industry to take a robust attitude towards the fraudulent firms encouraged by this easy money, even when goaded by the financial press. The collapse of such a firm, to which the Bank of England had been directing its pensioners, shamed the government into doing something about investor protection. This then got mixed up with the movement towards worldwide and uncontrolled financial markets, of which London constitutes one of the three largest centres. Not surprisingly the Financial Services Act is complicated.

There were perhaps three weaknesses of the previous insurance-dominated retail investment market. Practitioners were not required to have any investment training; there was no compensation fund to protect the victims of fraud; commissions were hidden. There is now an inadequate compensation scheme to pay investors defrauded by authorised firms. Commissions are to be disclosed, though in the teeth of life company opposition, but still no investment training will be required for those who sell us unit trusts and investment bonds. Despite the appalling losses of Barlow Clowes, incompetence probably costs us just as much as fraud.

So we must remain very careful with whom we deal. Specifically, we should always ask ourselves these key questions:

● Is this firm authorised by an SRO? If not, we should not deal with them, and 'interim' authorisation is not sufficient. Many such firms are presently so authorised, and that 'interim' does not give us the protection of the new laws.

● Does this SRO have a compensation fund? Is this firm covered by it, and does it also have professional indemnity insurance? Full compensation will be up to £30,000 only, and 90 per cent of a further £20,000. Unfortunately, this means that the TSA compensation fund has fallen from the present limit of £250,000 to the new industry levels, an excellent example of the modern business adage that 'better means worse'.

- Can we be sure that these firms are financially sound? To be fully authorised, and to maintain this status, firms must satisfy their SRO that the business is soundly financed, keeps client money separate from company money, has adequate administrative systems, and conducts business in a proper way. But 'interim' authorisation can mean that the SRO is still checking on this, while the adequacy of the monitoring arrangements will only be proved in practice. Only The Securities Association has practical experience of doing this.

- Must these firms prove their competence before they can advise us on investment? Only stockbrokers are required to show their knowledge of investment matters by passing examinations before being allowed to deal with clients. Firms authorised by FIMBRA and LAUTRO need only show that they are 'fit and proper' persons to run an investment business, and are covered by 'best advice' rules. If we feel our adviser has not given us 'best advice', we can complain to the complaints department of the SRO and then to the new 'Ombudsman' for investment matters. If we lose money through breach of SRO rules, we can later sue for compensation, and it is possible for the SRO to instigate an action on behalf of many clients.

- Do we have to answer all these personal questions, and sign these customer agreement letters? Yes, this is a key part of the new system and is the 'know your customer' rule. It is intended to prevent unsuitable investments being sold to us and, even more hopefully, to stop salesmen selling us the investment scheme with the highest commission. It also insists on 'best execution' and outlaws excessive trading to generate commission income. But rather than relying on this, we should understand what we are doing, and only go to those firms who openly disclose their terms of business.

- Can we trust the adverts? Yes: these are now controlled by the SRO rule books, and performance statistics can no longer be flagrantly abused. But remember there will always be 'lies, damned lies and statistics'.

- Are we getting independent advice? Yes, if we are dealing with a stockbroker, probably if we are dealing with an investment broker authorised by FIMBRA as an independent adviser. The answer is no if we are talking to a representative of an investment company. The key word is 'polarisation' – either a firm must offer products from the market as our agent, and is independent, or it sells only its own products, is not our agent, and acts in its own best interests. The principle, in practice, is not quite so clear cut. Many firms, and particularly the banks and building societies, are 'tied' to their own products but can pass us on to their 'independent' subsidiaries. We just have to ask the status of the firm, and then ask again how the adviser is getting paid and, if not by us, by whom and how much. Investment brokers displaying the CAMIFA logo are independent. The Campaign for Independent Financial Advice is a grouping of the major non-profit-making life assurance companies and dedicated to supporting financial advisers who act as our agent rather than as a representative of a specific company.

● Will I still get 'cold called'? Yes, but only by representatives of life assurance and unit trust companies. Now, though we may sign something to get rid of them, we have two weeks from the call to cancel the contract.

● Does this mean that the only people who can try to sell me investments are honest? No, definitely not! The SIB cannot stop the telephone salesmen from overseas territories, nor even crooked promoters who are prepared to take a risk by establishing 'unauthorised' businesses here. Investment is only safe if thought about beforehand, and then transacted by a properly authorised firm. The system is in place; we have to use it.

Checkpoints

● It's our money; many others would like it. Only we can look after it. Ignorance and greed are the allies of the fraudulent and incompetent. The SIB and the new SROs can help police the system but 'a fool and his money are soon parted' remains true however many laws are introduced. If in doubt, write to the financial editor of your newspaper for advice, talk to a solicitor, the Citizens Advice Bureau, your bank or building society manager.

- Make no investment decisions without checking the status of the adviser, and have as a general rule: 'If it sounds too good to be true, it probably is.'

- Investment is the purchase of income, which can lead to an increase in the capital value of an investment. Dealing is the pursuit of capital gains in the short term and, like betting on the horses, is generally better for the bookies than for the punters.

- Most investment pricing works on the assumption that promises for the future will obscure our interest in the costs of the present. Don't be fooled; use the new rules of the Securities and Investment Board and insist on being told.

- Investment policy needs to be developed on the basis that the worst can happen, and generally does.

Notes – know what we are paying!

SIB is initially making things more difficult. It has forced the unit trust companies to forgo some time-honoured ways of making money out of us, and their management charges are going up. While the SIB will require disclosure of commissions from 1990 onwards, this also means that the industry agreement to limit maximum commissions on unit trust and life assurance products will also become a dead letter.

We need to sort out what investment advice costs us. The differences between what we *ought to pay* and what we *actually do pay* are so large that these can make a considerable difference to the success of our investments. Do fees matter? The less we pay in fees, the more of our money is working for us in the stock market. Of course, investment skill is very important but it is sometimes difficult to know who is good in advance; it is easier to see who is taking twice as much as someone else for doing the same job.

Fees and financial services

Fortunately SIB now requires our advisers to tell us how much they are earning from us, if we ask. To do that we must understand how the investment management business makes its money so that we know which questions to ask. Some of the costs we cannot escape, but there are many we can reduce.

Comparative Costs of Investment Management Packages

	Inv Trust	*Unit Trust*	*Ins Bond*	*PEP*
Transaction Costs	1.7%	absorbed	absorbed	1.7%
Marketing Costs				
S.E.Comm & VAT	0.23–1.9%	absorbed	absorbed	0.23–1.9%
Selling Commissions	none	3% + VAT	4–6% + VAT	none
Management Costs				
Initial Charge	none	2–3% + VAT	see text	0–5.75%
Annual Fee	0.29–0.57%	1.15–1.72%	see text	0.57–1.72%
Total Initial Costs	1.93–3.6%	6–8%*	hidden	1.93–9.35%
Plus Annual Costs	0.29–0.57%	1.15–1.72%	hidden	0.57–1.72%

* This is the normal bid-offer spread on a unit trust price which includes cost of selling the units; for shares this is another commission plus VAT, or 0.23% to 1.9%.

Transaction costs are inescapable and comprise three separate elements:

Stamp duty is charged by the government on all purchases of shares – not sales – at 0.5 per cent.

The *touch* is the spread between buying and selling prices quoted by the market makers, or share dealers in the stock market. This depends on the size and importance of the share, and is from 1.2 per cent upwards for the most widely traded 'alpha' and 'beta' shares to 7 per cent to 8 per cent for the infrequently traded small companies in the 'gamma' and 'delta' categories.

The *levy* is charged at 0.60 pence per contract by the Stock Exchange to pay for special costs such as the Take Over Panel.

Marketing costs differ not only in amount, but also in whether we are told about them.

Stock exchange commissions are disclosed and, as the result of 'Big Bang' and the scrapping of Stock Exchange club rules, institutional investors such as unit trusts and pension funds can avoid these costs. They can go direct to a market maker. When they do pay commission to a stockbroker for economic and company research help, rates are about 0.2 per cent. If we wish to buy shares, we normally use the *discretionary* or *advisory* service of a stockbroker. Commissions, in practice, average 1.65 per cent on the value of the shares bought or sold, and VAT is added to this at 15 per cent. This makes 1.9 per cent for transactions up to £7000, while above this commission is reduced. Most stockbrokers have minimum commissions of between £15 and £30.

Discount stockbroking services give no advice on shares, and just buy or sell on our instructions. Minimum commissions start at £15 plus VAT and generally have a maximum of £100 or 1 per cent plus VAT of transaction value.

Selling costs or *commissions* are paid out of our capital to our advisers by the managers of unit trusts and all life assurance investment products. These fees are not normally disclosed by our advisers to us, although not kept secret within the industry. These commissions are likely to increase now that the maximum commission agreement of the life assurance and unit trust companies has been disallowed by SIB because life companies have always competed through commission levels. Advisers get from our capital the following payments:

- 3 per cent from unit trusts.
- 4 per cent to 6 per cent from 'life assurance managed' or 'broker managed' insurance or investment bonds.
- On average, the equivalent on one year of our premium payments on an endowment – or regular investment plan – policy taken out from a life assurance company.

Management costs consist of an initial *management charge* and an annual *management fee* and are charged by all providers of investment management services.

Investment trusts

Management charges as such are not levied because investment trusts have the legal structure of a quoted company, with shares quoted on the Stock Exchange, and investors therefore have to absorb the *touch* when they buy investment trust shares, and pay *stamp duty* and *stock exchange commissions*. However, most investment trust managers operate savings schemes which allow their shares to be bought directly from the managers at *reduced stock exchange commissions* of between 0.2 per cent and 0.3 per cent plus VAT. Otherwise, they must be bought through our own stockbroker. There are normally no marketing commissions of the type described above, though the Martin Currie management group and stockbrokers Robert White have attempted to encourage investment advisers to offer investment trusts by 'creating' marketing commissions from our capital similar to the level paid by unit trusts.

Management costs consist of an *annual management fee* only of between 0.25 and 0.5 per cent plus VAT of the value of the shares held as the assets of the trust, and are taken from the income of the trust.

Unit trusts

Initial management charges incorporate all transaction and marketing charges, as described earlier, together with a further initial charge of 2 per cent to 3 per cent plus VAT. The total of these charges, plus VAT on the fee element, are taken through the *bid offer spread*, or difference between buying and selling price of units. For every £100 we give to the manager, only £93 or so is invested. Unit trust groups keep these spreads to an average of between 6 to 8 per cent but they can increase them to a maximum of 12 per cent under Department of Trade and Industry rules.

Annual management fees have, until recently, averaged 1 per cent plus VAT a year but are now being increased to between 1 and 1.5 per cent plus VAT. These fees are deducted by the managers from the dividends paid by the shares held as investments within the unit trust.

Insurance bonds

Initial management charges incorporate higher selling commissions than unit trusts, though other costs are probably similar. Though the quotation of insurance bonds show similar *bid offer spreads* to those of unit trusts, these charges are made on the money allocated to investment; probably only £90 or £91 of our £100 is invested for us. The extra £2 or £3 is taken by the life assurance companies to cover the extra commission they pay our advisers, as well as the life assurance cover attached to the insurance bonds, and all have different and ingenious methods of describing how much of our money is kept back rather than invested for us. These costs are often described as *capital units* and the life assurance companies are fighting hard against disclosing its costs and commissions in the way that all other providers of investment services do.

Annual management fees are frequently 0.5 per cent plus VAT or so higher than on unit trusts, particularly on *broker bonds* which can have an additional 1 per cent levied on our income, and paid over by the life assurance company to our adviser.

Personal equity plan

There are over a hundred and thirty investment managers prepared to run a portfolio of shares for us even though we only have between £1000 and £3000 to invest. These plans are PEPs and the government gives us enough tax relief to pay for a large part of the fees of the cheaper schemes.

Management charges differ significantly between the cheapest – Lloyds Bank at the time of writing – and the most expensive which are the unit trust groups. Other conditions also vary, such as the number and choice of shares we can have, whether they are chosen by us or the manager, dealing costs on share purchase and sale, and the level of discounts available on managers' unit trusts bought within the scheme. Full details are listed by Chase de Vere Ltd, 63 Lincoln's Inn Fields, London WC2A 3JX. 01-404 5766 a FIMBRA broker who will supply its list for £2. They can also be reached on Freephone Chase de Vere. The best of these schemes offer the cheapest terms for a managed portfolio after an investment trust savings scheme.

Personal Equity Plans (PEPs) are the second stage of the government's encouragement of the private investor. Privatisation successfully introduced several million of us to the investment world. PEPs are to encourage us to buy and own shares in British companies already quoted on the stock market.

Each PEP is a miniature tax haven. While the PEP is held, no tax is payable, either on income or capital gains, nor need it be mentioned on our tax return. The principles are simple. Each of us can open one PEP each calendar year, and invest up to £3000 in it. This investment must be in cash, either by regular savings or by transfer of capital. This cash must be invested in the ordinary shares of quoted British companies although the greater of £540 or 25 per cent of the total subscription to the plan can be invested in unit or investment trusts.

No more than 10 per cent of the value of the portfolio may be held in cash after the initial year of investment. The PEP must be held for one full calendar year, in addition to the remainder of the year of opening, before money can be encashed without loss of tax relief.

The dividend yield on the stock market is 4.1 per cent but is expected to be between 4.5 and 4.7 per cent as a result of dividend increases. The average PEP investment is £2000 so this will produce an annual income of £90 or, at the basic rate of 25 per cent a saving of £22.50, and £36 at the higher rate of tax. This may be small but that saving pays Lloyds' management charge of 1 per cent (£20 plus VAT on the £2000 average) and some of the transaction charges, or a further £42 at 2.13 per cent.

Chapter Two

Fear and greed in the markets

Profits on the exchange are the treasures of goblins. At one time they may be carbuncle stones, then coals, then diamonds, then flint stones, then morning dew, then tears.

CONFUSION DE CONFUSIONES, *1688*

This was one of the key principles in the first primer to modern stock market practice, written by Joseph de la Vega and published 300 years ago. This was within a few decades of the founding of the Amsterdam Stock Exchange itself. De la Vega himself is reputed to have made – and lost – five fortunes on the Amsterdam exchange, which was almost as developed then as are exchanges today; perhaps the only difference was a more brutal terminology. In those days, 'futures' contracts were known as 'windhandl' or 'trades in air'. There is another similarity: de la Vega's personal history illustrates the perennial difficulty that investors have of following their own good advice.

Back to 1929 and the Great Depression?

The October '87 share crash immediately invoked half-understood memories of financial disasters such as the 1974 'meltdown' of the London market, and the Great Crash of 1929. Financial markets and disasters have long been bedfellows. Since we all need to establish patterns, in order to understand day to day reality, both financial analysts and the newspapers were soon at work comparing those earlier crashes with that of 1987.

The BZW chart shows a close similarity between London share price performance in 1987–88 and that of Wall Street in 1929–30, but the resemblances are even closer for the two Wall Street crashes. Investors there breathed more easily when May 1988 passed without another sharp fall in prices.

Figure 5: How the London Crash of 1987 began like that of New York in 1929.

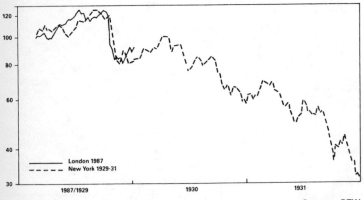

London 1987
New York 1929-31

Source: BZW

The fearsomeness of the 1929 crash for professionals was not the initial fall. Such falls are part of the investment game and, if they serve to transfer wealth from the ignorant to the wise, this is only reasonable: it is simply the working of the famous 'hidden hand' of free markets. But when the professionals, with all their experience, take advantage of such falls to re-enter markets only to see shares fall to less than a third of their new values – as happened in New York in 1930–32 and London in 1973–74 – then quite obviously the hidden hand has been nobbled, and cries of outrage are justified.

1987 may well be the harbinger of another savage bear market of the 1929 or 1972 type. Commentators may guess, but no one can possibly foretell what will happen. Generally, stock market prices presage economic events, rather than cause them. In hindsight the economic boom of the nineteen-twenties was already ending before share prices collapsed: the shock to confidence, worsened by the bankruptcy of so many banks and businesses as a direct result of the fall in share prices, definitely worsened the nineteen-thirties slump.

Figure 6: When things are bad they can be very bad.

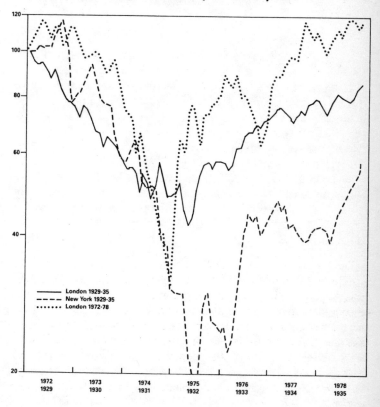

Legend:
— London 1929-35
- - - New York 1929-35
······ London 1972-78

Source: BZW

In 1987, monetary authorities around the world acted promptly
to secure the safety of the financial system. World economic
prosperity, for the moment at least, seems not to have been
influenced by the stock market crash. But then, just possibly the
function of the 1987 fall was to tell us that although individual
economies are doing well, without greater cooperation in the way
these are being run, the world economy as a whole will develop
major problems.

How safe are shares when everything goes wrong?

We, as private investors, should remember the uncertainty of
'profits on the exchange'. Our fundamental attitude must always be
to assume the worst while hoping for the best. If October 1987
signalled the start of a bear market with the possibility of further
falls in share prices, and if the economic situation does worsen, how
dangerous does that make our investment in shares?

Since not even the professionals with the benefit of expensive
and comprehensive research can foretell the future, we must rely
on history and probabilities. The figures below are based on
January 1973, before prices started the long fall which only ended
in January 1975, and December 1987 when shares were at their
worst after the crash two months earlier.

Security	Return 1973–87	Yearly rate of return 1973–87
UK equities	+ 715%	+ 15.0%
UK gilts	+ 502%	+ 12.7%
Deposit	+ 449%	+ 12.0%
Retail prices	+ 360%	+ 10.7%

Source: Phillips & Drew

Investors who timed investment badly and bought before the
1973–74 collapse and sold after the 1987 crash, still did better than
investors in government bonds – gilt-edged stock – or depositors in
building society accounts. An important reason for this is graphically shown by the regular increase in the dividend payments of
M&G's High Income Unit Trust.

Figure 7: A growing income supports the share price.

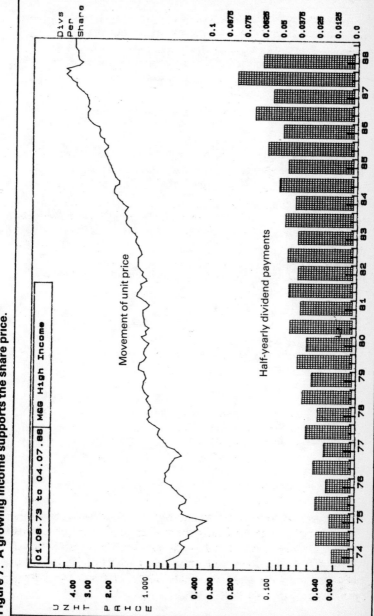

01.08.79 to 04.07.88 M&G High Income

Movement of unit price

Half-yearly dividend payments

Source: Micropal

For more than half the fifteen years since the end of the 1972–74
bear market, company balance sheets and our incomes alike were
savaged by inflation and high marginal rates of tax. Yet the steady
increase of income from the M&G trust, while not compensating us
fully for inflation, at least gave us the illusion that we were keeping
ahead of rising prices.

The danger of inflation to the value, or purchasing power, of our
savings is something that most of us now recognise. Only 'real'
investments, those with values that increase in line with rising
prices, have protected us. BZW has been tracking the performance
of the investment market in London since 1918 in an annual
publication called *BZW Equity-Gilt Study*.*

To own fixed-interest investments – such as government bonds –
has been disastrous. Between 1945 and 1980, adjusted for inflation,

**Figure 8: Inflation in the twentieth century has made shares a
better bet than bonds.**

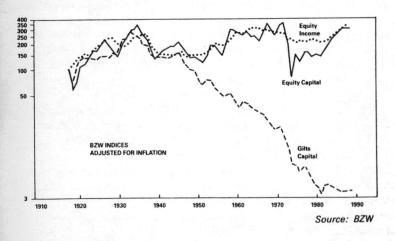

Source: BZW

---

* Barclays de Zoete Wedd Research Ltd, PO Box 188, 2 Swan Lane, London
EC4R 3TS, £15.00.

these lost the bulk of their value. The capital value of shares has also fluctuated alarmingly since 1918, but in real terms they have gone up more than threefold.

None of this should surprise us. Our century has been one of war, revolution, world slump, confiscatory tax rates, and double figure inflation. What is remarkable is that, despite this environment, shares have done so well. The income that we earn from owning shares has not only maintained its value in real terms, it has actually trebled. Why what are generally regarded as the most dangerous of investments, should have turned out to be the best needs a little explaining.

The function of financial markets

There have probably been 'financial markets' as long as some men have had money and a desire to make more, others have had ideas but no money, and middlemen have enjoyed 'making a turn' by bringing them together. The buccaneering voyages of Francis Drake were financed by selling shares in the ventures, to Queen Elizabeth amongst others; no doubt someone pocketed a commission for arranging this and the many other such enterprises of the early modern world. The first English 'joint stock company' was the Muscovy Company founded in 1555, and the first with what we would recognise as shares was the New River Company of 1605.

The commercially minded Dutch Republic formalised these functions by the creation at Amsterdam of the first modern bourse or stock exchange. Success was followed by others. The ability of the financial middlemen – or 'stock jobbers' as they were called – to tap investors for spare cash was crucial to the foundation of the Bank of England in the late seventeenth century. Despite the success of the Bank, both as a dividend-paying company and as the manager of the borrowing requirements of the government, for several decades afterwards land and property remained the favoured outlet for investment.

This was because of the financial speculation – or 'bubble' – associated with the South Sea Company. This company, founded in 1711, was initially successful and the forerunner of a series of new company formations. At much the same time the Mississippi Company, founded in Paris by Scotsman John Law, was developing the economic potential of the then French-controlled territory of Louisiana in America.

In 1719 the South Sea Company offered to take over the National Debt in return for further financial concessions from the government. There was a counterbid from the Bank of England, and a more than doubled offer was accepted in 1720. Amid wild speculation, which included a rash of fraudulent money-raising 'issues' of new companies, South Sea stock rose from 128 in January 1720 to over 1000 by July. Then prices began to fall. By November – this sounds just like the London market in 1987 – South Sea stock was back to 135 and Bank of England stock had nearly halved from over 260 to 145.

The spectacular end of this bubble, and a similar end for the Paris one built around John Law, meant the loss of much money, and many reputations. Both crashes came within a generation of the ruin of the Scottish gentry and trading classes by the Darien Venture, an earlier New World trading and colonising venture. Economic historians believe these financial catastrophes held back the development of joint stock capitalism in Europe by many years. Nevertheless, by the beginning of the nineteenth century, Jane Austen's heroines were as likely to have their 'modest competence' in government bonds as in land.

Greed, even in the era of fixed interest investment

The nineteenth century, with stable prices and rapidly rising family wealth based on successful manufacturing and exporting – very similar to Japan today – was the great age of fixed income investment. Well-bred young women needed to show not only maidenly modesty but also some thousands 'in the funds' if they were to attract the right suitor. The Consolidated Fund – 'funds' or 'consols' – was the major debt instrument of the British government. The great increase in the National Debt, consequent upon the funding of the First World War, led to a major expansion of this market, as well as the number and names of the debt instruments used. Because government stock certificates were finely printed on the best quality of paper, they later became known as 'gilt-edged' or 'gilts'.

But even in the nineteenth century, some investors wanted something a little more risky, and so potentially more rewarding, than British government debt. Naturally bankers, borrowers and investment managers all stood ready to oblige.

The entrepreneur used his own money as the 'seed' or 'risk' capital but looked to the stock market for loan capital: theoretically this was secure, and would be repaid, because the real risk was being taken by the 'share capital' of the business founder and manager. In practice, as investors repeatedly found, their loan capital was just as much 'at risk' – and often more so – than the owners' equity.

Fear also, despite the Pax Britannica

The merchant bankers and their satellites, the stockbroking partnerships, thrived by selling to their investing clients the fixed-interest stock of foreign governments and British companies. Opportunities abounded for the emerging Victorian middle classes to finance mines, railways, shipping lines, and what is today known as 'agribusiness' throughout the world.

There were some four or five major banking crises during the nineteenth century, the result of overexpansion by banks and the repudiation of debts by their customers, as well as several minor financial crises. These latter were generally caused by investing fashions such as railway mania. This led to over-enthusiastic trading in the stocks of railway companies, some of which existed only in the imaginations of their promoters. Though some investors lost, rather more gained.

It was also the age of the investment trust. These, formed initially to help investors to invest in a spread of risks amongst a variety of corporate and overseas borrowers, later helped them invest in the increasingly important equity – or share – issues. The oldest of these companies – Foreign & Colonial Investment Trust – was formed in 1868, and bought its first Japanese bond in 1887. It invested in British equities as early as 1926 when it bought the shares of British Gas – one of the constituents in the later nationalisation of this industry and now the name of the privatised corporation – and bought its first Japanese share in 1961.

Foreign & Colonial's actions reflected the post-1920 reality of a dying Pax Britannica and, with it, fixed-interest investment for Britons. Taxation and inflation killed this investment world, even though investors found it hard to face up to the change.

The end of one era, and the beginning of another

It was not until late in the nineteen-fifties that professional investors finally accepted that the world had changed from the one their fathers knew. It was then that something extraordinary happened. The yields that investors could obtain on British government bonds for the first time ever were higher than those from shares. Indeed, so strange was this that for some years afterwards the more traditional investment managers continued to expect this 'reverse yield gap' to disappear, and normality to return to the market place.

The reason for their confusion is understandable. Companies can go bankrupt, or fail to pay a dividend. So there is risk both to capital and to income in holding shares. Neither of these risks applies to the debts of the British government; because of this investors naturally pay a premium for what is a less risky investment. This premium is a higher price, or lower yield. To the traditional investor, to pay this premium for the riskier equity investment is to see the world turned upside down. But the world has indeed been turned upside down.

Some years ago the American investment magazine *Forbes*, with the help of statistics from economic historians, patched together a seven-hundred-year chart of price movements in England. Two periods stood out. The sixteenth and the nineteenth centuries were both periods of revolutionary change. Both were also periods of explosive increases in prices, compared to which all other historical inflation seems unimportant. Rising prices create problems for investors.

Investors are concerned to use their capital to purchase a regular income for the future. Maintaining the value of the capital and the income against diminution, or outright loss, is equally important. Dishonest trustees, crooked company promoters, incompetent advisers are misfortunes we all recognise, albeit often after the event when it is too late to take action. Valueless money is harder to accept. This is why it took so long for investors to recognise that the twentieth century was not going to be kind to savings invested in bank deposits or fixed-income securities such as gilts or the preference capital of companies.

Real before tax annual rate of return to London investors

Period	Years	Equities Before tax	Equities After tax	Gilts Before tax
1920–1936	16	+ 17.7%	+ 14.3%	+ 12.2%
1936–1952	16	− 1.9%	− 6.1%	− 4.7%
1952–1968	16	+ 12.3%	+ 7.6%	− 1.0%
1968–1982	14	0.0%	− 4.8%	− 1.0%
1982–1987	6	+ 20.5%	+ 17.1%	+ 6.0%

Source: BZW

The sixteen years from 1920 to 1936 – the period of the 1929 Wall Street Crash and the Great Depression – was the last period of stable or falling prices for investors, but even then equity investors did significantly better than those investing traditionally.

From the beginning of rearmament in 1936 to the reimposition of control over inflation in the early nineteen-eighties, even tax-exempt pension fund investors were unable to maintain the purchasing power of the funds they managed by investing in gilts. Interest rates were simply not high enough to compensate for the rise in prices. But for the private investor the outcome was much worse. Tax on investment income for much of this period was at a marginal rate of nearly one hundred per cent; it was what was left of 'after tax investment income' that then had to contend with rising prices. Not surprisingly, private investors spurned fixed-interest investment in favour of investments that could promise lower taxed capital gains.

Inflation does not only affect bond investment; it has a similar effect on shares. For share prices as a whole to increase in value, dividends must grow faster than inflation. It is this 'real growth' of income that justifies increased capital values. The control of inflation after 1980 turned higher profits into bigger share dividends, and so into 'real' income growth; this improvement in real income justified the rise in share prices.

The growth in real dividends

% per annum	Nominal dividend growth	Retail price index	Real dividend growth
Period 1968–87	11	10	1
Period 1973–87	12	11	1
Period 1978–87	13	8	5
Period 1983–87	15	5	10

Source: Phillips and Drew

Though equity investment has 'hedged' the capital of the private saver against the worst ravages of inflation, share investment has been at its best only when inflation was low or declining. The rise in share prices during the last decade was enjoyable for those who participated, but it was only restoring what investors had lost through the inflation of the nineteen-seventies.

Figure 9: The bull market of the eighties has only made up for the inflationary losses of the seventies.

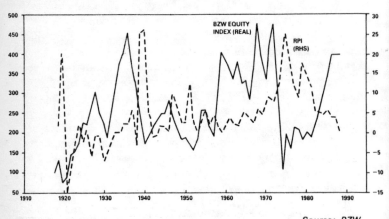

Source: BZW

The cult of the equity

The destruction of the returns available to fixed-interest investors was the major reason why this sector of the securities markets began to languish in Britain. But there is another reason. Even in the era of stable prices, investors were prepared to take risks for greater rewards. The truth is that most of us want to do more than maintain the value of what we have.

Though sometimes hard to admit to ourselves, we want more: greed is one of the two factors that motivate us as investors. Julian Baring for many years has been the gold guru of the London

Figure 10: Savoy dinners, gold and FT30 index.

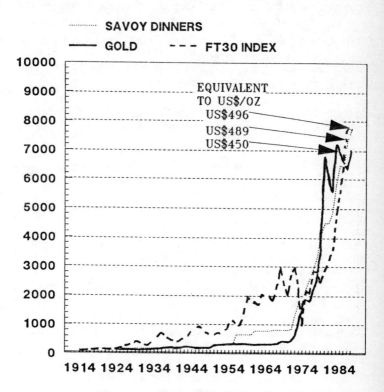

Source: Julian Baring, James Capel & Co.

market, and he has wittily developed the case for gold – and for equity investment – with his 'Savoy dinner' yardstick. In 1914, the price of an ounce of gold would have bought dinner for thirteen at the Savoy. By the nineteen-eighties life had got harder: an ounce of gold only bought dinner for twelve.

The real challenge for us as investors is not just to maintain the value of our capital in relation to a rising cost of living, but to maintain it against a rising standard of living. We want to have more friends at more Savoy dinners. This is difficult to achieve, but it is probably easier for us acting in a private capacity than it is for the professional managing other people's money. Such managers have too many career pressures to be able to escape the passing fashions of the financial markets.

It was appropriate that the fashion for equity investment should have taken hold between the two World Wars. For though popular memory is of world depression and the decline of the great nineteenth-century industries, these were also the years of new technologies, with the creation of businesses based on the internal combustion engine, synthetic chemicals, and popular entertainment in the form of the radio, gramophone and cinema.

The financing needs of the new companies were too great for privately held risk capital and publicly quoted debt. Shares in these companies' equity – or risk capital – had to be sold to investors, and that needed better-regulated company law. Slowly, legislation was introduced which made illegal the more obvious share ramping, and the associated imaginative company accounting practices.

The great economic boom, that started in the late nineteen-thirties as the nations rearmed for the Second World War, was encouraged in the post-war era by the formation of GATT – the General Agreement on Tariffs and Trade – with the express intention of encouraging international trade, and eliminating nineteen-thirties-style 'beggar my neighbour' trade protectionism. The development of regional economic groupings such as OECD – Organisation for Economic Cooperation and Development – and later the European Economic Community benefited the more efficient of the new companies, and enabled them to become international in scope.

Today, while not inconceivable, it is highly unlikely that any of the major world companies could be forced into bankruptcy by a deterioration in general economic conditions. Indeed, so concerned are most with 'investor relationships' that they are reluctant to reduce their dividends to shareholders, even when circumstances warrant such a course. This was certainly not the case in the nineteen-thirties.

Coming of age of the equity markets

Since the nineteen-fifties the 'cult of the equity' has been in full bloom, with institutional investors becoming the dominant force within equity markets. The 'institutions' are the life assurance companies and the pension funds and, although the 1987 equity figures are higher than average, the trend in favour of equity investment is clear.

Institutional portfolio preference – use of cash flows for investment

£billions	1963	1972	1978	1987
UK gilts	£0.1	£0.3	£4.2	£ 0.0
UK corporate bonds	£0.3	£0.2	£0.0	£ 1.7
UK shares	£0.3	£1.2	£2.1	£11.2
Property	£0.1	£0.3	£1.2	£ 0.5

Source: Phillips & Drew

Institutional needs, just as much as legislation itself, have ensured that stock markets are now as 'clean' as they are ever likely to be. Company accounts, given the desire of boards of directors to present the best possible image to their investors, will always be presented as creatively as possible. However, this manipulation of figures now has to take place within fairly strict guidelines, and under the eye of the company analysts and the financial press. The accounts are 'straight' or truthful in a way that many accounts in the nineteen-thirties, and even nineteen-fifties, were not.

The commissions that can be made from institutional business have created in the last twenty years a whole new 'research' industry. Economists, industry and company analysts, and currency commentators stand ready with instant advice for their investing clients upon any and every event in the real world, in terms of its likely impact on 'this year's earnings' of industry X and company Y.

Though it may be true that 'if you take all the economists in the world, and lay them end to end, they will never reach a conclusion' their efforts have made a difference. Most importantly, and in alliance with the financial press, regularly updated knowledge about companies and industries makes it hard for the dishonest to thrive. Despite the opposition of some of the practitioners, the major stock exchanges have been turned from well protected money-making clubs into important and serious money markets.

1987 changed markets, but not human nature

The shock of 1987 to the private investor was that, despite this greater professionalism, and wider dissemination of knowledge, the market still behaved as in the old, unreconstructed days. The shock to the professionals was greater.

Surprise and chagrin was part of their reaction. Most professionals felt during 1987 that equity prices were too high, but expected the crash to come in 1988, and in Tokyo. New York and 1987 were quite unexpected. The real shock was that share prices throughout the world fell simultaneously, and too fast for protective action to take effect. Though the majority of professionals have long known that most of the world's stock markets follow similar paths, they have never before known them to do so without considerable time lags. All carefully considered global diversification 'strategies' now lay in ruins. The universality of the '87 crash reflected two significant developments in the investment world.

The global market and new style 'stockbrokers'

The 'global' market is nothing new in itself, for our Victorian grandparents happily invested in Australian gold mines, American cattle ranches, and South American railways. Today, however, this international investment is transacted by investors through share dealing firms with branches in the world's major stock markets. What is different is the world-wide and integrated nature of these new-style stockbrokers.

Leading stockbrokers, if not themselves part of a large commercial banking group, now have as much capital as many banks. Their activities are concentrated on servicing professional investors, and making 'dealing profits' for themselves. Their 'market-making' function, with teams of dealers backed by salesmen, creates the 'liquidity' of the financial markets. The dealers' function is to buy from, or sell to, the investor. To do this they must often buy quoted securities for which they have no buyers or, more dangerously, sell securities which they do not own in the hope that they will later identify sellers and so 'cover, or square, their positions'.

The business objective of all international share-dealing firms is to reduce their exposure to loss by ensuring that their 'positions' – whether they are 'long' and own, or are 'short' and owe, securities – are passed from one trading centre to another as each opens for business during the twenty-four hours that the earth takes to circle the sun. Such continuous supervision should thus prevent, or at least alleviate, losses caused by misguessing market movements.

Still more a dream than a reality, these global connections have already meant a quicker transfer of market 'moods' – today's fall in Wall Street is immediately reflected by dealers in the Tokyo market. Tokyo's optimism or pessimism, as that market closes, is an important factor in the way that London sets its opening prices.

'Catch 22' for the investment manager

The roller-coaster of market demand is meat and drink to a dealer – the Porsche-driving, champagne-guzzling, overpaid 'yuppie' of the newspapers – but is poison to the institutional investor. The volume of funds controlled by these life assurance, pension fund and unit trust managers is such that their investment decisions dominate stock markets everywhere. Institutional decisions to buy or sell are the main influence on share price movements. They cannot insulate themselves from the short-term volatility of market prices because they themselves live in a competitive world.

Their performance as fund managers is under regular scrutiny by pension fund trustees, competitive investment managers, the financial press, and their own superiors. Success is doing better than similar portfolios managed by others, and not doing worse than the market 'indices' or price yardsticks of stock markets split into various business sectors. Failure to perform satisfactorily means a reduction of funds under management, and possibly the loss of the management contract itself.

If investors wanted protection from the volatility of share prices, of currencies, and of interest rates, there were ways of achieving this, even if those ways were not obvious to traditional security market participants. Manufacturers regularly 'hedge' their purchases of essential but price-sensitive raw materials through the commodity markets. Cable manufacturers, for whom copper is a most important metal, cannot simply buy the copper as they need it, but nor can they buy all their requirements in advance of manufacturing need. The supply and price of copper, like most other basic materials, is notoriously erratic.

Copper, bought at the wrong price, can make the cable manufacturer uncompetitive. So the commodity markets developed two main types of traded contracts to help manufacturers ease this problem. Option contracts give the right, though not the obligation, to buy or sell commodities at today's price but at some specified time in the future. Futures are actual contracts to buy or sell, but in the future rather than now.

The rise of the derivative markets

Commodity markets, faced with declining turnover as their customers became bigger, more efficient in their use of raw materials, and increasingly integrated in their structure, saw an opportunity. These 'hedging' techniques, that had for so long protected manufacturers and raw material suppliers, could do the same for investors.

So contracts were developed for options and futures both on currencies, on individual shares, and on share markets as a whole through the use of indices of different security markets. These are the 'derivative' markets, so called because most of the options or futures contracts derive from an underlying or 'real' activity such as the purchase or sale of a share at a particular price on a specific day, or selling dollars and buying pounds at a known exchange rate. Using such contracts, investors could protect their 'book' profits in existing portfolios, or 'hedge' holdings of foreign shares from adverse currency movements.

The existence of such contracts created further opportunities. The most natural was 'arbitrage' or the profitable exploitation of small price differences for the same product traded in separate markets or on different contracts. Initially used to describe trading in the price differences that occurred in bonds or shares traded in markets divided by space, time, currency and language, this is now used for the flattening out of price differences between the options and futures markets, and the securities and foreign exchange markets.

As traders used computers and employed PhDs in physics or mathematics – quickly dubbed 'rocket scientists' – arbitraging price differences between the various markets with their competing contracts soon developed into an enormous trading activity on its own account.

Arbitraging developed problems for the working of share markets. 'Triple witching hour' comes quarterly, when the rules of the New York Stock Exchange require members to square their books between these three different – security, option and futures – types of contract; late in the 1980s, this caused sharp and anomalous price movements on Wall Street. A change in settlement procedures cured this problem, but no such easy solution is in sight for the violence of volume and price movements caused by the development of 'programme trading'.

This is the use of computers to follow prices, and set in motion pre-programmed arbitrage trading strategies when certain price conjunctions occur. It is also a series of simpler programmes, used by those who believe that analysis of price movements can indicate when shares should be bought and sold. Since such price analysis is stultifyingly boring, even to price analysts, the computer is a godsend. It can be set to watch the prices, and give the orders, while the rest of us do something more interesting.

These derivative markets have linked security markets, trading in bonds and shares, with money markets which trade deposit and foreign currency contracts. All are 'deregulated' because no government can now, any more than they could in the nineteenth century, prevent money and capital going where it pleases. Though there is a world financial market, trading goes on in many separate markets, under varying national jurisdictions, and with widely different rules. One of the lessons of October 1987 was that these technical differences can cause dangerous trading imbalances when sentiment changes. These differences will neither quickly nor easily be resolved.

Eating your cake, and having it too

Deep in their trading strategies, not dissimilar to a complex football pool or 'tote' calculation but with more noughts, the market technicians began to glimpse the investment manager's nirvana.

The investment manager needs to keep clients and superiors happy. This means staying in the market while it goes up, and so not losing out in comparison with competitors or the indices. It also means following prevailing fashion since that is what makes prices move in the short term – and no investment manager needs to be told by followers of Keynes that 'in the long run we are all dead'.

Though directors and trustees sometimes forget, the investment manager knows that, at some stage, the music will stop and there will not be seats for everyone. Get out of the markets too soon, and you've realised your profits – but those who stayed in longer have made more. Leave it too late, and you've lost the profits and now have losses – but then you're not alone for many of your colleagues are standing with you looking equally sheepish.

But what if you could stay in the markets, and get out too? Oh, what joy – and what business too! Thus was portfolio insurance born. With the right combination of option and futures contracts against an existing portfolio, continually renewed and recalculated as time passed and markets moved, existing profits could be protected at a small cost. Then, when the markets should crack, exercising existing contracts and taking out new ones as prices fell would realise all those profits on the portfolio without the cost of selling shares.

The danger of forgetting Mr Murphy

Though an unfair simplification of some very complicated and painstaking work, the creators of programme trading and portfolio insurance, in the heady atmosphere of the bull market, ignored both Mr Murphy and the lessons of history. Mr Murphy's expurgated law is that 'whatever can go wrong, will go wrong' while history teaches that financial markets are prone to panic because when greed goes, fear comes. And a financial panic implies a shortage, and sometimes a complete absence of buyers.

During 1987 the problem of how the vast and growing American trade deficit was to be financed without recourse to inflation began to bother investors. The price of bonds not only in America, but also in Japan and Germany, fell heavily during the summer; investors demanded higher yields as they prepared themselves for higher interest rates. These were part of governments' attempts to control currency uncertainty and the plunge of the dollar against the Japanese yen and the German mark. Equity markets, which up to then had been roaring ahead, began to slow in sympathy with the fall in bond markets.

In the autumn Mr Murphy took a hand: the slanging match between the American and German finance ministers over economic policy became public in October. Nervous investors began to sell, share prices weakened, and the computers began to do their stuff. By Friday 16th – when the London market was closed because of the previous night's hurricane – falling prices in Wall Street were triggering more and more programme trades, and buyers were sensibly deciding 'to sit this one out'. When London opened on the 19th, already knowing that Far Eastern markets had been hit by a wave of selling, another financial panic was in the making. The rest is history.

Checkpoints

● Investment is at least as old as modern Europe, and so are financial 'bubbles', 'panics' and 'crashes'.

● Investors today, just as much as three hundred years ago, are concerned to protect what they have, and to make more.

Figure 11: The dollar collapses and bond yields rise during the summer of 1987.

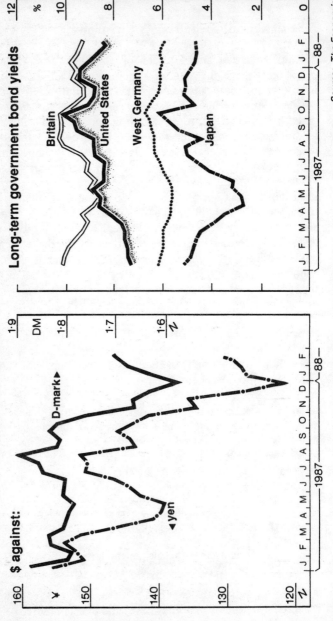

Source: The Economist

• Inflation during the twentieth century has made investment more difficult, but fortunately the development of international business and world trade has made equity investment – or buying shares – safer.

• Though the post-Second World War combination of tax and inflation made many investors forget that the purpose of investment is the purchase of future income, it has been the real, or after-inflation, growth of dividend income that has underpinned the rise in the capital value of shares.

Notes: valuing markets and measuring performance

There are some forty-five different indices that measure the London market, and many hundreds more to measure all the other security markets. The oldest in London is the *Financial Times* Ordinary Index, which measures the values of the thirty largest companies quoted on the London Stock Exchange. The American equivalent is the Dow Jones Industrial Average.

In 1962 the *Financial Times* and Institute of Actuaries developed jointly a more representative share index. This is called the *FT* –Actuaries All Share Index – FTA for short – which covers 730 or so companies divided into six main groups subdivided into thirty-four market sectors. An American equivalent is the Standard and Poor 500 index.

The options and futures traders needed quicker calculations of market movements, so in 1984 'Footsie' – or the *FT*–Stock Exchange 100 Share Index – was developed to calculate minute by minute the value of the one hundred largest quoted companies. These companies account for seventy per cent of the total value of quoted UK equities.

As investment managers became ever more international in their activities, they needed an equivalent to the FTA with which to compare their performance. The *FT*–Actuaries World Index covers 2300 shares quoted on 23 stock exchanges and dates from 1986.

These indices are published daily in the *Financial Times*. Because of the importance of the FTA to professional fund managers, who have to try to match its performance, this is also a key measure to us of the temperature of the market.

Chapter Three

Prices, reason and emotions

The expectation of an event creates a much deeper impression upon the exchange than the event itself. When large dividends or rich imports are expected, shares will rise in price; but if the expectation becomes a reality, the shares often fall; for the joy over the favourable development and the jubilation over a lucky chance have abated in the meantime.

CONFUSION DE CONFUSIONES, *1688*

The technical workings of the market are not sufficient to explain the '87 crash. Computers are programmed by human traders, who are still responsible for the majority of decisions made within the financial markets. Obviously, there was a change of perception by investors. Optimists began to temper their expectations of future profits, while pessimists became more certain that their favourite horror – whether inflation, recession, slump, or just the collapse of the financial system and civilisation as we know it – was about to overwhelm us all.

But perceptions are always changing: the economic world is a very complicated place, and our understanding of it is continually being modified. There are always optimists – bulls – and pessimists – bears – fighting to establish supremacy within the market trend. The question of what caused the change of perception comes second to why this change had such a devastating effect on share prices.

Ninety years ago Charles Dow, co-founder of the Dow-Jones

index of the US stock market, said: 'The market as a whole represents a serious, well considered effort on the part of far-sighted and informed men to adjust prices to values such as exist or which are expected to exist in the not too remote future.' This is an elegant wording of the Efficient Market Hypothesis – EMH – over which countless academics and market practitioners have waged war this last twenty years or so.

This hypothesis, and all the research effort of brokers world-wide, should mean that shares cannot be worth today only half of what they were worth yesterday. But indeed they can be, and often are. The trouble is that both Charles Dow and the EMH go only so far in explaining stock market behaviour – probably about as far as a production of *Hamlet* without the Prince of Denmark would go in meeting Shakespeare's intentions.

Though reason has an important part to play within the invest-ment world, all too frequently it is completely overwhelmed by emotions of greed or fear. Prices are made by the interaction of what we think should happen – we as rational theorists – and what we wish or fear might happen. The successful investor is the one who can more frequently than most use reason to control expecta-tions. It is not an easy fight, and it never stops, for markets are driven at least as much by the heart as by the head.

This should be an important advantage for us as private inves-tors. Professional and private investors alike are prey to the same anxiety about investment decisions and their timing. All are under the same emotional pressure to 'gain' and not to 'lose'. All know that the market judges investment decisions each and every trading day. Because we do not have the career concerns of professional investment managers to add to these already intense pressures, we should be better able to act with a little extra objectivity.

Good investors generally follow simple disciplines. These stop us doing silly things, and though such rules will not necessarily make us money, at least they should stop us losing it. This, after all, is the first, necessary step towards success. What these rules are is the substance of the second part of this book, but their importance springs from the theory and practice of investment pricing, and what light this throws on market behaviour.

The theory of value – how it should work

A 'share' is a piece of paper which entitles us to a share in the profits of an enterprise. It has no intrinsic worth, except what might be left as equity – or shareholders' funds – if the business was closed down, creditors paid, and long term debts and preferred capital (ie preference shares) redeemed. Today's price of a share, or equity investment, should represent the value of its entitlement to that part of a company's profits which we can expect to be paid out as dividends.

Money today is more valuable to us than money next year, because we can spend it now or, more usefully for value calculations, deposit it and earn some interest. Ten pounds promised to us in five years' time is not as valuable as £10 today. We cannot earn any interest on it, nor can we spend it. Its value can be calculated. The method of doing this is known as 'discounting'. In other words, that £10 today is worth £10 less the interest we would have earned on it over the next five years.

Dividends, to which a share entitles us provided the business makes profits, are paid out over many future years and so must be discounted to give today's value of a share. This calculation is notoriously subjective since the future cannot be known but only guessed – what will the dividends be? If they are to increase, by how much and when? What rate of interest should be used to discount those future dividends to determine present value?

Other than this dividend flow, theoretically an equity has no value so, though most investors do, no investor should buy equities for capital gains. Capital gains only come about because investors revalue those expected dividend flows, or dividends turn out to be more than investors expected, so the shares are then worth more, or another company buys our company expecting to make more income out of the assets than the existing management, and so on.

In the end, all reasons come down to the same. As money is worth what it earns for us – for some wine and song, for others leisure, yet others power or more money – so shares are only worth what they will earn. This is why actuaries never value pension or life funds by looking at market prices for the shares. Instead they calculate the future income flow, based on past experience and current interest rates, and this enables them to calculate a capital value for the fund. At all levels money is what money earns.

Relative and not absolute values

Because the value of shares depends on the income they will produce, there is no absolute standard of value. Values are always relative, either to other types of investment such as cash or bonds, or similar investments such as another share. Indeed, one of the central functions of stock markets is to ensure that the decisions of many investors with varying investment needs ultimately equalise the returns available on all types of investment.

Whether we hold cash, bonds or shares, the returns that we can expect should be the same after taking into account the varying levels of risk the different types of investment incur. So, in theory, to compare the value of a share against that of a bond is easy. We know the rate of interest on the bond, and the length of time over which we will receive those annual payments.

The discount rate is a matter of personal investment judgement, but is related to current and expected interest rates. Provided we can then decide the amount by which dividends on shares will increase, and the size of the risk premium that we and other investors will want to persuade us to buy shares rather than government bonds, a simple equation gives the answer. This risk premium is important; it is because dividends, and particularly their rate of increase, are uncertain while companies have also been known to go bust.

As American investment bankers Goldman Sachs say, these two calculations are what the investment game is all about. Fundamental share analysis, theoretically, should help us to decide the rate at which dividends will grow. This is not as easy as brokers' circulars might suggest. Deciding on the risk premium seems even harder. Both turn out to be moving targets.

The trouble is the subjectivity of our judgements. As we develop greater optimism about business conditions, and the state of the equity market, the more sure we become that company profits will grow and dividends increase at a faster than normal rate. The better this outlook, the lower we feel the risk premium ought to be. Since we are confident that nothing can stop dividends increasing, where

is the risk in owning shares rather than bonds? Over-optimistic
assumptions about dividend growth translate into super-optimistic
valuations of equity yields compared to bond returns.

An inbuilt tendency to exaggeration

That BZW chart of the inflation-adjusted performance of equities
and gilts – see Figure 8, page 30 – shows that dividend income from
shares has grown in a much more stable fashion than equity values.
Though these have also shown the same increase in real terms as
dividends, prices have fluctuated a lot more than dividends.
Goldman Sachs* were curious as to why this should be so, for the
function of the market is to adjust returns on all investments, given
the necessary risk premia, to parity.

The market has plenty of historical probabilities to work on.
During the nearly seventy years since the bottom of the 1920
market crash shares have had an inflation-adjusted dividend
growth of 1.5 per cent a year, or slightly less than the growth of the
economy as a whole. The total return from equities over this
period, after inflation but before tax, has been 7.5 per cent a year.
The equivalent figure for gilts is 1.5 per cent a year. Equity prices
have risen ninety-nine times while retail prices have risen only
fourteen times.

Had the market used these probabilities to dictate its pricing
decisions, would the trend of share prices have been so unstable?
The Goldman Sachs chart shows that, if the market had 'known'
the course of future dividends, a 'rational' market would have
followed a path far smoother than the one it actually took. Though
the market obviously cannot ever know the future, it can rely on
probability. The future is likely to repeat the past, and change
slowly within socially acceptable limits; it is unlikely to change
radically and quickly, whatever current circumstances make us
feel.

Yet the actual graph of equity prices suggests that for long
periods the markets ignore probability. To explain the difference

* *Valuing UK equities against gilts – theory and practice*, Gavyn Davies and Sushil
Wadhwani, Goldman Sachs International Corporation, London 1988.

between actual and theoretical behaviour, Goldman Sachs suggest that: 'Equity markets are subject to extremely prolonged "fads" during which they lose touch with valuation benchmarks.'

In other words, the relationship of equity prices to dividend yield, and the parallel relationship of bond yields to equity yields goes haywire. Markets forget everything that has happened in the past, and the lessons of probability, and concentrate instead on imaginative projections of the immediate past into the distant future.

Figure 12: The 'rational' line of share price movements is very similar to the line of dividend payments shown in Figure 8.

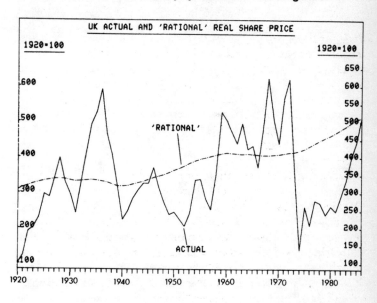

Source: Goldman Sachs

Practical application – the theory of analysis

Today, the market thinks more about determining the growth rates of individual companies than price relationships between bonds and shares. The analytical work needed to value a share, and so estimate likely dividend growth, was first and best developed in an American book called *Security Analysis*,* originally published in 1934.

Fundamental share price analysis

Share price analysis, which theoretically everyone follows even today, requires an exhaustive investigation into the capacity of a business to earn money. This analysis requires detailed investigation of a company's

● accounting practices, to determine if any of the various creative tricks are being used and why.

● financial strength, based on various banking-type ratios, and needed to determine the company's ability to survive hard economic times.

● basic profitability, assessed on the record of the last ten years, and a qualitative view of the strength of the company within its market and the prospects of the industry in which it operates, together with an estimate of the stability of profit margins.

● forecast of future earnings based on all the above information, and covering the next seven to ten years.

The appearance of the desk-top computer has made this mammoth task a little easier, except that now general economic forecasts need to be inserted into the equations in order to give 'sensitivity' analyses of future profits in the light of alternative growth rates for the economy. Economic forecasting has not helped, as economists

---

* *Security Analysis*, Benjamin Graham/David Dodd/Sidney Cottle/Charles Tatham, 5th Edition, 1988, McGraw-Hill. The private investor version is *The Intelligent Investor*, Benjamin Graham, 2nd Edition, 1955, McGraw-Hill.

spend a good deal of their time trying to estimate how close to reality are current government statistics and, if they are accurate, what do they actually mean in terms of the economy here and now. Though getting all these relationships right is near impossible, they do determine what profits actually will be.

The yardstick of value

'It cannot too often be said that the stock market reflects all everybody knows about the business of the country,' once said the *Wall Street Journal*. Good analysts help that knowledge to be more formally presented, and more widely spread. The leading research brokers are keen to get publicity for their views, and increasingly sell their work to firms which no longer carry out this fundamental research for themselves.

The summation of their work is in their estimate for company 'earnings' and this, together with all other knowledge held by the

Figure 13: Glaxo's better earnings growth enabled its dividend to overtake that of Thorn.

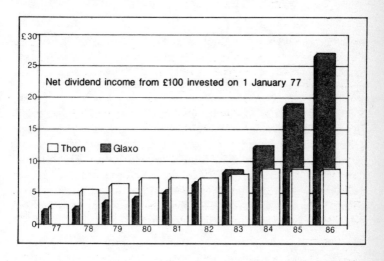

Net dividend income from £100 invested on 1 January 77

☐ Thorn ▩ Glaxo

Source: Investors Chronicle

market and the hopes and fears of all participants, come together in another figure called the 'price to earnings' ratio. The importance of these key figures cannot be overemphasised.

During the sixties and early seventies Thorn was one of the stock market's favourite shares, while Glaxo was a worthy, but dull, pharmaceutical company. Sir Jules Thorn's successors lacked his magic, while Glaxo changed and became a very much cleverer marketer of drugs. A decade ago, dividends paid out by Glaxo were lower than those paid out on an equivalent investment in Thorn but the changing business success of the two companies soon reversed that as the chart shows. This relatively faster increase in earnings and dividends is the grail for which analysts and investors search.

Earnings are not the same as profits: they are the profits available to shareholders, after tax and other 'prior charges' such as a share of profits to minority partners in some aspect of the business, or dividends due on preference share capital, have been paid. Earnings are what is left to maintain the business and pay dividends to equity shareholders.

Very many companies increase profits without improving earnings. They do this by buying other companies through the issue of shares, or raising more money from shareholders to increase the size, but not the profitability, of their business. Profits increase, but not 'earnings per share'. Profits without increased earnings are of little value to us as they do not allow the company to increase dividends. We should invest for such increases.

Earnings without increased profitability are sometimes not much use either. Profitability is the efficiency with which companies use their assets to make profits. Some companies become trapped in industries – textiles, paper manufacturing and heavy electrical engineering are notorious examples – with so many competitors that they cannot improve profitability. The company makes good earnings each year, but those earnings have to be ploughed back into new equipment to maintain efficiency and competitiveness and so stay in business. They are not available to pay higher dividends to shareholders.

The temperature of the market

The price to earnings ratio – PER or sometimes PE – is shown in the financial pages of newspapers. This figure is the ratio between the last-disclosed profits of a company after tax – earnings per share or EPS – and the market valuation of the company as shown by the current share price. Most brokers also publish a prospective PER – what they calculate this will be at the present price, but based on their estimates for company profits in the current year, and possibly next as well.

Put simply the PER expresses the number of years that an investor must wait until the addition of these 'earnings per share' total the price paid for the share. The more attractive we think an investment then, in theory, the higher this 'purchase multiple' that we should be prepared to pay. The PER of any company, in theory at least, summarises the market's view of the profitability of the company, the speed with which earnings are expected to grow, and the availability of those earnings to finance higher dividends.

The most authoritative historical figures are calculated for the *Financial Times*–Actuaries indices (see notes). Individual figures for companies are shown in the *FT* share price tables, which also include dividend yields, and the summary table gives the average PERs for different business sectors of the market as well as for all quoted companies used in the FTA – ie the market itself. For these figures alone the serious investor must buy the *FT*, if not on every day of the week at least on Saturday. PERs are the market's temperature and, in particular, show which industries and companies are 'in fashion'.

Share analysis in practice

The company researcher has a hard enough job to produce an historical analysis on the lines described above, generally between journeys to visit companies and talk with management. Theoretically, the analyst can then value one share in comparison with another by:

● estimating future earnings and dividend growth of one company against another, with forecasts anchored firmly to past records.

● comparing financial strength, net asset values, market position, and management experience and record of the potential investments.

● assessing 'value for money' on the basis of current price, dividend yield, and PER.

In the world where most analysts live, conclusions need to end with a 'buy' or 'sell' recommendation if their employers are to earn a daily crust. Their customers, haunted by the quarterly review of their own investment performance, want rather less of the historical facts, and somewhat more of the crystal ball. Ideally, they want to have 'growth' companies pinpointed – those occasional magic companies that make us rich because of the speed and size of their earnings and dividend growth – but will accept recommendations of companies that are expected to outgrow their peers in the short term.

The search for growth

If straightforward analysis is difficult, growth analysis is doubly so. The key to all is – why is the company doing so well? Is it because it has a unique product, market position, management team or is it just lucky with economic and business conditions? The management will assure us that it is their skill at developing a strategy, and exploiting opportunities. Then they would, even though case history after case history shows that luck plays an important part in business success. Generals are much more honest: they talk openly of the 'fog of war' and the great value of their opponent's mistakes to their own victories. And business is much the same as war.

The output of analytical work is generally most impressive, and the columns of figures are of such precision that it is easy to believe that the future can be foretold. Unfortunately, any analyst knows how very difficult it is to uncover the real 'why' to a company's profitability and success.

GIGO is used by computer users as a shorthand description to explain that if the initial key assumptions of a programme are wrong – Garbage In – then however beautiful the resulting figures look, it will still be Garbage Out. The record of analytical success in estimating company results is not particularly good, not for lack of effort but because foretelling the future is beyond us.

Difficulties with growth analysis

Analysis of company profits – and profitability, or why profit margins are as good or bad as they are – requires us to think in ways that seem not to be very easy for humans, or so say the psychologists. We are excellent at linear thinking: working out a route from a map at a simple level or, a more complex task, designing aeroplanes or computer software. Linear thinking is a logical path, however twisty, but with each move we take one definite step further forward. Analysis of company profits and share valuations requires interactive, rather than linear, thinking.

We all know the difficulties of getting our parties to go with a swing. Success requires a mixture of people who will get on well with each other, and so have everyone 'sparking'. The party needs listeners as well as talkers. Pleasant surroundings are helpful, good food and drink important – if bad enough they can destroy the pleasure, however attractive the guests – but equally one wrong guest can quickly and effectively ruin the occasion for everyone.

This is because life is interactive – we are affected by our surroundings, and by others, and we affect them. Our judgements of our fellow guests, together with the part we play in the party, are continually changing and evolving.

Now think of the interactive relationships that can influence company profitability. Our party room has become the world economic scene, and the food and drink the political and economic conditions that face the companies in which we are thinking of investing; the guests are the companies themselves, trading and competing with each other, as well as with overseas companies establishing a foothold in Britain, just as our guests form and reform conversation groups at our party.

Company analysis requires a judgement of the importance of hundreds, if not thousands, of such interactive economic and financial factors. The values of many of these factors are not known – some cannot be known – but judgements must still be made as to their importance to the whole. Even with computers, we are not equipped to handle this level of conceptual complexity. So we take short cuts. Much analysis becomes either simple extrapolation from the current short term trend, or the assumption that trends which can be calculated in detail for parts of the company are also true of the business as a whole.

A case history: growth analysis of the pharmaceutical industry

The pharmaceutical industry is an excellent example of growth analysis. The companies are large, the industry is worldwide, we all spend more on health as we get richer, and patent protection means those companies that develop the wonder drugs can make untold millions. But these can be a long time in the proving, and mistakes either in drug-development research, or the marketing of the developed drugs, can cost a company dearly.

Competition and drug development costs are rising, reflecting the increased scale of the research effort required. Spending on research and development has risen over the last decade from about ten per cent of company sales revenues to over twelve per cent and is set to rise to fifteen per cent. The marketing effort needed to make a return from that spending – and put more aside for further development – has also increased more than proportionately in cost.

Neither the costs nor the risks of this business are about to decline. The applied research of the companies depends on the basic research of the universities; reduced government funding of the universities means the replacement of research grants with research sponsored by the drug industry. This will add to company costs. Whether it will produce as good results as university-funded pure research will only be known from the industry's success in the years to come.

A risk area is the natural desire of governments to hold down their health costs. Ten per cent of the National Health Service budget goes on the purchase of drugs. So Britain and other countries attempt to impose price freezes, or limit the patent life of drugs, or recommend approved lists of cheaper drugs. Various governments have tried these different solutions, though nothing is as simple as it seems. The new blood-clot-dissolving treatments, only recently introduced, cost over £2200 a shot. While that seems expensive, is it really so if heart attack patients only spend seven or eight days in hospital, and not nine or ten?

So there is plenty of meat here for research. *The Economist* reported twenty brokers in London alone following just eight drug companies. Though many of these analysts were reported to have scientific qualifications – essential to understanding the risks and opportunities faced by the companies in their research efforts – apparently only half of them have been doing the job for longer than two years. Yet developing and bringing a new drug family to market can take decades rather than years, and research is a continuous process.

Share prices in what was once a relatively humdrum and solid industry sector have now become more volatile. Regular and frequent reports on the medical success and profitable marketing of a range of unpronounceable new drugs is one factor causing this. Currency movements are another. As a worldwide business, health profits are affected by currency changes. Companies take different approaches to this problem. Some believe that attempts to manage 'currency risk' are as likely to end up wrong as right while others take a more determined approach. It certainly adds to the complexities of forecasting profits for finance directors, let alone analysts.

The effects of fashion on prices

Market sentiment is equally important in deciding on who is 'in' and who 'out' as the pharmaceutical companies clearly show. Fashion should never be forgotten for it is the unmentioned but potent element in the pricing of any security. Fashion has become even more important with the increased international ownership of the larger companies. Wellcome and Glaxo are two of Britain's best-known, and most heavily traded, pharmaceutical companies.

AIDS has done wonders for the Wellcome share price, and they are now selling on a PER of 44 or nearly four times more than the PER of 12.89 for the industrial sector of the market, and two-and-a-half times the 17.52 PER for the health and household sector. This price is based on the expectation of an explosive growth in profits from Retrovir, which is not a cure but only an ameliorative treatment for AIDS, in the next few years.

But will these profits, when they do arise, persuade the market to maintain this rating, improve it, or decide that Wellcome has gone 'ex-growth' – that although profits are growing these are not increasing fast enough to justify the price? Will no better solution for AIDS appear over the next year or two, and put at risk this source of monopoly earnings? Who can possibly tell – certainly not analysts since they are no more blessed with the powers of the soothsayer than any of the rest of us. If historical probability is our best guide, then the omens are not hopeful.

So bright did the future of Glaxo appear two years ago that the market was prepared to buy the shares on a PER of over 25. The company produced the results promised by it, but the market decided they were not as good as expected, and that the company had misled it. Now Glaxo is selling on a 14 PER, not much above the market as a whole and a twenty-five per cent discount to the health sector.

As the Datastream price chart shows, the market certainly marched Glaxo right up to the top of the hill – and then all the way down the other side. Yet Glaxo has not changed, and still remains an excellent and highly profitable drugs company. Sooner or later this lovers' tiff will be made up, and Glaxo will again be selling at the sector average. Why should this same fate not await Wellcome? All market probabilities say it will: only hope says that Wellcome will buck history.

Analysis and the investor

The Goldman Sachs study showed how equity markets as a whole seem to lose contact with valuation benchmarks on a regular basis. This is even more the case with individual shares because the very quality of company analysis suggests that the future is known, is profitable, and will become even better.

None of this is so. It is just that we want to believe that it is. It makes investment decisions that much easier for now they seem 'scientific' or logical, and a long way removed from putting a fiver on the favourite for the Gold Cup.

Figure 14: Comparative share price performance of Wellcome and Glaxo.

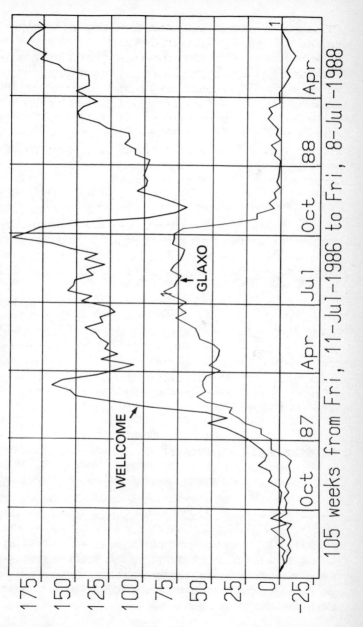

105 weeks from Fri, 11-Jul-1986 to Fri, 8-Jul-1988

Source: Finstat

What goes up must come down

A friend, and most successful investor, trained his juniors by asking them to choose between two possible investments. One had an exceptional five-year record of earnings and dividend growth, was seen as a leader in an attractive industry, and was highly rated by investors. The other, the major company of its declining industry, had shown little growth in earnings and, because of its unpopularity with investors, was selling on a high dividend yield and low PER.

Nearly all chose the first company, with good conformist reasons on why the lower dividend yield was perfectly acceptable because of the greater growth prospects. My friend would then show them how over the next five years the shares of a revitalised Imperial Tobacco – the second company – performed very much better than those of Marks & Spencer. These remained virtually unchanged because, although M&S profits continued to grow, the share rating was so high that all this growth was already discounted in the share price.

The moral of this story is that life contains a particularly unpleasant statistical pothole called 'regression to the mean'. Some of our friends are exceptionally tall, and some short. Generally, the children of very tall parents are shorter than their parents, while the opposite is true of the children of short parents.

In financial terms, regression to the mean ensures that, while companies can produce extraordinarily high returns for some time, they will not do it for ever: sooner, rather than later, their return on assets will fall to the average for industry. The same is true of companies that produce below average returns. Competition sees that this is so. In one case new entrants will increase competition while in the other new managers or owners will improve efficiency.

What is true today is not necessarily true tomorrow

Regression to the mean suggests a need for caution in our assumptions about the future. Extrapolating present trends forward is all too easy to do unconsciously, simply because of the amount of data that a company researcher must handle. This has further dangers for the investor.

To do this is to allow present-day fashion to influence our judgement. We ignore past probabilities, and the outcome of similar cases to the one we are studying, and concentrate all our efforts on the particular facts of the case in front of us. By concentrating on present activities, and projecting them into the future, we rely entirely on our perceptions. These are influenced by the perceptions of others.

Less than twenty years ago, the largest US banks and trust companies decided there was only one way to invest. This was to pick the best capitalised, and most significant companies in selected industries – or the 'nifty fifty' – out of the twelve thousand or so quoted US companies. PERs for these 'champions' were driven to 40, 50, even 60 and, naturally, research brokers supported such valuations with forecasts of exceptional profit growth.

Alas for hope – reality intervened, profits were ordinary, the bear market of 1973–74 arrived, PERs went back to long run averages of 12 to 14, and the 'nifty fifty' cost their illustrious investors eighty per cent of their capital.

And does analysis actually work?

There is another problem with analysis of future earnings. No one likes to talk about this as some desirable and well paid jobs depend on believing the contrary.

Some years ago Professor Ian Little* of Oxford, later followed by American researchers, investigated the relationship of previous year profits with current year out-turns. It seems that, statistically, there is no evidence that what a company made last year has any relevance to what it will make this year. Sad for analysts, if true, and no one has yet refuted these findings.

The investor through the looking glass

But let's assume the analyst can actually identify those companies which will increase their profits significantly faster than the average. Even this is not sufficient, for the analyst must both identify a

---

* *Higgledy Piggledy Growth*, I M D Little. Oxford Institute of Statistics 1962.
Higgledy Piggledy Growth Again, with A C Rayner. Blackwell 1966.

growth company and also outguess the market. Will investors, when they see the figures, decide to maintain the current ranking of the shares? Will they re-evaluate the company and, if so, will this result in a higher or lower rating for the shares?

Many an investor has been disappointed when the share price of a company goes down, despite better than expected results, but this is a central part of that pricing process. What has happened is past; the only relevance of these figures is in the help they may give in assessing future profitability.

This factor is based both on market reason and market emotion. Its workings can be seen particularly clearly with mining companies, whose shares seem to do so much better in the exploration phase, than when they have a working mine. The reason is that our dreams – the expectation of the profits that will be made – are always more intense than reality can ever be. Though it is reality in the end that sets the level of prices, it is the dreams that fuel the activity between times.

Analysts, like any other investor, are influenced by the general mood. In the context of the financial markets, this is known as market sentiment. Our decisions about possible investment action are shaped by the way we habitually think. Our thinking is influenced by the immediate past, and the views of others. The mutual dependency of our thinking creates market sentiment. Market sentiment is based on either fear or greed.

The strength of such raw emotions ensures that we forget past probabilities, and so the influence these should have on our judgements of present and future values. In short, sentiment steamrollers common sense into oblivion. As the Burmese proverb has it: 'Man fears the tiger that bit him last, not the tiger which will bite him next.'

The danger is not of buying some comparatively over-priced shares. This is bound to happen to all investors. The real risk for us, as investors, is of being deceived by a financial bubble. This happens quite regularly, and the rise in the first months of 1987 was a mild example of how the madness of crowds can make even the most sensible of us do foolish things. When perceptions change, panics follow. This is why investment disciplines are so important.

Checkpoints

• Regression to the mean tells us to treat all forecasts with respect, but also some scepticism, and not to believe in futures that look too exciting and profitable. Reality will never match our dreams.

• Remember that stock markets never deal in absolute values, only relative values, and our investment choice should always be based on the best return we can get for our money.

• Since share prices depend on future dividends then 'a bird in the hand is worth two in the bush' often applies to stock exchange investments, so we need to understand earnings per share.

• We never need to justify our actions to superiors or customers, so we have no excuse for losing money by following the 'in-crowd' and will not do so provided we understand PERs as a standard of relative value.

• KISS is American management shorthand for 'Keep It Simple, Stupid' and, if we remember that, we can stay in control of our investments. Control is the beginning of investment success.

Notes: interpreting the FTA

The table shows the categories into which all quoted shares are classified, but many large companies are too complicated to be easily categorised while small companies are generally *sui generis*. So don't take sectors too seriously. The numbers in brackets are the number of companies within each sector, whose shares are used to compile the index.

The first column is the index for yesterday, followed by the change that day from the previous day. The last four columns are for the index over the last three trading days, and a year ago.

The third column is the earnings yield; this is earnings per share expressed as a yield on the market price of the share, and is comparable to the dividend yield. It is what the company could theoretically pay to us, without reducing the value of its assets, if the directors felt very generous and had neither the desire nor the need to spend money on new buildings and machinery over and above 'tax depreciation' or what the Inland Revenue think they need to spend.

Figure 15

FT – ACTUARIES INDICES

These Indices are the joint compilation of the Financial Times, the Institute of Actuaries and the Faculty of Actuaries

EQUITY GROUPS & SUB-SECTIONS	Thursday July 14 1988						Wed Jul 13	Tue Jul 12	Mon Jul 11	Year ago (approx)
Figures in parentheses show number of stocks per section	Index No.	Day's Change %	Est. Earnings Yield% (Max.)	Gross Div. Yield% (Act at 25%)	Est. P/E Ratio (Net)	xd adj. 1988 to date	Index No.	Index No.	Index No.	Index No.
1 **CAPITAL GOODS** (208)	808.23	−0.1	9.89	3.92	12.54	13.72	809.16	804.80	810.59	1038.07
2 Building Materials (29)	1016.69	−0.2	11.07	4.16	11.10	18.34	1018.31	1013.35	1030.05	1381.08
3 Contracting, Construction (36)	1577.20	....	10.39	3.41	12.58	26.35	1577.46	1584.48	1593.52	1951.50
4 Electricals (12)	2183.31	+0.3	8.65	4.57	14.30	48.13	2176.21	2157.43	2159.36	2706.42
5 Electronics (31)	1757.53	−0.6	9.70	3.38	13.24	21.30	1768.05	1749.30	1749.88	2205.81
6 Mechanical Engineering (56)	428.23	+0.1	9.46	4.08	13.09	8.05	427.80	426.03	427.51	541.14
8 Metals and Metal Forming (7)	509.92	+0.8	9.11	3.67	13.53	7.95	505.87	500.88	505.64	588.17
9 Motors (14)	286.01	+0.3	11.44	4.48	10.12	5.22	285.19	286.23	288.71	406.20
10 Other Industrial Materials (23)	1332.41	−0.2	8.75	4.16	13.64	25.61	1334.73	1323.61	1338.61	1712.49
21 **CONSUMER GROUP (187)**	1102.04	−0.2	8.93	3.56	14.15	16.74	1104.60	1096.90	1107.60	1406.32
22 Brewers and Distillers (21)	1114.86	−0.9	10.67	3.65	11.83	15.97	1124.47	1120.03	1134.18	1269.35
25 Food Manufacturing (22)	1001.05	....	8.67	3.61	14.76	17.07	1001.59	996.90	997.92	1092.25
26 Food Retailing (16)	2024.22	+1.2	8.57	3.29	15.45	21.46	2000.41	2002.24	2021.06	2649.96
27 Health and Household (12)	1878.17	−0.4	6.62	2.60	17.52	17.98	1886.17	1876.60	1906.54	2699.85
29 Leisure (30)	1347.20	−0.2	8.52	3.70	14.77	24.33	1350.45	1345.48	1360.27	1480.59
31 Packaging & Paper (17)	530.51	−0.6	9.18	3.79	14.00	9.15	533.50	529.40	536.35	739.48
32 Publishing & Printing (18)	3518.33	−0.1	8.08	4.34	15.61	70.60	3520.67	3502.52	3539.45	4564.47
34 Stores (34)	813.93	−0.6	10.21	3.95	12.94	14.50	818.85	801.53	806.74	1157.89
35 Textiles (17)	607.20	....	11.35	4.48	10.35	12.34	607.19	604.69	612.29	864.21
40 **OTHER GROUPS (93)**	914.31	−0.1	10.66	4.27	11.51	12.00	915.02	909.93	917.26	1192.30
41 Agencies (19)	1177.95	−1.1	7.40	2.31	17.06	12.99	1191.07	1194.11	1204.59	1785.00
42 Chemicals (21)	1088.13	−0.4	11.10	4.52	11.01	22.34	1092.98	1084.65	1097.84	1471.02
43 Conglomerates (13)	1218.81	+0.2	10.18	4.36	11.36	20.98	1216.77	1206.14	1224.40	1546.12
45 Shipping and Transport (12)	1925.93	+0.5	11.11	4.65	11.91	34.04	1915.66	1901.19	1908.47	2497.85
47 Telephone Networks (2)	994.16	....	11.20	4.48	11.59	2.32	994.04	991.43	993.03	1164.15
48 Miscellaneous (26)	1198.59	+0.1	11.22	4.30	10.17	20.41	1197.50	1188.28	1198.43	1711.29
49 **INDUSTRIAL GROUP (488)**	987.01	−0.2	9.66	3.85	12.89	14.90	988.57	982.49	990.94	1268.86
51 Oil & Gas (12)	1833.20	−0.7	10.92	5.81	11.77	39.80	1846.28	1830.50	1855.22	2458.68
59 **500 SHARE INDEX (500)**	1058.80	−0.2	9.84	4.12	12.72	17.04	1061.30	1054.40	1064.20	1369.88

EQUITY GROUPS & SUB-SECTIONS	Thursday July 14 1988						Wed Jul 13	Tue Jul 12	Mon Jul 11	Year ago (approx)
Figures in parentheses show number of stocks per section	Index No.	Day's Change %	Est. Earnings Yield% (Max.)	Gross Div. Yield% (Act at 25%)	Est. P/E Ratio (Net)	xd adj. 1988 to date	Index No.	Index No.	Index No.	Index No.
61 FINANCIAL GROUP (121)	714.73	−0.7	–	4.76	–	15.23	719.65	715.92	717.01	882.11
62 Banks (8)	683.67	−0.7	20.94	6.14	6.40	18.03	688.51	682.75	683.85	898.38
65 Insurance (Life) (8)	1063.36	−0.5	–	4.72	–	24.97	1068.79	1064.46	1068.34	1190.53
66 Insurance (Composite) (7)	555.53	−0.4	–	5.33	–	13.82	557.88	557.43	557.19	647.13
67 Insurance (Brokers) (7)	1010.63	−0.2	9.53	6.30	13.55	31.54	1012.98	1000.60	1007.09	1365.34
68 Merchant Banks (11)	363.13	+0.1	–	3.98	–	7.03	362.71	J55.86	355.59	489.75
69 Property (50)	1230.60	−1.3	5.02	2.62	25.55	13.26	1246.89	1244.86	1250.17	1374.86
70 Other Financial (30)	394.62	−0.2	9.93	4.78	12.62	8.97	395.42	394.21	391.39	603.48
71 Investment Trusts (78)	934.07	−0.2	–	2.92	–	11.85	935.58	931.14	931.77	1149.12
81 Mining Finance (2)	522.70	−1.1	9.16	3.60	12.34	8.12	528.39	523.13	532.27	622.46
91 Overseas Traders (8)	1183.00	+0.2	9.74	4.72	12.07	29.22	1180.35	1173.34	1193.37	1197.17
99 ALL-SHARE INDEX (709)	969.47	−0.3	–	4.18	–	16.35	972.51	966.41	974.10	1238.57

	Index No.	Day's Change	Day's High	Day's Low	Jul 13	Jul 12	Jul 11	Jul 8	Jul 7	Year ago
FT-SE 100 SHARE INDEX	1863.3	−8.0	1875.6	1863.3	1871.3	1858.5	1876.8	1877.2	1855.5	2443.4

FIXED INTEREST

PRICE INDICES	Thu Jul 14	Day's change %	Wed Jul 13	xd adj. today	xd adj. 1988 to date
British Government					
1 5 years	120.71	−0.06	120.78	–	6.14
2 5–15 years	136.60	−0.02	136.62	–	7.17
3 Over 15 years	147.12	+0.03	147.08	–	6.88
4 Irredeemables	163.02	+0.02	162.98	–	7.30
5 All stocks	134.05	−0.02	134.08	–	6.81
Index-Linked					
6 5 years	128.08	−0.02	128.11	–	1.12
7 Over 5 years	119.76	−0.07	119.84	–	1.89
8 All stocks	120.29	−0.06	120.36	–	1.82
9 Debentures & Loans	117.69	+0.01	117.68	–	6.47
10 Preference	93.03	−0.59	93.59	–	3.31

AVERAGE GROSS REDEMPTION YIELDS			Thu Jul 14	Wed Jul 13	Year ago (approx)
British Government					
1 Low		5 years	9.56	9.54	8.08
2 Coupons		15 years	9.46	9.46	8.85
3		25 years	9.22	9.22	8.86
4 Medium		5 years	10.03	10.01	8.96
5 Coupons		15 years	9.69	9.69	9.08
6		25 years	9.41	9.42	9.09
7 High		5 years	10.13	10.09	9.13
8 Coupons		15 years	9.85	9.86	9.23
9		25 years	9.49	9.50	9.04
10 Irredeemables			9.63	9.60	8.77
Index-Linked					
11 Inflation rate 5%		5 yrs.	2.69	2.67	2.35
12 Inflation rate 5%		Over 5 yrs.	3.91	3.90	3.74
13 Inflation rate 10%		5 yrs.	1.74	1.72	2.08
14 Inflation rate 10%		Over 5 yrs.	3.75	3.74	3.69
15 Debs &		5 years	10.84	10.83	10.12
16 Loans		15 years	10.79	10.80	10.12
17		25 years	10.79	10.80	10.12
18 Preference			9.67	9.62	10.24

Source: FT

Some investors feel that when the earnings yield is less than the yield on the 'long, or twenty-five years and over, bond' the equity market is cheap. They believe that the correct market comparison is between the earnings yield – or what a company is earning for us and could pay out – and the gilt yield. Others consider the only true comparison is between what we actually get: that means the dividend yield is the comparison as there are too many unknowns for us ever to be confident that we will get our hands on a company's earnings.

The PER is, in theory, the reciprocal of the earnings yield. However, the FTA calculates PERs net of tax while earnings yields are calculated before tax so simple conversion won't do.

The fourth column is the gross dividend yield, or yield before Advanced Corporation Tax at twenty-five per cent. Non-taxpayers can reclaim this tax on their dividends. This is an important comparative for anything we think of buying: the dividend yield on the market has averaged 4.3 per cent over the last five years, and 5.3 per cent over the last fifty. By dividing the earnings yield by the dividend yield we get the 'cover' or leeway of safety before earnings drop so much that the dividend is in danger of being reduced. 'Cover' figures for individual shares are given in the *FT* price tables.

Next comes the PER for sectors but not the 710 shares of the FTA All Share; PERs are not published for some of the Financial Group, though calculated by analysts. The figure most commonly used is the PER of the Industrial Group though sometimes the '500' is used. The former, together with the Health and Household sector PER, was the comparative used to look at Wellcome and Glaxo.

The remaining column no doubt has a value but not one that I have ever understood. It shows the needed adjustment to the index, from the start of the year, to account for shares going 'ex-dividend'. This is the moment a company pays its dividend and, in theory if not in practice, share prices should fall by the amount of the dividend paid out.

Finally, the bottom of the table shows index values for gilts and corporate fixed interest issues – debentures, unsecured loans or corporate bonds, and preference shares – and also redemption yields by class of bond. A fuller description of this market is in Chapter Seven.

Chapter Four

A spectre haunts
the markets

Another toreador appears on the scene, earnestly trying to keep composed. He wavers as to how best to secure a profit, chews his nails, pulls his fingers, closes his eyes, takes four paces and four times talks to himself, raises his hand to his cheek as if he had a toothache, puts on a thoughtful countenance, sticks out a finger, rubs his brow, and all this accompanied by a mysterious coughing as though he could force the hand of fortune. Suddenly he rushes with violent gestures into the crowd, snaps with the fingers of one hand while with the other he makes a contemptuous gesture, and begins to deal in shares as though they were custard.

CONFUSION DE CONFUSIONES, 1688

Uncertainty as to the future, and fear of its possible outcome, remain as potent today as when, three hundred years ago, Joseph de la Vega was placing his orders on the floor of the Amsterdam Stock Exchange. Today's dealer sits in front of a computer screen, but in all other respects behaviour has remained constant. When this anxiety is combined, as it is in stock markets, with large numbers of people and intense excitement, then the possibility of a 'bubble' and its subsequent panic is always present.

Crowds do not always go mad over financial matters,* but money

---

* *Extraordinary Popular Delusions and the Madness of Crowds*, Charles Mackay 1841. Farrar Strauss & Giroux, New edition Farrar Strauss & Giroux, New York 1986.

and madness certainly seem to have an affinity. This may be for the reasons given by French psychologist Gustave Le Bon* some hundred years ago. According to Le Bon, once we become part of a gathering, we begin to lose our individuality and in the emotion of the moment 'a collective mind is formed, doubtless transitory, but presenting very defined characteristics.' Once this 'psychological crowd' is formed, then it 'thinks in images, and the image itself calls up a series of other images, having no logical connection with the first' and 'accepts as real the images invoked in its mind, though they most often have only a very distant relation with the observed facts.'

These images, and Le Bon likened them to magic lantern slides in a darkened room, are simple, dramatic, and apparently infallible. The combination creates enormous emotional energy, for good or bad, which is hardly to be gainsaid by cold and precise reason. Crowd behaviour analysed by Le Bon appears so frequently amongst the faithful – whether of a church, political party, football team or fighting unit – that it excites little comment.

What more enticing an image than instant riches, or more terrifying than immediate ruin? None of us should be surprised that 'only capable of thinking in images [we] are only to be impressed by images.' Indeed, stockbrokers have long recognised that a 'story' sells a security more satisfactorily than comparative figures and a market saying goes: 'It's ideas which fuel the market; the figures can always be made to fit the ideas.'

The need for belief, and validation by experts

Stock markets operate for much of the time on belief. The past, whether of an economy or a company, can be dissected and examined; the present can be assumed to be a little better or worse than the past depending on current political and economic policies; the future can only be guessed. Only astrologers claim expertise in foretelling and, though it is rumoured that a surprisingly large number of bankers and stockbrokers use such occult aids, there is no evidence that they are any better investors than the rest of us.

---

* *The Crowd*, Gustave Le Bon, 1895.

Naturally, in this uncertainty, we look to experts to validate our hopes or fears even if, in our ignorance, we accept as 'experts' those with a glibber tongue or louder voice than the rest of us. Even professionals fool themselves this way, for analytical work is only as good as the assumptions made, and analysts are subject to the same emotional pressures as the rest of us – indeed, probably more so.

Few of us really wish to be 'loners', and there is considerable pressure to ascribe to the values of the group, particularly for those who have careers to mind. So the psychologists say that, as soon as we find ourselves in emotionally intense but uncertain circumstances, we suspend our own judgement. We know that to be flawed; we assume others know more than us. Sometimes we are right, and they do. More often, they just seem more authoritative, and talk loudly to maintain their own courage and beliefs.

Bankers who were old enough to know better, and certainly senior enough to have no career worries, defended in front of the US Congress their investment policy of the 'nifty fifty'. Today few research brokers can be found to doubt the value of Wellcome on a PER of 44. This is possibly correct for their own career: investment managers who pursue their own investment course, even if later proved correct, often lose their clients, for though their policy is right, their fashion is wrong. So validation of our belief by experts frequently turns out to be a case of:

> Dogs and cats have fleas
> upon their backs to bite 'em
> And greater fleas have lesser fleas
> and so *ad infinitum*

One of the more noticeable aspects of 'bubbles' is the willingness of everyone, not so much to forget the past, as to use it to show that conditions have changed fundamentally, and that former valuation systems no longer have validity. It always happens, partly because the images are so strong that it is impossible to fight them so our reason forces us to justify them, and partly because we do not want to be the outsider.

Only the most emotionally masochistic amongst us wishes to be a Cassandra while everyone else is rejoicing – she, after all, had an excuse, for the Gods had laid a curse upon her. It is not only that

that sort of spectre is unwelcome at the feast: even worse, when things later do go wrong, our gloom is remembered and held against us even more. Financial success bought at the cost of friendship can seem expensive indeed.

Not everyone gets carried away by the mood of the moment, but this should worry us even more. Professional investors, particularly, continue to buy when they know that prices are too high. They operate the 'bigger fool' system: while the price is ridiculous, they can still take a profit from the market's euphoria because there will always be a bigger fool to buy from them. For the professional dealer we are the bigger fool.

The pricking of the bubble

1987 was a good bubble. Commentators predicted, with the most scientific of arguments, that valuation standards had changed because of the investment needs of the Japanese economy. The effect of this 'wall of money' would fundamentally change American and European investment returns.

This argument conveniently ignored the experience of Victorian Britain. Proportionately, this had an even bigger difficulty than Japan has today in finding a home for its savings. However, that experience showed that young and vibrant economies have no problems in finding ways to invest. Stock exchanges only become really important when banks and businesses no longer handle efficiently the conversion of savings into productive manufacturing capacity and the development of new markets. There is no sign of this happening in Japan.

By summer 1987, equity markets had risen by about fifty per cent in six months. Market prophets were promising further substantial rises in the indices. It is not true that we never learn: last year the prophets were protecting their backs with the bigger fool hypothesis. The markets would rise until, in 1988, the bull market 'topped out' but their followers, forewarned by them, could safely ride the updraft until told to bale out.

Preparations were already in hand to switch one of Le Bon's 'magic lantern slides' and with it the crowd's master image. There has been a worm at the heart of the nineteen-eighties economic expansion. But because the situation is so new, and there is neither agreement on what the problem is, nor how to deal with it, no one can predict the resolution of the difficulties that have now surfaced.

The dollar was weak for most of 1987. Japanese private investors refused to countenance further losses on their portfolios of US bonds, and stopped buying at the regular auctions held by the US Treasury. Governments stepped in to fill this vacuum; central banks supported the dollar, and bought US Treasury bonds instead. There was a cost to this, for the support of the dollar put the anti-inflationary policies of the German and the Japanese governments at risk.

Then, during the summer, bond prices around the world suddenly fell. Investors panicked as they began to comprehend the weakness of the dollar, and wondered how much longer world economic expansion could continue. This was bound to spell trouble for equity markets since the relationship of equity to bond yields had already become strained.

According to Goldman Sachs, the dividend yield of 2.9 per cent on the London market had never been lower since the nineteen-twenties. The gilt yield was 6.6 per cent more than the equity yield; the difference between the two yields had only been greater in seven of the last sixty-four years. Economic conditions were good, but future expansion scarcely justified this level of expectation.

The changed economic reality

The early nineteen-seventies saw the end of the great economic boom which had transformed most of our lives. The oil price rises of 1973 onwards, together with a continuation of economic policies which had outlived their usefulness, ushered in several years of fast rising prices which destroyed savings and threatened living standards. This inflation also had a serious impact on company balance sheets, particularly those of the banks.

So, by the end of the nineteen-seventies, most Western governments knew they had to act to get inflation under control. The rallying cry was 'supply side economics'. By this was meant a reduction of government regulation of the economy, taxes which were neutral rather than designed to bring about socially desirable ends, privatisation of government-owned businesses, and strict control of government spending. There was a scrapping of financial controls.

Removing restrictions on the freedom to move money to wherever the owners wished would ensure that capital went to the most efficient, or profitable, markets. Freely floating currencies would penalise those businessmen who allowed their costs to get out of hand, as foreign firms moved into their markets with the advantage of lower costs. This would also put pressure on uncooperative work forces, as ultimately employers could move their activities to countries with more efficient labour markets.

Increased business competition would stimulate efficient production, and this more productive supply of goods and services would bring prices under control. The short term cost might be high – the bankruptcy of individual firms and higher levels of unemployment as greater competition bit – but in the long term a healthier economy would benefit everyone. That was the theory and, to a great extent, it worked. However, reality, and particularly the financial markets, had a few tricks the theorists overlooked.

The debt crisis and the threat to the banking system

This leaner and more efficient developed world bit particularly hard at the under-developed world, and especially the countries of Latin America. Slower world growth stifled the exports on which their economic prosperity depended, and lowered their foreign currency earnings. At the same time, these tighter money policies increased interest rates. Countries which had borrowed from the international banking community when rates were negative – in other words when the rate of inflation was higher than the rate of interest charged on the loan – now found themselves paying real rates of interest.

Furthermore these real interest rates – ie the cost of the loan less the rate of inflation – were well above both the long-term cost of capital and the economic growth rates of the borrowing countries. The effect of this meant that debts were soon increasing faster than they could be repaid. The banks, who had encouraged their customers to borrow in the expectation that loans would never be recalled but 'rolled over' into new ones, now wanted their money back.

The home of supply-side economics was America, and 'reagan-omics' was the name given to it. Latin America has always been North America's backyard, the natural trading partner and largest user of North American manufacturing skills and capital. So, when a full-scale debt crisis surfaced in 1982, American banks were more deeply involved than all others. New York looked set for a repeat showing of a typical nineteenth-century London bank crisis, even down to the same Latin American countries repudiating the same type of international debt.

The heavy commitments of all the major US banks to these countries made such a resolution unthinkable. The over-exposure of many of them to this type of business was such that repudiation of these debts would have bankrupted several, with unknown consequences for America and the rest of the world. The damage inflicted on the American economy could have crippled the West, and would have made the 1929–32 banking crisis seem minor by comparison.

Control of the American money supply was eased. Some brutal arm-twisting by the US government persuaded the banks to make further loans to these less developed countries – LDCs in banking jargon – so that outstanding interest could be paid. This meant that all involved could then pretend that the loans were good. Given time, and some economic improvement, these countries should be able to get their finances back into shape.

Just in case this happy scenario turned out to be over-optimistic, the banks got down to making some serious money so that they would be able, in time, to write off these debts. This seemed relatively painless to do. The dollar was at an all-time high as, with the new economic policies in place, America became the 'in-place'.

Investors the world over bought dollars to invest in America, either directly in property and businesses, or indirectly through the security markets. While some gloomy economists argued that this high comparative valuation of the dollar was damaging America's productive capacity, at least as many could be found to argue the other way.

Dollar strength, and the perverting of the American boom

No one listened because everyone benefited. The American government, despite the rhetoric of 'reaganomics' did not actually cut spending and, with the further loosening of money supply necessitated by the debt crisis, the economy began to grow rapidly. The dollar was high compared to other currencies, so foreign goods and holidays looked cheap to the American consumer.

The high dollar made the American market irresistibly attractive to overseas manufacturers because of the profits they could make. The rest of the world concentrated on supplying the inexhaustible appetite of the American market for foreign goods, and the banking system financed this consumer boom.

American industry lost out. By 1982 Wall Street had been going gently sideways, with the occasional sharp downward collapse, for sixteen years. It was 22 per cent lower than the 'high' of 1964 and, adjusted for inflation, lower than it was in 1951 or even December 1929. Major American companies were selling on dividend yields of 7 per cent or more, with PERs as low as 3 or 4, and often at less than net asset value.

Buying assets cheaply, splitting them up into smaller lots, and selling them on more expensively is one of the classic manoeuvres of stock exchange activity. The banks were willing to lend, so takeovers flourished. Since the high dollar made it hard for US companies to compete in their own home market, let alone anywhere else, companies with unwelcome bidders found it difficult to fight them off with promises of better profits. All they could do was to cut back on spending for the future, and make themselves look as good as possible. Share prices began to go up, and investors finally felt richer.

Then the corporate raiders had a brilliant idea. Buying and reorganising companies takes time, and is hard work. Since neither boards of directors, nor senior managers, like losing their jobs and perks, why take over the company when its managers could be forced to do it for you? Companies were blackmailed – though the term used was 'greenmailed' – into 'restructuring' themselves by increasing indebtedness, reducing their equity by buying back their shares, and selling off assets.

'Greenmailing' was profitable for banks, stockbrokers and

shareholders. 'Risk arbitragers' built up positions in a company, and then forced it to borrow enormous sums from the banks – often the same as those financing the arbitragers – in order to buy back its own shares at greatly increased prices. Rather more than 10 per cent by value of the equity quoted on Wall Street disappeared this way during these years. This was good, too. The price of what was left went up even more. Everyone felt richer still, and went out and spent more.

There was a disadvantage. Part of the economic justification for bull markets is that they allow companies to raise new capital cheaply, with which to pay off outstanding debt, improve the efficiency of factories and machinery, and invest in new products and markets.

But at the very time that corporate America should have been strengthening balance sheets and competitive edge, it was forced to do the very opposite. As the great boom rolled on, foreign competitors captured more and more American markets. The trade deficit got bigger as American firms sold less at home and abroad, while American consumers became hooked on imported goods.

Disenchantment with America

As the decade grew older, so America's budget deficit, which is the difference between what is raised in taxes and what is spent by the government, got bigger. So did the trade deficit or the difference between what is earned in foreign currencies and what is paid. The fact that there is a budget deficit means there is a shortfall of 'savings' within the economy, so the current account deficit has to be financed by attracting overseas investors instead. In the early years, such investors queued up to finance the trade deficit by buying US Treasury bonds.

The years went by, and the two deficits continued to increase. From 1985 onwards America ceased to be the world's major creditor and instead became the world's largest debtor. As the size and permanence of these deficits became obvious, overseas investors lost their enthusiasm for US bonds and the dollar.

Interest rates were increased to attract more investors, but a 50 per cent decline in the value of the dollar against the yen and the deutschmark in a period of two years more than wiped out the extra interest for non-dollar investors. Other countries could not stand idly by as the value of the dollar declined. It put their exports to America at risk and if, in consequence, their exporters did worse, then it increased their already high unemployment.

When her allies remonstrated with America over these 'imbalances' on the trading accounts between them, the American answer was that there would be no problem if only they would expand their own economies. Then either America would sell more to them, or their manufacturers could concentrate on their home markets and so sell less to America: either way, these current account imbalances would then disappear.

This meant other countries, and particularly Europe, expanding their economies in the old nineteen-seventies style. They saw this as putting their anti-inflationary policies at risk. Their view was that America should increase taxes, and cut back on government spending. Then the imbalances would disappear without causing inflation for other countries. It is not only that America and its allies disagree on the solution to the problem: they find it hard to agree on what the problem is.

If the world's banker is imprudent, who is safe?

Solutions are complicated also by America's role as the home of the dollar. At the end of the Second World War this took over from the pound sterling as the world trading and reserve currency. Since a reserve currency is that in which other central banks hold their 'reserves' – or national cash balances – this means that if America feels like printing more dollars to pay its debts, it does so.

Nor can a balance of payments crisis of the sort that plagued Britain (until the development of North Sea oil) influence America. Holders of the pound sterling – and most other currencies – can if they disapprove of government policy buy dollars (or deutschmarks or yen) and sell sterling. Most governments have to remain conscious of the effect their policies will have on the world financial community.

There is, as yet, no alternative to the dollar as the 'world' currency. In the past governmental authorities were constrained by national legal requirements that they back the issue of printed money with gold. American governments many years ago got rid of any constitutional requirement to back the dollar with gold. About the only thing that can influence American policy is an investors' 'strike' of the sort that took place in 1987.

This is less than satisfactory for, unable to finance the deficit, America would be forced back onto policies that would disrupt world economic growth. So the strike meant that the central banks of the leading industrial countries had to finance the American trade deficit instead. No one likes feeling helpless, and this certainly worsened relationships between legislators and central bankers, particularly those of America with the only other two economic superpowers – Germany and Japan.

Economic power and the financial markets

Investors strive for certainty, even while they know it is beyond their power to achieve it. Dividends depend upon earnings. These company profits are the result of national prosperity. This depends upon a peaceful and cooperative world with free flows of trade and finance between all areas. Such a world has, in the past, revolved around a particular currency and country.

During the nineteenth century, Britain was this power, and gold-backed sterling was the currency. Though other countries developed strong economies, and investment markets of their own, London was the piper to whose tune all others danced. This was because London was the creator of the savings that flooded out to finance the first stage of the world's industrialisation.

By the beginning of this century British industrial vitality had declined, and America and Germany were evolving as the new superpowers. The First World War showed up the serious weaknesses of the British economy, and its inability to support a modern war. Britain was forced to look to America for the money and the weapons needed to hold back German expansion.

Between the two world wars, though America and Britain battled for financial supremacy, there were few doubts about the outcome. Wall Street and the dollar became influential in world financial affairs. Any remaining doubts were resolved during the Second World War. By 1945, America was preeminent industrially and financially. American savings and know-how reconstructed a devastated world. Since then it has been Wall Street's financial chills that have given the rest of the world influenza.

New investment uncertainties

The post-war reconstruction propelled Germany and Japan into economic superpower status. In the last five years Japan has become the vital nucleus around which the Pacific economies are developing. Germany is the economic and financial heavyweight of a Europe which, in contrast to the Pacific and even to America, seems to be suffering from 'eurosclerosis'.

Japan has also become banker to America and in three years has accumulated more overseas assets than Britain did in three hundred. Although today's money is worth rather less than Victoria's sovereigns, that is still a most remarkable achievement.

There is no evidence that the American economy shares the deep-seated social and educational weaknesses that destroyed British economic power and will in the twentieth century. Indeed, the Americans show no real desire to share financial or political leadership with Japan or Germany let alone abdicate present authority because of current financial weakness.

American attitudes to foreign capital a century ago, when Britain was America's banker as Japan is today, were very hostile. The battle for economic supremacy, if economic struggle rather than cooperation it is to be, will last well into the next century. Though such questions seem far removed from which share we should buy, the answers will help determine the profitability of that choice.

To which centre must investors now look for a lead? Can America, Japan and Germany run a world in which there is no leading economic power? If there is increasing tension between these economic superpowers, will that mean an increase in trade protectionism, and a return to the economic nationalism of the nineteen-thirties?

Might increased currency instability bring back a return of high inflation? Will this mean an end to economic expansion? What will that mean in terms of company profits, and unemployment? If employment suffers further because of slowing economic growth, could this bring a return to political extremism, and instability? There are many matters here to give investors sleepless nights.

How long will the bear market last?

Bernard Jones is an historian of stock markets, as well as an experienced analyst. As head of the technical analysis department at Kleinwort Grieveson, he has examined the London stock market since the First World War for 'bear market' behaviour. Interestingly, he found no definition of a bear market; up to the nineteentwenties, falling markets were described simply as 'panics'. 'Bear' then came to be used and understood but never described. He has now defined a 'bear' market as a period of declining prices exceeding six months, and has reviewed the twelve that have occurred since 1920.

The average bear market is of a price decline of 35.1 per cent with an average life of 23.5 months. Since the '87 crash can be seen in hindsight to have started from its high in July 1987, this bear market has lasted only a third of the average life – eight months – but has already shown the average price fall. However, it has recovered somewhat (July 1988) since its low in November and Jones is not convinced that this is a bear market. It could be a panic similar to that of 1982.

According to Jones: 'No one can forecast in advance how long a bear market may last or how far it may fall. It all depends on the underlying reasons. Once these become known the bear trend is often in the terminal phase.' But he also says: 'Bear markets and panics are not always associated with business recessions as popularly supposed. Changes in monetary conditions, or even wars, which sometimes exert powerful pressures on securities markets are of varying significance.'

Maybe October's crash was started by political fears. Searching for its justification in signs of an economic downturn could be looking in the wrong direction altogether.

A village parable

Since the Second World War, the world economy has become rather like a village of the pre-industrial world. Each of us, rich or poor, depends on the village remaining successful and happy. The Squire lives in the Big House on the hill overlooking the village and, as Squires will, has become a bit lazy about maintaining the

Estate. Also his ne'er-do-well cousins, who used to buy a lot of the Estate's produce, are now so hopelessly in debt that he has refused to help them with any further credit.

Fortunately the Squire has not had to cut back the style in which he lives. This is partly because the villagers are dependent upon the Big House for employment, and as the buyer of their produce. They are accustomed to waiting for their money. More usefully, one of the most industrious and frugal of the villagers has been able to go into the money-lending business. He has helped the Squire with some temporary loans. But now all these relationships are getting a little fractious.

The villagers (the main European economies) have begun to realise, when they do get their money, that the Squire (America) has clipped the edges of his silver coins, so they are getting paid less than was agreed; moreover though the Squire promises to stop doing this (devaluation), in practice he keeps on doing so. Since he owns the local mint, they can't prevent him doing it, even though the practice is causing prices to rise in the village as people become confused by the different value of the coins now circulating amongst them.

The moneylender (Japan) is not very happy either; he has lent so much money to the Squire that he can't afford to stop in case the Squire devalues his silver coins even more. On the other hand, he can't afford to continue lending without thought of the cost either. But when the moneylender, supported by some of the other villagers, suggests to the Squire that he solve his problems by exchanging the debts for some of his orchards and farms (foreign investment in real American assets such as land and companies) he gets very upset.

The Squire does not like the idea of upstart villagers thinking they are as good as he is and, if only they would buy some of the goods that he used to sell to his cousins (Latin America), he would not be in the pickle he is in.

The habit of deference is sufficiently strong that the villagers are reluctant to upset the Squire by pushing this issue, or telling him that the Estate's produce is no longer as special as it once was. They know he is still powerful enough to hurt them very seriously if he is crossed, by becoming choosy over who he deals with (trade protectionism) or refusing to send his sons to help them against the local bandits (cutting back on military bases and support for NATO).

But the villagers know, even though no one dares admit it openly, that things can't continue as they are. So they carry on talking (G7 meetings). The Squire promises that he will economise sensibly, and organise the Estate more efficiently. Then, if the villagers will spend just a little more with the Estate, and are patient for only a little longer, everything will work out for the best (this is the 'soft landing' for the dollar and a minor recession in 1989–90).

But he also implies that, if they continue to bother him, he will really tighten his belt and sort his finances out once and for all and, though he won't enjoy it, they will like it even less (the 'hard landing' or severe US recession, and major economic setback for the rest of the world).

But can the villagers trust these promises of gradual reform? Even if they do, can they afford to wait or will the hotheads amongst them (the financial markets) take precipitate action by raiding the Big House for the silver (another share market collapse) and so force the Squire to cut back his spending (further loss of business confidence leading to severe recession)?

Has the world learned enough from 1929?

It may be hard to believe that this is the way that economic leaders think. The inside story* of the meetings of the Group of seven finance ministers suggests that this is so. These G7 ministers are the principals behind the Plaza and Louvre accords on the international coordination of currencies. The meetings of the seven largest economic countries are not so much about cooperation to solve the problems of world economic growth and 'imbalances' as about 'squaring' the ministers' respective electorates.

We should not be surprised by this. Ministers are in business to be elected, and need to consider our prejudices and concerns. If, in looking after these, some of the economic problems that cause international difficulties can also be resolved, then that is a pleasant

---

* *Managing the dollar: from the Plaza to the Louvre*, Yoichi Funabashi 1988, Institute of International Economics, 11 Dupont Circle NW, Washington DC 20036.

bonus. For though we do live in a 'global village' we, the villagers, seem reluctant to accept the need for compromise and cooperation. Though Britain is one of the largest buyers of other countries' companies, we still squeal as loudly as any when a British company goes to an overseas buyer.

The policy-makers of 1929 thought that they were acting for the best, as do those of today. Hindsight shows us that their actions in 1929 and 1930 worsened the crisis. Only hindsight will tell us whether our national interests will be the same as those of the 'global village'. Until that outcome is clearer, security markets will be haunted by the fear that we have not learned as much as we ought to have from the events of sixty years ago.

So it is quite unimportant which particular event it was that switched the magic lantern slide during that October weekend. The slide was switched, and fear is now the dominant emotion in the market place. If the fall was more than a 'panic' how much worse are really savage bear markets?

The five worst lasted between two and a half to three and a half years compared to the average life of just under two years. The price decline of the three worst – 1920–21, 1929–32 and 1972–74 – was between 50 and 70 per cent. These, Jones points out, took place against a background of monetary disorder – severe deflation for the first two and 20 per cent-plus inflation for the last.

Jones ends his study on an encouraging note for, he says, the decline of insider trading has made the stock market less effective as an economic bell-wether and 'what remains is a more egalitarian system in which professional money managers, appointed to husband the savings of the many, are making their decisions on the basis of information which is freely available.'

However, 'investment performance statistics show that few managers achieve consistently smarter-than-average results. In fact, the need to conform is so strong that the danger of being left out of a trend is to risk losing the client to a rival. Such circumstances may lead to the dominant influence in markets becoming the popular or crowd opinion, not previously noted for the ability to forecast events ahead . . . the crash of '87 may have been purely an example of crowd hysteria.'

Each of us will have to make our own subjective judgement on the world outlook. Will the Squire be forced to tighten his belt –

then the 'panic' will certainly turn out to be a 'bear' and a grizzly at that. Or will the Squire sweet-talk the villagers into holding on, and so produce a 'soft landing'. The size of the American deficits are awe-inspiring, but then America is still so much richer than the rest of the world. As percentages of the size of the economy, these deficits are no bigger than those run by most European countries.

Demographics are also part of the problem. We save when we are young, and again when our own families grow up and leave us. In between we borrow, for homes, education, business and the building up of our personal assets. Few Americans die in debt; the post war 'baby-boomers' are now entering their forties, with children educated, mortgages reduced and boats and second homes almost paid off. The speed with which the American savings scene turns around could surprise us all.

The concern over current account balances reflects past 'beggar my neighbour' trade attitudes, as well as our political failure to recreate the financial freedom common until 1914. Back in Queen Victoria's days, with steamships rather than satellites, and quill pens for computers, Argentina could borrow more cheaply on the financial markets than Germany today. Few bankers, even then, described Argentina as a 'good' name.

Developing countries then had ratios of debt to trade which make current Latin America figures look positively miserly. That world ended in 1914, and all efforts to replace it have failed. Maybe the 'global yuppies' playing in the newly integrated financial markets will force politicians to do what reason never could.

If we are optimists at heart – and who else invests in shares? – then Jones has further words of comfort:

> The concept of 'sideways' markets does not exist [in stock markets] as in other markets such as currencies, commodities and real estate where often for long periods of time the trend is neither up nor down . . . [nevertheless] the next few years may see a period of consolidation in equity markets . . .
>
> [this] . . . they did between 1959 and 1966 when, after more than doubling in the previous bull market, the stock indices remained in a narrow range of 20 per cent for the next seven years making no overall gain. This period was very fruitful for active investors concentrating on stock selection but very

unprofitable for those trying to forecast overall levels of the market.

How we can ensure that this period, if it comes, is equally fruitful for us now becomes the major theme of this book.

Checkpoints

• Conventional wisdom is nearly always wrong in the stock exchange; if it was right, we'd all be rich. It isn't and we aren't.

• Since for every buyer of a share, there must be a seller, the chances are that we will be right only half the time. If we remember that most investors are cleverer than us, we won't so often be 'the bigger fool'.

• 'No man is an island,' said Donne of our heart, but this is also true of our business affairs. Though London is one of the three world financial centres, Britain is now an 'also ran' amongst economic powers. What goes on in the rest of the world will affect the profits of our company, and the dividends we can expect from our shares.

• In almost any year since 1920, the current view of the economic and political future looked dreadful. Shares still did well as an investment. The outlook now seems clouded; can the future be any worse than the last seventy years? Investment in shares, like anything else, requires moderation and control if the experience is to be successful and enjoyable.

Chapter Five

The practical investor – setting objectives

> *One has to pay attention to the different tides, and to trim one's sails according to the wind.*
>
> CONFUSION DE CONFUSIONES, *1688*

January 1987 was an important month for Mr Andrew S. Contracts were exchanged then for the sale of his hotel, which he had bought in a very run down state some ten years earlier. For the first time ever, he had substantial capital of his own.

Andrew had become an hotel-keeper after successfully building up, and then selling, his own accountancy practice in the home counties. The appeal of doing something 'real' had been part of the decision to give up accountancy. Living in the beautiful Welsh border country, and with more time for his family, was the other. Nevertheless, even with the house owned outright, five children at state schools, and £300,000 Andrew had no wish to retire.

Andrew had maintained an interest in accountancy and wanted to develop an accountancy-based management consultancy. He saw good opportunities for such a business in the new 'enterprise' culture, particularly with his practical experience of building up two such different small businesses as a professional practice and an hotel.

To avoid capital gains tax, Andrew had to invest in another business and so gain 'rollover' relief. He also needed income to maintain the family. In practical terms, he would have to find a business to buy – or set up – during 1989 at the latest. That gave him two years with his new-found capital, and the opportunity to indulge his wish to be an investor. Indeed, it seemed to him not so much an indulgence as a necessity.

From all sides – including the government with its privatisation programme – came the messages: Buy shares – only wimps keep their savings in the building society! Forget income – capital gains are what it's all about! Why work – you make more investing in the stock market! Andrew needed little persuading. The bull market had been going for five years, and the performance figures he studied showed that unit trusts had grown in value by 20 per cent a year.

A cautionary tale

Andrew was not an accountant for nothing. Though he knew little about practical stock-market investment, he understood that there was risk attached to it, and that he should invest the money needed for his new business in such a way that it was readily available. He was also aware that there are 'advisers' and 'advisers' so he used his connections within the accountancy profession to get the right introductions and establish what he considered to be a properly diversified portfolio.

Despite all these precautions, he wrote to me in January 1988 'in the hope that you will be able to advise me where I go from my current position. I am not asking for a detailed appraisal or review of my financial affairs, as clearly that would be too much to expect, nor to appraise or criticise the action and advice of others, as perhaps I should have been less trusting and more forward thinking.'

In twelve months the value of Andrew's fortune had fallen by £90,000 (see box). Furthermore, he was getting no income from his investments. He needed cash – both for day-to-day living expenses and to buy a business – so when he wrote to me he knew that these 'book' losses would have to be turned into 'real' losses by selling some or all of his investments. He had not kept back any cash reserves to weather this type of setback.

Andrew's investment plans and advisers

Long term money

£50,000 in private, unquoted business investments
£4800 in Save & Prosper Personal Equity Plan

Short term money

£50,000 in Hoare Govett Managed Unit Trust Portfolio. These were worth £41,500 in March 1988 when he sold them
£50,000 in Parker Munroe (Birmingham investment broker) Managed Insurance Bond Portfolio. These were worth £42,600 in March 1988 when he began to sell them.

According to Andrew: 'These two plans were specifically designed for capital growth, with no income, so as to guarantee my investment in my future business. [The managers] . . . were given written instructions . . . and told to plan for no longer than a two-year period. I made it clear I was not interested in income but what I wanted was complete security.'

Speculative money

£100,000 on a full discretionary account with I A Pritchard Stockbrokers of Birmingham. As Andrew says: 'These were known to me, and understood my financial affairs. The intention was to give me a return of £20–25,000 a year from dividends and dealing profits. Unfortunately at no time did they, or I, question this figure prior to October, and at no time did we consider that if this dried up I would be without income.'

£50,000 on an advisory account with Quilter Goodison Company, London stockbrokers owned by the French Paribas banking group. This was for trading in equities, 'based largely on my own ideas, City comments, and a number of recommendations from London accountants and chartists with stock exchange connections. I used this to invest in sectors not covered by Pritchards – oils, commodities, property – and wanted to add to the success of the Pritchard account. But though things started well in the summer, never was the difference between 'advisory' and 'discretionary' explained to me, and with all the changes of staff and lack of information, this turned out very badly.'

'My share portfolio peaked at £170,000, but is now worth only £81,000.'

As Andrew's letter said:

My advice came from a number of sources, including a well-known City firm of chartered accountants, but at no time did I go to one single person for a complete global picture of my affairs. Sad to relate, therefore, no adviser warned me of the fact that I had become very heavily exposed, and no adviser ever gave me the slightest indication that there could be the stock market crash.

As a chartered accountant, I clearly knew certain basic elements about investments, but perhaps it was the case that a little knowledge is a dangerous thing, and it was the first time in my life I had personally ever had a lump sum of capital of my own. I am far more used to running a business with overdrafts, staff and customers and targets to achieve – and helping others do the same!

I felt that if my investments were spread over insurance bonds, unit trusts, UK and overseas, and a very broad portfolio of stock-exchange investments, I should be safe. Though I had discussed various aspects of my investments with certain people, I did not want to get involved in things I didn't know anything about like gilts, traded options, etc. But what was hammered home to me by all and sundry was the one thing I was not to do was to put my money in a building society.

After the crash Andrew's advisers had no answers to his very practical concerns. Indeed, one of Andrew's complaints was that he was getting no replies to or even acknowledgement of his letters, or telephoned requests. He wrote to me asking:

> How best do I increase my income? Is time too short, with my cash needs for 1989, to do anything with my investments or should I realise them for as much as I can get now? Should I place my affairs with one firm? Can you give me some general guidelines on these questions, or advice on who I should discuss them with?

Why disaster was inevitable

Andrew failed to establish any clear investment objectives for himself. In consequence, he was unable to resist the emotional pressures to 'get into' the market, nor was he able to assess the level of 'risk' he was taking for the 'rewards' promised in the proposals made to him. Professional advisers can become just as much affected by bull-market euphoria as amateurs, so Andrew launched himself onto a course that would have led to disaster sooner or later. Fortunately for him, the crash came early. His losses, though painful, are not crippling.

Basic principles: the investment policy

None of us should become a stock market investor until we have clearly thought out what we want to achieve with our savings, and the level of risk that we are willing to run. Even more important, we must write these down, and regularly remind ourselves of them. Such investment objectives are the only sure way of inoculating ourselves against the emotions of the stock market. Two elements make up this investment policy – a target for the income we need from the portfolio, and another to establish the risks that we are prepared to take.

The importance of income

Investment is about purchasing a flow of income and one that, if we are both lucky and clever, will increase faster than either prices or the cost of our own improving standard of living. Since the war, this key objective has been obscured by tax considerations. Tax is no longer a problem in setting investment policy. Capital gains, other than our annual exemption of £5000 each, are now taxed on the same basis as income. Investors can concentrate on value in the stock market.

Even when tax was a problem to investors, the dividends paid by equities were essential to their capital performance. It is the reason that 'income' unit trusts have done better in capital value than 'growth' trusts which are managed simply for capital growth (Figure 16).

An equity investment that pays no dividends has done little better than a deposit. This helps explain the paradoxical behaviour of 'income' compared to 'growth' trusts. Dividends are 'real' money with which we can buy the groceries; capital gains, for which so many of us search, are 'maybe' money. We will only get those gains if we can gauge share price levels correctly. Because the stock market trades on greed and fear, estimating what the value of shares might be is very difficult for it depends both on the mood of investors, and current fashions.

The value of alternative investments 1955–1987

£1000 invested in	Before inflation	After inflation
Equities including dividends	£94,600	£9800
Equities excluding dividends	£15,600	£1600
Gilts including interest	£ 9,900	£1000
Deposit including interest	£13,800	£1400

Source: London Business School/Hoare Govett

The lesson of these figures is that we should invest for good immediate income as compound interest does more for growth of capital values than all the tip sheets in the world. An income of 7 per cent a year reinvested will double the value of our portfolio in ten years – even if none of the shares we hold increase their

Figure 16: Compounded income is the key to investment success.

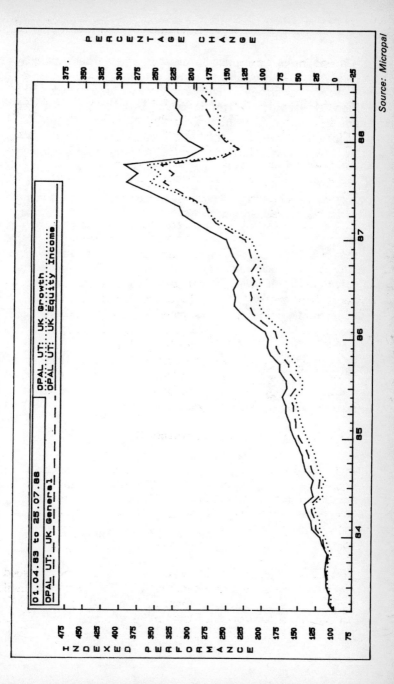

Source: Micropal

dividends, or go up in price during these years. That is unlikely unless we are really terrible pickers of investments.*

When we as private individuals invest, we have to look at the different risks and rewards of shares, bonds and cash, and compare them to our personal financial needs. From these three investment categories, we need to formulate an investment policy that will meet our income objectives, and enable us to sleep soundly at night. This is not easy but historical probabilities show that:

● equities are best in the long run, and are the only investments which will increase our income – though we know share prices are very volatile and that stock markets cannot be relied upon in an emergency.

● bonds, of which gilts are the largest sector, are affected by market movements as well as interest rate changes, and have been even more vulnerable to inflation than deposits – but we know that they guarantee us a high and fixed level of income for years to come.

● the income from cash deposits is not fixed, and cannot be trusted for living expenses, and is also vulnerable to rising prices – but we know that in an emergency we can get back what we put in.

Portfolio choice and income needs

Market yields		Sept '87	July '88
Shares	FTA Index	3.12%	4.18%
Convertible bonds	Market range approx:	5.5/7.5%	6.5/8.5%
Gilts	5 years	9.5/10.4%	9.6/10.1%
Gilts	5 to 15 years	9.8/10.3%	9.5/9.9%
Cash deposit	90 day BS a/c	10.65%	8.67%

Note: income needs should determine portfolio structure

---

* The rule of 72 says that 72 divided by the interest or growth rate – 7 per cent here – gives the number of years over which a sum will double in value. This is useful when looking at some of the 'offers' we receive.

The object of portfolio planning is to earn sufficient income from shares, bonds and cash to match our needs. Obviously, the higher we set our income level, the more of the portfolio that must be invested in the higher-yielding bonds.

Even though we may not need this income, we should still establish a figure. It is our performance target. It also creates a straitjacket which helps to keep our investment policy from being affected by market emotion. We also need to establish two other figures that we never alter. These control the 'risk' in our portfolio.

Investment policy: controlling risk

The first of the figures we need to establish is the *maximum percentage of the portfolio that we will invest in shares*. We do not have to – indeed should not – invest up to this percentage if we think the market is too high. We should never invest above it. In terms of price volatility, convertible bonds and preference shares are more stable than ordinary shares, but lack the marketability of government bonds in a crisis: in risk terms, they are part of our equity percentage.

The second is the *minimum cash holding in the portfolio*. This can be much higher if we are worried about price levels but it should never go lower, however enthusiastic we become as investors. The actual amount will depend upon our personal circumstances, but the minimum should be sufficient to cover three months' living expenses together with any immediate cash liabilities such as educational fees. This is our liquidity reserve.

Market risk, and absolute and relative loss

When professionals talk about 'risk' they often mean not so much 'risk of loss' – which we naturally take it to mean – as 'risk of being wrong'. The most general 'risk' is 'market risk', or misguessing the direction (up or down) or level (too high or too low) of the stock market as a whole. Institutional managers accepted the 'market risk' of stock market investment in summer 1987 because of the expected 'reward'. Though share prices were high, the economic outlook was good, companies were making excellent profits and increasing their dividends, and investors were bullish.

Despite high market levels, share prices seemed more likely to stay up – or even go up further – than go down. So the 'risk' for such investors of being in the market was outweighed either by the expected 'reward' of further price rises or the 'risk' incurred by getting out of the market and producing worse results than competitors.

Institutional investors can take a relaxed view of 'market risk' because each month they have more cash coming in to invest. When markets change direction, and institutional managers see that their strategy is wrong, they then use their cash flows to restructure their portfolios. Since the crash, they have been building up cash holdings and not buying shares. This is why share prices have been drifting sideways.

The question for private investors

Private investors rarely have a cash flow with which to adjust portfolios. Our funds are limited. When we get it wrong, if we have no cash reserves or an inadequate income, we have to take action. That action turns theoretical losses within our portfolio into real losses in our bank account. Last year the risk/reward ratio was not favourable to the private investor; if we had asked ourselves: 'Do I have more to win, if I am right, than I stand to lose if I am wrong,' we would have had to answer 'no'.

Share markets were at historically high valuation levels and yields were very low. More worryingly, yields on bonds were high while those on equities were low and the reverse yield gap was over 6 per cent. Institutional investors were bullish about the market, but only for the immediate future. Newspapers commented that many professionals thought markets were close to their 'highs' and investors work on the assumption that what doesn't go up must be coming down.

The intensity of 'market risk' changes, as economic or financial conditions change. There is more risk in buying shares when equity markets are at historically high levels – as they were in 1987 – than when they are low because everyone is fearful for the future. Gilts are probably safer bought now, when rates of interest are high, than back in the nineteen-fifties when interest rates were very low and no one worried about inflation.

Classic mistakes of new investors

So Andrew, abetted by his advisers, made most of the classic mistakes of new investors:

● he thought, on the basis of a rapidly rising market, that making money in the stock market is easy. Historical probabilities, and folk memory, say that it is not.

● he ignored his family's need for income, having been assured that he would make dealing profits instead. If it was that easy, none of us would work.

● none of his advisers warned him of 'market risk'. When the crash came, he had neither the income nor the cash to ride it out, and what he thought was 'diversification' was 'overexposure' to equity markets.

● his advisers were hopelessly optimistic, for they too were carried away by bull market enthusiasm, and he lacked the practical knowledge to know that this was so.

● he never thought that his policy might be wrong, and developed no contingency plans in case things did not go as he hoped. The one sure thing about financial markets is that nothing is sure.

Investment policy: theory into action

Ignoring the income function of investment is especially dangerous when market sentiment turns from optimism to fear. Quite how dangerous was discovered by Jenny Prudence. She is one of my mythical *Sunday Times* investors, though with real and typical investment problems.

Jenny is divorced with two young children. She has a good job, with reasonable prospects, and it is pensionable. She considers her long-term financial future to be fairly safe. Nevertheless, she does not have as much as she needs, with two young children to support and little help from her former husband. A legacy of £30,000 from the sale of her aunt's house faces her with a decision.

Jenny could use her inheritance to pay off her mortgage of £25,000. She knows that if she does this, she loses her tax relief and will not be able to get it back without moving house. On the other hand, if she holds the money as cash, the deposit interest she will earn will, after tax, only just cover her mortgage payments. So she must either repay the mortgage or invest in the stock market.

Jenny does not want to forgo the chance of bettering her financial position. She was prepared to risk investment in the stock market to increase the value of her capital, and the income she earns from it, and was clear about her own investment objectives. These can be shown in a matrix which illustrates the constraints that Jenny has imposed upon her managers.

She wants to keep £2000 in a building society as a cash reserve, she needs an income of £2400 a year which she hopes will increase over time and so protect her from inflation, and she does not want to risk any speculative loss of her capital. The difficulties faced by her managers is also shown by the matrix; she needs a yield of 8 per cent when shares are yielding less than half that, yet she must have shares if her income – and ultimately her capital – is to increase.

Jenny's investment policy

Security	Invested	Approx yield: market	Portfolio	Annual income
Cash	£2000	10%	10%	£ 200
Gilts	?	9–10%	?	?
Cv Bonds	?	6–8%	?	?
Shares	?	3–4%	?	?
Total	£30,000		8%	£2400

Jenny, by investing rather than paying off her mortgage, is choosing a 'high risk for a high reward' investment policy. How did her advisers solve her income problem, did their solutions increase her risk 'profile', and how did their answers work out in 1987?

Bilmes Financial Management is an investment broker, of the type now authorised by FIMBRA and to be found in the high streets. They persuaded Jenny not to keep a liquidity reserve, and go for an all equity portfolio. This was a high-risk strategy on top of a high-risk policy for the portfolio produced only £1000 of the income needed, but Bilmes reckoned to make this up by realising capital gains of £1400 a year.

Jenny's money was invested in large and well managed unit trusts though costs are high at over 6 per cent of her capital. International diversification and capital gains did not stand up to October. Now Jenny has to realise capital to make up her income needs, at a time when the price of her units is very depressed, and so convert book losses into real losses.

Penney Easton has now merged with Parsons, another Scottish stockbroker, and both are part of Allied Provincial Securities. They invested two months later than the other managers, in February, and after the stock market had already risen sharply. Penney Easton chose a lower risk strategy than Bilmes.

£8500 of Jenny's money was kept in cash and bonds. These yield Jenny £900 of her needed income. A similar sum from her share holdings gives her some 75 per cent of her annual income requirement. The shares are in large British companies that will do well, even if there is an economic downturn, so Jenny can expect some increase in the £880 of dividend income that she gets from these.

The shortfall of £600 was to be covered partly by dividend increases but mainly by capital gains taken on the £21,500 invested in shares. As a result of the crash, there are 'book' or unrealised losses of £3000. Fortunately, some £2578 is in the building society deposit, so she will not have to sell shares to raise money to supplement her living expenses this year. But even dividend increases of 10 per cent a year over the next two or three years will not make up the existing income shortfall. So, unless the prices of her shares recover, she will have to economise or continue to spend her capital.

Robert White, the former private client department of research broker and investment trust specialist Wood Mackenzie, is now part of the Trustee Savings Bank. They followed traditional practice – and apologised for being so old-fashioned and Scottish at the time – by designing a portfolio to meet Jenny's income needs. Two-thirds of her capital is in cash and bonds with the remainder in the shares of investment trusts. Though they hoped for capital gains from these, they did not rely on such gains to meet Jenny's income needs which are covered by dividends.

The table below shows Jenny's costs. These are the transaction and unit trust costs and, in Robert White's case, a portfolio management charge as well. The last column shows the income that Jenny can expect from her portfolio while the middle column shows what her £30,000 was worth after the crash.

How the managers performed for Jenny Prudence

Portfolio managed by	Costs to date	Value at 30 Nov 87	Estimated income per annum
Penney Easton	£ 673	£26,860	£1782
Bilmes Financial Management	£1912	£25,149	£1029
Robert White	£ 519	£28,895	£2338

Robert White did not forget the fundamentals of investment during the height of the bull market. Their low-risk investment strategy insured Jenny against her own high-risk policy when it had to – during a major market collapse. Her other two managers compounded the risks inherent in her policy with their investment strategies and now face her with real losses.

The Robert White portfolio has other advantages. The first column shows Jenny's investment at cost, while the second column shows how much of the investment has been absorbed in transaction and other management charges. These charges are lower than Penney Easton's because Robert White, as an investment trust market maker, could deal as a principal and avoid VAT. More importantly, investment trust shares give Jenny active management of an equity portfolio at significantly lower costs than unit trusts, and also ensure that very little activity will be needed on her account. This keeps commissions down. Although the value of the portfolio has fallen slightly, Jenny does not need to sell because the final column shows that she is getting her needed income. The losses can remain 'paper' losses, and not real ones.

How Robert White did it

Security	Cost including expenses £	Expenses to date £	Value at 30 Nov 87 £	Estimated income £
Abbey National ChequeSave a/c	1893	nil	1893	115
Exchequer 11% 1991	7382	102	7767	798
Treasury 12% 1995	7830	103	8208	864
Cash and Gilts = £17,105 or 57% of the portfolio at cost				
British Assets 6% Convertible	2528	46	2112	144
Convertible bonds = £2528 or 8% of the portfolio at cost				
First Scottish American	2597	55	2573	136
Govett Strategic	2474	54	1926	50
Murray International	2603	55	2121	98
Securities Trust of Scotland	2635	56	2295	133
Shares = £10,309 or 34% of the portfolio at cost				
Management Fee	58	58	*	*
Total	30,000	529	28,895	2338

Checkpoints

• It's our money – remember Jimmy – and only we can look after it. Our responsibility is to establish an investment policy, and ensure that our advisers stick to it.

• Establish minimum cash needs within this policy: never invest these however good the outlook or attractive the investment.

• Fix the maximum policy percentage for share investment: never exceed this percentage however certain we may be that the market is going up. If the market always reacted the same way to a given set of circumstances, everyone would be rich. It doesn't and they aren't.

• Invest the portfolio to meet our needed or target income level. That is 'real' money; everything else is only 'maybe' money.

• With a high risk investment policy, choose a low risk investment strategy. Always remember that we might be wrong.

Notes: financial planning and how to do it

Many investment brokers were originally established to advise on the use of life assurance products to mitigate the harshness of the personal tax regime. As this was softened, they became more interested in personal asset management, a subject which many stockbrokers were inclined to ignore. The best of them have considerable expertise in this, and have developed alliances with stockbrokers to invest that part of their clients' assets devoted to investment in shares and, sometimes, bonds.

Nevertheless, investment brokers thrive on public ignorance of the development of life assurance from an industry primarily concerned with 'protection' to one now selling 'investment'. The difference both to us and to them is marked:

Yearly cost of providing £10,000 life cover*

Man aged	29	39	44	54
Term assurance	12.20	27.80	45.80	127.00
Whole of life with profits	209.80	288.60	341.80	491.00
Endowment with profits	710.60	718.20	728.60	774.20

* *Life Assurance: Which?*, September 1987.

A useful rule of thumb is that brokers receive, as commissions, the equivalent of one year's premiums of a life assurance policy. Not surprisingly, little term assurance 'protection' is sold compared to endowment and whole of life 'investment' policies. Life protection is essential for most of us, but regular savings are a different matter, often best not carried out within the rigid discipline of a life policy. How to calculate how much, and what sort, of life protection we need is very well covered in the edition of *Which?* already mentioned.

If we prefer life assurance company investment management to that of a stockbroker or fund manager, then the monthly *Money Management* has regular surveys comparing the performance of life companies. The difference between best and worst is very great, and investment returns vary by more than 100 per cent, so past records do need to be checked.

Advisers cannot be trusted absolutely. Commissions vary, and are hidden with all life assurance products. Despite the new investor protection rules about 'best advice', commission levels will influence advisers. Britain's oldest life company also has one of the best performance records, but Equitable Life happens not to pay commissions so is rarely recommended by advisers. We can do our own financial analysis, or go to an independent CAMIFA adviser who sometimes has the advantage of greater objectivity and professionalism. Either way, we must be aware that commissions are paid and influence judgement. The advice from a company salesman or representative cannot be relied upon to be in our best interests.

Check amongst local solicitors and accountants by telephone to see whether they have financial planning partners, that the initial appointment is free, and that their hourly fee charges – depending upon the part of the country between £30 and £70 – will be offset against commissions earned.

An investment broker, who must now be fully authorised by a self regulatory organisation set up by the Securities and Investment Board, can often be more knowledgeable and imaginative. The best of these are beginning to function as fee-charging firms. Telephone first, to get a feel for the firm; don't give your address or telephone number until you are sure that they are not a hard-selling sales organisation.

The essence of financial planning is an analysis of what we earn, and what we spend, and how these elements may change in the future. Such an analysis is essential anyway to define the income objectives for our investment policy.* A good financial planner will carry this analysis into the future, questioning the safety and value of our job, future calls on this income such as children's education,

---

* Useful software for those of us with Amstrad PCW or IBM PCs and no liking for accountancy is *Money Manager Plus*, Connect Systems, 3 Flanchford Road, London W12 9ND 01-743 9792.

the support of relatives, any need to supplement existing pension schemes, regular savings plans or finding capital for business ventures.

This revenue analysis will be supplemented by a review of our assets and liabilities such as outstanding mortgages and other loans compared to the value of our property, the possibility of raising capital by downgrading our housing, expectation of legacies, value of pension rights and life assurance contracts, and the type and size of other assets such as stock-exchange investments, other property, and personal assets such as jewellery, fine furniture or paintings etc.

From all of this come recommendations for the organisation of our financial affairs designed to give us as much as possible of what we want for the least risk. Within this overall scheme, life assurance and stock market investment both have a role. The encouragement of the new individual pension plans makes this type of financial review more important since poor planning, or a bad choice of manager, will hit us hard at retirement; in company pension schemes the contributions of others can help to gloss over expensive investment or funding mistakes. Nevertheless, the size of commissions available – out of our capital or savings – makes this a market where it must be *buyer beware!*

Chapter Six

The practical investor – managing market risk

I said indeed that ruin must soon come upon us but I owe it came two months earlier than I expected.

James Milner, MP, commenting on the collapse of South Sea Company shares, and his personal bankruptcy

The luckless Mr Milner discovered the hard way that stock markets never do what is expected of them. Since it is hard to amass capital in the first place, we as private investors must make the protection of our existing wealth our highest priority. This means investing in the stock market. Whether the threat that we face is of a resurgence of inflation, or another nineteen-thirties-style slump, the best probability is that a well balanced portfolio of equities and bonds will see us through whatever comes.

The BZW chart shows that since the mid-nineteen-seventies gilt prices have stabilised. Now, with the new personal tax system and assuming no more than 3–5 per cent inflation a year, bonds are safe for private investment. The better inflation outlook has also resuscitated the corporate bond market, particularly convertible bonds and preferred shares, so that the private investor again has a proper choice of investments.

This is fortunate. Bonds are important in successful portfolio construction. Correct portfolio balance will keep our capital safe and allow us to participate in the market. Peter Thompson of BZW Gilt Equity Study may be right – the crash of '87, just like that of '29, could turn out in hindsight to be an unpleasant hiccup in a bull market with half its life still to go. Bonds will help insure our portfolios against hindsight telling us we were over-optimistic.

Figure 17: By the 1970s, inflation had done its worst and gilts became a reasonable investment again.

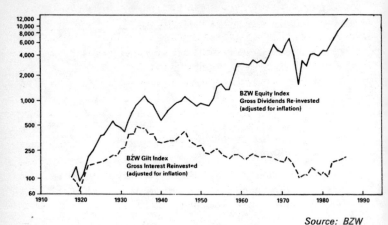

Source: BZW

Basic principles: investment strategy

The actual structure of a portfolio depends on our investment objectives, and attitude to risk. The level of income we need sets the proportion of the capital we have to invest in bonds. Our attitude to current market price levels should determine the percentage of cash and bonds we choose to hold. Such a portfolio strategy will require time to mature and, even if prices move faster than a decade ago, investment still takes three to five years to pay off. It is not for the impatient.

As with roulette, luck rather than skill is required to pick the top-performing trust or share of the year. Profitable share trading requires a particular mentality, as well as time and up-to-the-minute information. This puts it out of court for most private investors. Successful investment, on the other hand, needs skills and attitudes which are not the exclusive property of the professional manager.

Investment skill is the design of a portfolio structure to achieve specified ends. It is also 'stock picking', or buying good value in the individual securities chosen to make up the portfolio, but this comes second to the overall design. Establishing and maintaining a balanced portfolio structure is only partly about getting our needed yield.

Portfolio structure has a more important role. Investment policy is the straitjacket that stops us joining in the madness of the market. Investment strategy is the armour that protects portfolio income in a stock market crash. Together, straitjacket and armour ensure that we never need to sell shares at distressed prices. (Yes, this does seem very rigid, but our emotions encourage us to be all too flexible in our investment actions.)

Market risk, according to the statisticians who put together Modern Portfolio Theory (MPT), constitutes somewhere between 30 and 50 per cent of the risk of investment. Market risk simply means that, when the market collapses, all shares go down in price simultaneously, irrespective of the size, quality or prospects of individual companies.

A balanced portfolio is designed to maintain, except in paper prices, the value of family fortunes in difficult markets. Management of this portfolio structure is more akin to garden planning and maintenance than a day at the races. It is, together with necessary, regular and judicious pruning and improvement of the individual holdings within it, what investment skill is all about. Designing and maintaining the right portfolio structure is our most important investment decision, both for the safety of our capital and the performance of our portfolio.

At any time, but particularly during a bear phase of the market, the way to safe investment is to assume that we will get market timing wrong. None of us, however clever, can eliminate market risk. When markets collapse again – and probability tells us they will sometime – all shares will go down in price. No one knows when the worst is over but with a properly constructed portfolio, a market collapse is at worst a missed opportunity, not a disaster.

Offsetting risk through portfolio balance

The secret of portfolio structure is balance, or the offsetting of different types of risk. Change in this balance allows us to follow more or less adventurous investment policies, as economic and market conditions suggest. The Phillips & Drew matrix establishes a yardstick; in these very uncertain times, they recommend that their institutional investors be slightly on the 'bearish' side of a 'neutral' portfolio. They define 'neutrality' as the portfolio split an institutional investor would have regarded as natural before the latest 'equity mania' overtook the markets.

P & D recommended asset allocations (spring 1988)

	Current	Neutral	Maximum ever	Minimum ever
Equities	50%	60%	80%	30%
Bonds	40%	35%	50%	25%
Cash	10%	5%	20%	0%
Portfolio	100%	100%	—	—

Source: Phillips & Drew

This is a starting point, though we need to remember that institutions have a positive cash flow. We cannot afford not to have some cash in our portfolio. Income requirements have already established our basic portfolio split, and our knowledge of our future financial requirements has identified minimum cash holdings and maximum share percentages. Now, depending upon our view of the market, willingness to take risk, and need for income we can move our own portfolio from a more to a less defensive state by increasing the holdings of equities and reducing the bonds.

Each of us must discover that investment strategy with which we will be most comfortable; the table below suggests some options.

	Current	Normal	Bullish	Bearish
Equities	40%	60%	80%	30%
Convertibles	20%	15%	10%	20%
Bonds	20%	15%	0%	30%
Cash	20%	10%	10%	20%
Portfolio	100%	100%	100%	100%

Bonds ballast portfolios. They guarantee a high income while the certainty of their returns helps protect portfolio values when markets fall, and gives extra liquidity to a portfolio in difficult times. Gilts can always be sold, however bad the market conditions. Income is one objective of the portfolio but the other, equally important determinant of portfolio structure is risk.

Without risk, there is no reward. Each of us has a different capacity for taking risk. So our risk tolerance helps fix our spread of investments. Investors with a low tolerance of risk will probably regard the 'normal' structure as dangerously speculative; the sanguine 'high risk' investor will regard it as old-fashioned and fearful. Probably the best way of deciding on this very subjective matter is through the 'sleepless' night test.

Personal choice for risk exposure

The 1987 crash saw share prices – but not bond prices – fall by 30 per cent, while between 1972 and 1974 they fell 70 per cent. Now imagine an average of those two collapses, with our portfolio as it is and our expenses and income as they are. When do we stop sleeping through worry? Once we do, then we are over our risk tolerance, and should restructure our portfolio to a lower risk level. Remember also that we are talking about a trade-off between risk and reward; we should only take the risk when we are pretty sure the odds favour us getting the reward.

We should never overstep the agreed maxima and minima within the investment policy, however bullish or bearish we feel, and whatever others say. One way lies loss from market over-exposure, the other from inflation. It is this matrix of figures that we first calculate, then discuss with our family, later consider with our adviser, and finally type out, and permanently keep – probably in front of our investment records, but certainly where we cannot avoid seeing it whenever we think of buying or selling securities.

Investment strategy: theory into practice

Later we will discuss how the bond and equity sections of a portfolio must also be balanced. Now, it is worth considering a practical example of this approach, and how it protected the wealth of Margaret Wise, another mythical *Sunday Times* client.

In her early sixties, and recently widowed, Margaret faced a reduction in her income as her husband's retirement pension dropped to a third of its former level. She needs at least £5000 a year from her £100,000 of capital to make up her income to a total of

£9500 a year. But Margaret, like so many living on fixed incomes, is very worried about inflation. So she also wants her living standards protected – that is the purchasing power of the £9500 – and hopes to improve the value of her capital for her children and grand-children.

Roddy Macleod is a very experienced stockbroker, and now runs the Ipswich office of Gerrard Vivian Gray. Margaret's require-ments are for £10,000 as a liquidity reserve, and a £5000 annual income, but Macleod also considered that she would not be comfortable with a high-risk strategy. So his management of the portfolio, despite the euphoria at the time he started to invest, followed the classical pattern and the matrix originally looked like this:

Macleod's investment strategy for Margaret

Security	Invested	Approx yield: market	Portfolio	Annual income
Cash	£10,000	10%	10%	£1000
Gilts	£20,000	10%	10% +	£2300
IL Gilts	£10,000	2–3%		
Convertible Bonds	£10,000	6–8%	8%	£ 800
UK Shares	£20,000	3–4%	4.6%	£ 920
Foreign Trusts	£30,000	0–3%	1.4%	£ 430

Macleod's strategy was to invest in three roughly equal blocks of bonds, British shares, and overseas unit trusts. The yield on the cash and gilts virtually covers Margaret's immediate income needs and enabled Macleod to invest some money in his favourite Far Eastern markets. These, though very low yielding, are markets that he has followed for years.

The government bonds have high nominal interest rates which promise capital gains if interest rates fall but, if interest rates rise and bond markets fall, then the high 'coupon' and early redemp-tion – or repayment – of Exchequer 1990 will support its capital value. The Treasury 2003 will be more volatile because redemption is so many years away, but that gives time for the price to recover if interest rates do rise sharply.

Some £10,000 was earmarked for a possible purchase of an index-linked gilt. Macleod felt that ordinary gilts, given the expected level of inflation, were significantly cheaper than their index-linked equivalents. These index-linked gilts were never bought.

Instead, since Macleod was confident of the UK economic outlook, he purchased British & Commonwealth convertible preference shares later in the year rather than another gilt. Together with the Hanson Trust convertible, these benefit the portfolio with a good income now, and the opportunity to convert into the shares of two large and aggressively managed companies.

After two months this strategy, despite its very conservative approach during the early part of the 1987 bubble, was paying off. The columns of the table show how much Macleod had invested by

Portfolio for Mrs Margaret Wise by Roddy Macleod of Gerrard Vivian Gray, after two months

Security	Purchase cost including expenses £	Expenses to date £	Value at 30 Jan 87 £	Estimated income pa £
Cash – S&P HIBA a/c	10,766	NIL	10,766	1073
National & Provincial BS 90 day a/c	10,000	NIL	10,000	1302
Exchequer 12½% 1990	10,000	NIL	10,204	1206
Treasury 13¾% 2003	10,000	25	10,634	1179

Cash and gilts = £40,766 or 41% of cost and £4760 income.

Hanson Trust 10% Convertible	9966	126	9920	800
Britoil	5037	117	5700	338
W Canning	4997	117	6560	200
Courtaulds	4935	115	5890	144
Dee Corporation	5053	118	5334	236

British shares and bonds = £29,988 or 30% of cost and £1718.

Govett Euro Growth UT	4997	263	4791	11
N.P.I. Overseas UT	5000	263	4928	65
Sons of Gwalia	9250	175	9750	349
Henderson Japan UT	5000	263	4976	0
GT Far East UT	4999	263	4946	5

Overseas trusts and shares = £29,246 or 29% of cost and £430

Total	100,000	1845	104,399	6908

the end of January 1987, how much of Margaret's investments had been swallowed up in costs, the value of the portfolio, and its expected income.

The income from the cash and bonds almost covers Margaret's income requirements, so Macleod could pick equity shares on the basis of their present values and long term growth prospects, not immediate dividend yields. This policy keeps dealing costs low, since only 'pruning' changes will then be needed within the portfolio. Notice, however, that the British shares all yield better than the market as a whole.

The only disappointment Macleod had amongst his individual share choices was Dee Corporation. He sold them in the summer for a loss of £258, and switched into Pilkington. Pilkington had originally been chosen for the portfolio, but the attempted take-over by BTR in late 1986 intervened, and Macleod then felt the shares had become too expensive.

The Australian Sons of Gwalia gold mine was bought as a hedge against a recurrence of inflation or political change. Though hindsight can say the Conservative victory of 1987 was certain, that is not the way it seemed in late 1986. To prepare for the worst while hoping for the best should be an essential element in private client management. When these, and other commodity stocks, suddenly became fashionable in spring 1987, Britoil were sold, and also 1000 of the 2500 Gwalia shares.

The realised profits on these two sales, less the small loss on Dee, totalled £5625 and were within Margaret's capital tax exemption limit of £6600 for the tax year to April 1988. During the summer, the value of the portfolio increased to nearly £140,000 but then the crash came. The table summarises the main blocs of the portfolio at their values at that time.

Margaret's income at this post-crash valuation was 40 per cent higher than she needed. Her capital is down by less than £400 and the portfolio with £60,000 in cash, gilts and bonds is well placed to see Margaret through the bear market, and recession if it comes.

Unit trusts costs are £1188, or over 40 per cent of total costs, and represent both initial costs and annual management fees. Their low yields made them particularly vulnerable and they are valued at £4000 less than their purchase cost of £20,000. By contrast, the

Post crash valuation for Margaret Wise

Security	Purchase cost including expenses £	Costs to date £	Value at 30 Nov 87 £	Estimated income pa £
Cash – S&P HIBA a/c	13,031	NIL	13,031	1104
National & Provincial BS 90 day a/c	10,000	NIL	10,000	1027
Exchequer 12½% 1990	10,000	NIL	10,377	1207
Treasury 13¾% 2003	10,000	25	11,087	1179

Cash and bonds = £44,495 or 45% of value and £4517 income

Hanson Trust 10% Convertible	9966	126	9200	800
B & C 7¾% Convertible	7147	97	5150	388

Convertible bonds = £14,350 or 15% of value and £1188 income

W Canning	4997	117	7040	218
Courtaulds	4935	115	5115	205
Hillsdown Holding	5013	117	4012	89
Pilkington Bros	4990	116	3149	167

British shares = £19,316 or 19% of value and £679 income

Govett Euro Growth UT	4997	293	3497	52
N.P.I. Overseas UT	5000	294	3843	55
Sons of Gwalia	5550	106	5475	192
Henderson Japan UT	5000	295	4493	0
GT Far East UT	4999	298	4174	8

Overseas trusts and shares = £21,482 or 21% of value and £307

Realised capital gains	(5625)	669	n.a.	n.a.
Total	100,000	2668	99,646	6691

solid yields of the British shares have helped them keep their value.

In fact, had Macleod continued to run this portfolio in the *Sunday Times* he would have sold the Canning shares and Govett European unit trust. At the prices he dealt for his real clients, this would have raised £11,500, which had a dividend yield of only £333. Half the proceeds were then invested in BP New at 72p; the attraction of these is that they pay the full dividend on shares priced at only a third of the full cost; the remainder of the price is to be paid in two instalments in August 1988 and 1989.

The other half of the money was put into Willis Faber on a yield of 7.5 per cent, which reflects current City disenchantment with insurance brokers. These two investments bring in dividends of £1292 and increase the yield on the portfolio to 8 per cent – within only two percentage points of the yield she would get from the building society today, and this within a year of first investing.

Investment strategy: the need for discipline

It is hard to insulate ourselves from market euphoria without a yield requirement and an overall matrix for the portfolio. Enthusiasm was the downfall of Bryan Johnston of Bell Lawrie. Johnston had a harder *Sunday Times* client in Roly Chancer.

Roly is a rich man who wanted to turn his £250,000 into a lot more, quickly. No constraints were laid on Johnston. This can make it harder for a manager because we are always pushing for 'performance' and there are no objective standards such as Margaret Wise's need for income and safety.

Edinburgh stockbrokers Bell Lawrie are traditional private client stockbrokers, who believe that their main function is to manage their clients' wealth with the least risk and at the lowest cost. Such a policy requires continuous monitoring of the portfolio, together with regular pruning and reshaping. This initial cultivation worked well.

Johnston's cautious policy in December 1986 had some £45,000, or 18 per cent of the capital, in bonds and cash. This gave liquidity and flexibility to the portfolio in a market worried by political and currency uncertainties. For the same reason, another £72,000 went into unit trusts for overseas diversification.

With the rest of the capital, Johnston concentrated on picking good British 'blue chips' and got Roly's portfolio off to a cracking start. Johnston took profits whenever prices became too high. Barrow Hepburn was on the initial list and this was sold, together with some of the Wellcome shares, when AIDS hysteria drove Wellcome's price to unsustainable peaks. These realised gains of over £13,000.

Johnston had the same trouble as Macleod; the unit trusts were costly underperformers and one of the worst was GT German Fund. He sold these one day, and bought them back the next. This 'bed and breakfasting', as it is called, turned the 'book loss' on these units into a real loss of about £2300. This loss in turn offset some of the Wellcome gains. By summer 1987, with further disposals, net capital gains were up to £15,000 with some of these converted into a tax efficient personal equity plan. The portfolio was valued at over £300,000.

Portfolio valuation for Roly Chancer by Bryan Johnston of Bell Lawrie & Co of Edinburgh after six months

Security	Purchase cost including expenses £	Expenses to date £	Value at 29 Jun 87 £	Estimated income pa £
Cash	16,686	0	16,686	0
National Savings Certs 32 Issue	5000	0	5000	0
S&P Int DM Bond Fund	9729	534	9316	419
Exchequer 3% Gas 90/95	9957	53	10,756	399
Treasury 2% IL 1996	9939	53	10,532	168

Cash and bonds = £51,311 or 20% of cost and £986 income

BAT Industries	9453	193	12,080	403
Coloroll Group	9239	191	13,806	307
Dee Corporation	18,502	382	17,840	877
Harrisons & Crosfield	8988	188	12,540	603
Heywood Williams Group	9281	191	16,965	491
Hanson Trust	8826	186	10,500	349
Thos Locker Holdings	6759	159	6600	355
Low & Bonar	8336	181	9415	264
Quadrant	9069	189	8460	197
Racal Electronics	9207	190	13,377	222
Christian Salvesen	8341	181	10,380	298
Trafalgar House	14,979	324	19,600	925
Ultramar	8599	184	14,960	396
Wellcome	4433	187	9000	58
Personal Equity Plan	2400	67	2761	0

British shares = £136,412 or 51% of cost and £5745 income

Portfolio valuation for Roly Chancer by Bryan Johnston of Bell Lawrie & Co of Edinburgh after six months – cont.

Security	Purchase cost including expenses £	Expenses to date £	Valued at 29 Jun 87 £	Estimated income pa £
GT German Fund	6390	450	7040	64
Dunedin Euro Growth UT	9810	539	9945	78
BG: America UT	17,300	888	17,155	0
M&G American Recovery	9111	500	9366	41
Henderson Hong Kong Fund	8868	488	9848	159
EFM Tokyo Fund	8995	500	10,530	0
Baring Japan New Gen Fund	8250	453	7935	76
S.U.T.M. Scot Pac Fund	9144	507	10,668	34
Foreign trusts = £77,868 or 29% of cost and £452 income				
Realised capital gains	(15,591)	1326	—	—
Total	250,000	9284	313,061	7183

The election over, and believing that the outlook for both the British economy and its stock market was attractive, Bell Lawrie changed their tune, and joined the optimists. Johnston committed the bulk of Roly's capital to the UK market. Cash and bonds went down to less than 7 per cent of the value of the portfolio, and the cash was to be reduced still further by paying for rights issues on existing shares.

Initially this paid off. By autumn the portfolio was valued at over £330,000. This was due entirely to Johnston's stock-picking of British shares, for the unit trusts, as with Macleod, have disappointed. The crash hit the portfolio badly. The table shows the portfolio valuation at 30 November 1987 with the costs of the unit trusts shown at 15% initial charge and 10% annual management fee.

Post crash valuation for Roly Chancer

Security	Purchase cost including expenses £	Expenses to date £	Valued at 30 Nov 87 £	Estimated income pa £
Cash	3008	0	3008	0
N.S.Certs 32 Issue	5000	0	5000	0
Treasury 2% IL 1996	9939	53	10,836	168

Cash and bonds = £18,844 or 8.5% of value and £168 income

BAT Industries	9453	193	7900	419
British Petroleum	9518	194	6100	428
Coloroll Group	9239	191	7410	325
Dee Corporation	18,502	382	11,760	877
FKI Babcock	10,222	201	5760	132
Harrisons & Crosfield	8988	188	10,140	658
Heywood Williams Group	12,769	191	12,904	732
Hanson	8826	186	7320	257
Thos Locker Holdings	6759	159	6200	355
Low & Bonar	8336	181	6090	261
March Group	9736	196	5300	305
Quadrant	9069	189	7680	214
Racal Electronics	9207	190	10,829	222
Christian Salvesen	8341	181	8160	308
Trafalgar House	14,979	324	15,150	993
Ultramar	8599	184	7810	418
Wellcome	4433	187	7480	77
Personal Equity Plan	2400	67	1881	0

British shares = £152,736 or 69% of values and £6981 income

GT German Fund	6390	450	5255	62
Dunedin Euro Growth UT	9810	539	6510	22
BG: America Unit Trust	17,300	888	10,180	0
M&G American Rec Fund	9111	500	6452	95
Henderson Hong Kong Fund	8868	488	5778	49
EFM Tokyo Fund	8995	500	8425	0
Baring Japan New Gen Fund	8250	453	6974	69
S.U.T.M. Scot Pac Fund	9144	507	8118	0

Foreign trusts = £57,692 or 26% of values and £297 income

Realised capital gains	(15,191)	1967	—	—
Total	250,000	9929	221,630	7464

Johnston's misfortune neatly illustrates market risk. Chancer's portfolio is in no way speculative, and all the companies are known and substantial, with good stock-exchange marketability and above average yields. The unit trusts all come from good managers, with straightforward objectives, and invest in the major economies of the world. Though during 1988 the portfolio has recovered somewhat, its quality failed to save it during the crash. Like Andrew S, Johnston had gone all 'equity'. Both discovered, as Mr Milner had before them, that: 'Ruin . . . came two months earlier than I expected.'

Checkpoints

● Develop an investment strategy to take account of the temperature of the market, with a risk exposure with which we feel comfortable.

● Though the market is driven by fear and greed, it is also influenced by man's craving for security. By maintaining our pre-set risk limits, and never going outside them, we will give ourselves that security.

● A high-risk investment policy combined with a high-risk investment strategy can, and probably will, lead to disaster; remember Murphy's Law that: 'Whatever can go wrong, will go wrong.'

● Be optimistic but also be mean. Are those promised rewards big enough to justify those real risks?

● If we bought a share for one reason, which does not work out, we should not hold on to it for another reason altogether. Accept that we will often make mistakes.

● When we do find ourselves with a big, quick profit, realise part of it. It may not be there to take in six months' time.

● Never expect a bell to ring to sound either the top or bottom of the market. We have to make up our own minds as to what is a fair buying or selling price.

Chapter Seven

The practical investor – control and choice

> *The bulls are like the giraffe which is scared of nothing, or like the magician of the Elector of Cologne, who in his mirror made the ladies appear much more beautiful than they were in reality. The bears, on the contrary, are completely ruled by fear, trepidation and nervousness. Rabbits become elephants, brawls in a tavern become rebellions, faint shadows appear to them as signs of chaos.*
>
> CONFUSION DE CONFUSIONES, 1688

Mr Kenneth M gave up full-time surgery some years ago, but developed an equally intense interest in his share portfolio. He doubled its value between January 1984 and 'Black Monday'. But successful and active dealing in a bull market, unless practised within tight discipline, often results in messy portfolios, and lost coherence. This is what has happened to his portfolio. At the time of the crash he had over sixty separate investments spread amongst twenty-two different managers.

Kenneth's portfolio at November 1987 values

Security type	Numbers	Values
Unit Trusts	24	£137,000
'Insurance Bonds'	9	£145,000
Equities	25	£ 75,000
Gilts and Fixed Interest	5	£ 31,000
Deposits	2	£ 20,000
Total	67	£408,000

Kenneth developed his dealing as he began to follow a less active professional career. He was a name at Lloyd's and needed to understand the investment management of his Lloyd's insurance reserves. He has the right mentality to be a good investor, and is not afraid to take profits or losses. In fact, he pays capital gains tax most years.

The family do not need any income from the portfolio, and Kenneth treats it as an inheritance to be developed for the children. Though he regards himself as a cautious, rather than an optimistic investor, he likes to win, in the short term as well as in the long term. He does not wish to be out of the markets.

Kenneth found it difficult to find a satisfactory adviser, possibly because like many of us he never decided precisely what he wanted. Instead he relied on his own reading and research, and concentrated on unit trusts rather than shares. Like most investors, Kenneth thought investing was about finding 'stars' rather than developing a team. His portfolio did well, but may have done even better with a smaller and more controllable list of investments.

Basic principles: the need for a theme

The opportunity was there. Lloyd's requires certain types of securities to be held as reserves. These are gilts and shares in major companies, and should have been the core of Kenneth's portfolio. The rest of the capital could then have been used for active trading in fashionable 'blue chips' and unit trusts, which Kenneth enjoys doing, with perhaps 10 per cent of the capital kept for 'penny stocks' and third market gambles. A portfolio that lacks a theme and is of the size and spread of Kenneth's is impossible to control. It was poorly positioned when the crash came.

The managers asked to review this said: 'The holdings are random and concentrated in small companies with high hopes, or unit trusts with very specialised objectives. This is classic bull-market investment policy . . . and is no longer prudent. It is time to look for quality management, good yields, well covered dividends, strong cash flow and the ability to withstand a possible recession.'

Clear policy allows clear judgement on performance

Thornton Management was started by Richard Thornton after he had sold out of his earlier successfully quoted investment firm. It has grown over the last three years to become a major fund manager, and is now part-owned by the German Dresdner Bank.

Early devotees of Japan and the 'Tiger' economies of South East Asia, Thornton believe these markets should have at least 25 per cent of Kenneth's capital. With 30 per cent in direct UK 'blue chip' shares, and another 30 per cent in cash and gilts, they consider the portfolio would then be aggressively positioned for whatever befalls financially.

Rensburg also advise direct UK investment for Kenneth, keeping unit trusts only for overseas markets. They recommend a rather different asset allocation – more Europe than Far East – and propose a two-stage restructuring. This may be necessary for Thornton as well. Neither firm likes single premium 'insurance bonds' but getting Kenneth out of them quickly may be expensive. The same will also be true of the third-market stocks.

Rensburg are Big Bang in reverse. After a century as successful Liverpool 'market makers', the last decade has seen them become an efficient and low-cost private client agency stockbroker. They

Proposed asset allocation of Kenneth's portfolio at December 1987

Security	Rensburg Stage 1 %	Rensburg Stage 2 %	Thornton %
Cash	8	20	20
Bonds and Fixed Interest	13	30	10
UK Equities	29	35	30
European Equities	24	15	5
North American Equities	0	0	7
Far Eastern Equities	0	0	15
Japanese Equities	0	0	10
Gold	0	0	3
Insurance Bonds	26	0	0
Total	100	100	100

follow their own list of one hundred securities in great depth, and claim to be able to make money, either on an advisory or a discretionary basis, from clients with as little as £10,000 capital. They are now merging with Wise Speke of Newcastle to become one of the country's largest broking businesses.

Both firms have established a strategy; the theme of both is major companies in the UK and, for Thornton, the Far East and for Rensburg, Europe. Risk can now be controlled, and potential rewards identified and taken. But establishing a strategy is one thing, ensuring that we control our portfolio, and not it us, is another. Investment is a great creator of paper.

Control and management of cash

This is the beginning of administrative and investment control. First, we need a 'capital account' into which both our savings and capital go, and through which all security transactions are made. The High Street banks offer several purpose-built models for this, but these are just expensive current accounts. What we need is a free current account.

Both the Save & Prosper and the MIM-Britannia High Interest Current/Bank Account do the job perfectly if we have several thousand to invest. If we are still working on the thousands, then either the Nationwide Anglia FlexAccount or the Abbey National current account is the answer. None of the four make any charges whatsoever, produce full and regular statements, and pay interest on cash held in the account.

Those of us who are very efficient, or have few transactions, can then use this capital account to receive dividend payments. I prefer to have a separate income account – for this one or other of the building society accounts as they pay interest on all balances, however small – and arrange for share dividends and bond interest to be paid directly to this account. Arrange this with the broker when buying shares or bonds.

These monthly bank statements, recording all capital and in-come transactions, broker's contract notes, and interest or dividend income certificates show us what has happened, and enable us to produce a tax statement without too much loss of hair. Our broker should produce regular valuations, splitting the portfolio between bonds and shares, shares between different market sectors, showing cost price and current values of all holdings, performance of the portfolio against the index, and actual and projected income. Increasingly, we should expect to be charged for these if we want them more frequently than half yearly.

Those of us with home computers – Amstrad PCW, BBC Micro, or IBM PC clone – can do the job at home. There are two cheap and easy to use portfolio management software packages.*

Both are comprehensive. Either is worth having though *Personal Investor* gives greater analysis of the portfolio, while *Stockmarket* ties share transactions more conveniently into deposit and bank accounts.

If we are this far into technology, the Bank of Scotland Home and Office Banking System (HOBS) is great fun. There is a monthly £2.50 service charge for running the account which is accessed through Prestel. This costs a further £6.50 quarterly subscription but other charges can be avoided by using the system out of business hours. This keeps telephone bills down too. With this we can run all our own banking from home and, sooner or later, such systems are bound to include share buying.

Cash as an active component of the portfolio

Cash is really the most 'aggressive' portion of our portfolio. Part is the 'emergency' fund or liquidity reserve which is never invested. The other is the cash we keep for opportunities. A high level of cash implies uncertainty about price levels, and an unwillingness to commit ourselves to either bonds or shares until a more certain trend can be seen. Never be worried about high cash levels within the portfolio, particularly when sentiment has been bullish for a long time, for when markets collapse cash is king.

---

* *Stockmarket*, Meridian Software, 39 Balcaskie Road, London SE9 1HQ. 01-850 7057; *Personal Investor*, Micro Investor Software, Orchard Chambers, 4 Rocky Lane, Heswall, Wirral L60 0BY. 051-342 6482.

For higher-rate tax payers, National Savings certificates have tax advantages, though these have to be held for their full life of five years for all the benefits to be obtained. Local authorities still offer deposit rates fixed for one to ten years ahead but early repayment is generally difficult, though 'Yearling' bonds have a twelve-month life, are quoted, and pay interest six-monthly.

The building societies will continue to offer the best and most convenient method of earning from the cash part of our portfolio. However, the best rates are never available from the high street names, but from local or regional societies. There is an independent building society 'broker'* which gives free advice on rates, to both resident and expatriate depositors. Statutory protection of 90 per cent covers deposits of up to £20,000 with any building society, and there is now an 'Ombudsman' to handle customer complaints.

An alternative, and more aggressive way of holding cash is through a currency deposit. While this can be arranged through a bank, an easier way is through a currency fund. These operate from the Channel Islands, and are run by banks and fund managers. They should either be subsidiaries of quoted UK companies, or part of world-wide banking groups; otherwise we need to be wary, as these offshore managers are not always covered by UK or EEC investor-protection laws.

We have a choice with these accounts. Either we make our own decisions so that, if we believe that sterling is too high compared to the deutschmark, we have our deposit account in DM and earn the going rate but also hope that, as the pound falls, our DM deposit becomes worth in pounds; or we get someone else to do this for us.

Currency managers with their current rates and past performance, their charges and their addresses are shown each month in *Money Management* magazine. Interest rates are good, compared to the equivalent rate in a bank branch, because these 'pooled' funds operate in the wholesale money markets, lending short-term money to governments and major banks and industrial corporations. The managed funds, in addition, attempt to improve on the

---

* The Building Society Shop, City House, Maid Marian Way, Nottingham NG1 6BH. 0602 472595.

interest rate by their choice of currencies – sterling, yen and DM deposits rather than dollars, for instance.

However, the attractions of foreign currency accounts depend, for a sterling investor, on the weakness of the pound. Good capital performance of these funds has reflected the historical weakness of the UK economy, with its tendency to higher inflation than other countries. If we believe that this is now past history, and that the pound is likely to improve in value relative to other currencies, then we should use these off-shore funds as a sterling account depositing in the wholesale money markets, and possibly getting a better rate of interest for us, or keep our cash at home in a building society.

Bonds for high and certain income

Because cash gives us liquidity – the ability to get back immediately what we put in – it cannot be relied upon for yield. The best way of purchasing a certain flow of income for the foreseeable future is to buy bonds, either of governments or of companies. These are IOUs of the issuing organisation, with a fixed rate of interest, and normal quotations show two different yields – a 'flat' or 'running' yield and a 'redemption' yield.

The flat yield is the income that we will get if we buy the bond today. It is the 'coupon' or rate of interest written on the 'face' of the bond – gilts always have a 'face' or 'nominal' value of £100 – multiplied by one hundred and divided by the price of the bond. The market price will rarely be the same as the face value, and because most bonds are, in the end, repaid 'at par' or face value, there is also a 'redemption yield'.

This redemption yield is the actual rate of interest – or yield – earned by the investor who holds the bond to maturity. Sometimes it will be higher than the flat yield because the bond can be bought 'below par'. But at other times, when bonds are trading above par, the redemption yield will be lower. This is because the loss of capital between the purchase price, and the redemption value at par, must be deducted over the remaining life of the bond from the actual income being earned. Fortunately, these figures are now worked out by computers.

Interest rates, bond yields and prices

The relationship between bond prices, and interest rates, is inverse. When interest rates rise, bond prices fall – and vice versa. The reason is, again, the purpose of investment. We are buying a stream of future income. When interest rates rise, £100 will buy more income. The stream of income bought yesterday when interest rates were lower can today be bought for less than £100, so bond prices fall to reflect this. The opposite happens when they rise.

More importantly, the longer into the future that stream of income stretches, the greater the change in capital value today. This is the discount factor mentioned earlier – money now is always worth more than money next year, and a lot more than in thirty years' time. In general, gilt prices are more stable than those of shares, as is seen from the chart.

This relationship of the value of money today compared to money tomorrow creates the opportunities and complexities of the gilt market. Because government borrowing requirements are so enormous, and investors so diverse in their needs, the Bank of England issues many different categories of bonds to be traded in the market. The market consists of nine basic types of bond, together with two 'specials' which represent the far and recent past.

The government wants to appeal to as many different types of investor as possible. Low-coupon gilts produce most of their return as a tax-free capital gain; high coupons give an immediate high income from the interest rate but probably little capital gain. Some of the high-coupon gilts, particularly those issued when inflation was worst during the nineteen-seventies, now sell well above their face values. Buyers of these are getting high-running yields at the expense of their capital.

Equally, short gilts appeal to investors who want something with characteristics close to a deposit; because redemption dates are close, the price will vary much less than for those with redemption dates much further into the future. All investors can mix and match their needs from this combination of different coupons and different maturities.

How do we make our way through this jungle of types? With

01.06.87 to 01.06.88

OPAL UT: International Growth RI NX STG
OPAL UT: UK Growth
OPAL UT: Gilt & Fixed Interest

Source: Micropal

difficulty used to be the answer until Jeannette Ruttaford of CL-Alexanders Laing & Cruickshank showed in her decision tree which of the jungle trails skirted the crocodile pools.

Notice that she uses 'risk' in its investment sense. The risk is not of loss in the normal sense, but of price movement that may result in loss. This price movement can be up or down, depending upon the market's expectation of interest rate movements, and its assumptions about how tough or weak is the government's attitude to inflation. This is an attractive investment medium, for there is no capital gains tax on gilt transactions, and at a maximum income tax rate of 40 per cent the income helps boost our portfolio return.

The decision tree also mentions the 'specials'. These are the undated or 'irredeemable' gilts – such as the much-despised War Loan – issued when neither investors nor governments knew what inflation was, and 'index-linked' gilts. These last were issued when neither governments nor investors thought that inflation could ever again be conquered.

These IL gilts offer the traditional nineteenth-century coupons of 2 per cent to 2.5 per cent, but promise to make up, on maturity, the loss in the purchasing power of the capital. Yields on these gilts are normally shown at an assumed rate of either 5 per cent or 10 per cent inflation. They were designed on the assumption that most investors are concerned with the protection of 'value' rather than income here and now. As a result, they have never become popular amongst most private investors; other than the very rich, most of us do need a regular investment income.

If we buy gilts speculatively, or without thinking through our investment policy, circumstances may force us into realising 'book' losses. Long dated gilts can be volatile even though absolute price changes are much smaller than those of shares. The chart shows the long index-linked gilt; its volatility makes it a good dealing stock against expectations of changes in interest rates. Alternatively, it is a core holding for the very rich who need no income now but who wish to guarantee part of their wealth against inflation and tax.

Figure 19: How to buy gilts.

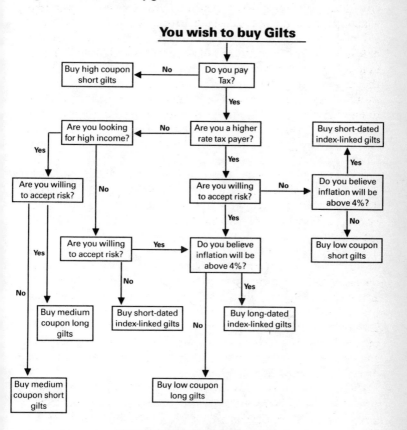

Maturity	Years	Coupons	Per cent
Short	Under 5	Low	Under 8
Medium	5 - 15	Medium	8 - 10
Long	Over 15	High	Over 10

Source: FT/CL-ALC

Figure 20: Long gilts are more volatile than short or mediums, and index-linked long gilts are exceptionally volatile.

MARKET PRICES OF TREASURY 2½%

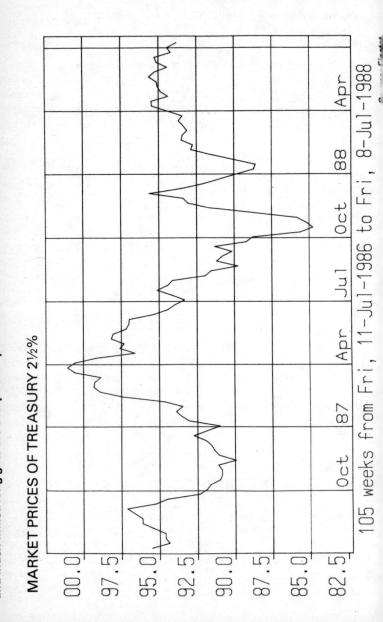

105 weeks from Fri, 11-Jul-1986 to Fri, 8-Jul-1988

Convertibles – the security designed for the private investor

Investors' demand for convertible bonds and convertible prefer-ence shares has grown rapidly with the slowing of inflation and of government spending. Since the crash, companies have preferred this way of raising money from shareholders for the expansion of the business; more new money has come from convertibles than from rights issues of ordinary shares. There are now over four hundred issues with a market capitalisation of £12 billion. This makes it bigger than the unlisted securities market (USM). It should also be a more important market to us as private investors, for it is the 'designer' investment for hard times.

All too often we shy away from this hybrid security. Since a convertible is designed to give an investor safety, income, and capital growth, it is worth a little effort on our part to understand it. In many ways the convertibles market, which is dominated by institutional investors, should be the main home of the private investor.

Safety

The nature of the security gives the 'safety'. It is either a debt obligation of the company – in other words a bond – or preference capital. In either case, the fixed yield is paid first – or in preference to – the paying of dividends to ordinary shareholders. So it is a safer security to hold in difficult times when companies may find it hard to maintain their previous profit levels.

Income

Because a convertible is first and foremost a fixed interest security the income, in order to attract buyers, has to compare with what investors can get from buying government bonds. Initially, a convertible will always pay the investor more than the yield available on ordinary shares. But, over the years, the dividends paid by successful companies should grow until the shares yield more than the fixed return on the convertible. That is the signal to convert.

Growth

This is where the growth comes from. Companies find it hard to get investors to buy their fixed-rate securities. The government is obviously a safer borrower, and generally pays a rate of interest that industry finds difficult to match. So companies offer investors a sweetener. In addition to the interest paid on the security, they also give the right to convert the bond – or preference share – into ordinary shares when it is profitable to do so.

The terms of this conversion are fixed when the convertible security is first created. Each £100 of stock can be exchanged for a specified number of shares at some future date, and this right can then be exercised for several years after that date. So convertibles offer investors the ability to buy shares for a long time in the future at today's price, while getting paid now a return nearer to a bank deposit rate than a share yield.

The compromise between yield and growth

For most of us, needing high income now but also determined to protect the purchasing power of our income in the future, the convertible is the ideal compromise between bonds and shares. It also offers simple and high-yielding insurance to those of us who are high-risk investors – keen to stay in the stock market but nervous about the risk of another crash.

Dealing costs for convertibles are the same as for equities. Many of the issues are large and very marketable and most can be bought in lots of £1000 upwards. We have to do our homework and be prepared to monitor our investments. We have to follow not only the company, but also the price performance of the ordinary shares as well as the convertibles.

Investing the indirect way

If we are not prepared to do this, we can buy indirectly. Many investment trusts with income investment objectives are keen buyers of convertibles, as a part of their portfolio, while there are an increasing number of unit trusts concentrating solely on convertibles. Investing through some of the trusts has other advantages. In addition to the domestic – or London – market, there is a euro-convertible – or international – market. This has become very important in recent years and accounts for about a third of the market.

This euro-market allows British companies to raise money at lower rates of interest than through London, but they have to give something in return. Generally, it is to allow the investor to 'put' these euro-convertible bonds back onto the company. This means that if investors feel that the share price is not going as well as expected, the company has to redeem the convertible bond. This is done at a price calculated to give investors the same return they would have got from buying a government bond of comparable maturity.

Obviously this facility is useful in a bear market but it is not for private buyers as the 'bargain' size in euro-convertibles is £25,000. What these developments demonstrate is that buying and holding convertibles is about assessing alternative returns – from the shares, the convertibles, gilts or a combination. It reinforces the point that investing is about achieving return and that the most certain part of this is the income of the coupon or dividend.

Possible drawbacks to convertibles

A convertible is a hybrid. It does not yield as much as a straight bond, nor will it grow so fast as an ordinary share. In a bull market, the investor looking for income growth may well do better in the shares rather than the convertible of a chosen company. But in volatile or 'sideways' markets, the fixed-interest yield puts a floor under the price. For many of us the price of slower growth for more capital security is worth paying.

Convertibles can become overpriced relative to the bond market. They then lose much of the appeal of a good yield, and some of their defensive qualities. This happened in 1987, and the price behaviour of Baillie Gifford's Convertible and General Trust shows this graphically (see overleaf).

What happened was that investors pushed shares in 1987 to such high levels that yields became negligible. Investors began to switch into convertibles. This was partly for yield, but it also reflected that convertibles had become a cheap way into the ordinary shares. The rise in the price of ordinary shares was so furious that it took time to be fully reflected in the convertible bond price. So, with the final charge of the bull, BG's trust outperformed the market as the price of convertibles was re-adjusted to reflect that of the underlying shares.

As a consequence of this, the yields on convertibles fell compared to straight – or non-convertible – bond yields. As the price of a convertible bond followed upwards in the wake of the related ordinary share, the increased price meant that the yield fell. As with gilts, the interest paid on a bond or preference share is fixed – so the higher the price, the lower the yield.

Convertibles were vulnerable to the crash, as the chart also shows, but they did not fall as badly as shares world-wide, or the

Figure 21: The price of convertibles can get out of line with bond prices.

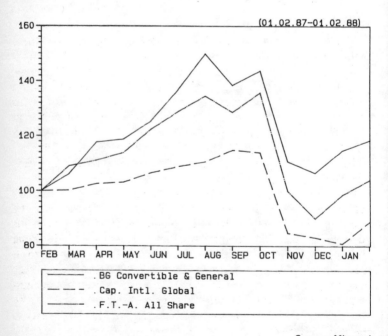

Source: Micropal

average of all UK unit trusts. Now that their yield basis is once again in line with the bond market, the defensive characteristics of convertibles will be to the fore if there is another setback in share prices.

Shares for growth of income

Share trading on the London Stock Exchange now takes place by telephone and the market is a computer screen. This has brought us two great advantages. One is that our local broker is now as well placed to deal, and as up-to-date with prices, as any City broker. The other is that we can now tell in advance how marketable our shares are. Marketability is important, as many of us found to our cost in October. Prices mean nothing if no one will trade the shares.

Shares to own

The most marketable shares are the 'alphas'. There are 136 of these at the moment, consisting of the largest British companies including all those that constitute the *Financial Times*–Stock Exchange 100 Index (Footsie). There is no exact definition as to what an 'alpha' stock is, but market makers must show actual dealing prices for them on the screen, together with the number of shares in which they are prepared to deal at that price; the screen also shows the price of the last trade done. The next 540 shares are 'betas'. These must have at least four market makers willing to quote dealing prices in order to qualify.

Most of our share portfolio should be selected from these two categories. Marketability is important. It has practical uses, for the 'touch' – or difference between buying and selling price – is determined by marketability. It defines quality, for institutional investors like to deal in big quantities and not feel 'locked-in' to an investment. It ensures widespread knowledge, for it is these very marketable stocks which the analysts follow since, if the fund managers like their recommendations, enough business can be done to justify the costs of the research. All of that spells security to us as private investors.

Shares for buying and selling

The 'gamma' stocks need only two market makers, and these only 'indicate' prices. After our broker has disclosed the size of the proposed transaction, then the haggling over actual dealing prices begins. Nearly all the smaller companies quoted on the USM – called the unlisted securities market because quotation standards are not so onerous as on the main market – are gammas. Finally 'deltas' are everything else, including the nursery companies quoted on the Third Market. It was companies such as these that Kenneth had, and both deltas and gammas have been very difficult shares to sell since the crash.

Gamma and delta shares, if held at all, should make up only a small part of our portfolio; they are fun gambling stocks in which we might do well, and equally lose our shirt if the company goes bust. By the time we learn which way things are going, it will be too late to act.

And shares for idiots

It should go without saying that only shares listed on one or other of the three 'official' markets should be bought by us. Nevertheless, it has to be said. It is easy to lose money buying shares on the official exchanges. It is certain that *we will lose all our money* if we buy shares any other way. Yet the gullibility of normally sensible people confronted by smooth talkers on the telephone never ceases to amaze anyone involved in the financial world.

Most such UK operations have been put out of business by the Securities and Investment Board, but many 'boiler-room' share-pushing companies are now based in Gibraltar, Spain and Switzerland. Several of the most notorious of these are reckoned to have earned at least £350 million over the last five years – and from whom? Why us, for who else is stupid enough to believe that a perfect stranger, telephoning out of the blue, will sell us the right to untold riches for just a few pounds?

Checkpoints

● **The American stockbrokers Shearson Lehman Hutton have a** slogan 'Minds over Money'. Let's adopt it for ourselves and develop both a strategy, and a theme, for our investments.

● Before we start investing, we must know how to organise the paper work. If our portfolio controls us, and not us it, then we will never do well.

● We must remember that investments for private investors comprise four different sections of the financial market – cash, bonds, convertibles and shares. Each has its place and function in our portfolio, and if we wish to be successful we must also learn how to use them at the right time and in the right way.

● Contrary to public belief, not all cats are black in the dark, and we will get badly scratched if we ever come to believe it. The core of our portfolio should consist of alpha and beta shares, and the gammas and deltas make up the marginal fun stocks bought with the capital we are prepared to lose. As for any other share offer, remember the professionals' view that: 'If it sounds too good to be true, it probably is.'

Notes: how to choose and price a convertible

There is one cardinal rule – only buy convertible securities of companies in which you are happy to be a shareholder for many years. Buying a convertible is taking a long-term view of an equity investment.

The other rules are easier:

● look for the longest possible conversion period

● go for the highest available nominal interest rates; they maintain their price better in bad times

● don't buy unless there is a substantial gap between the yield on the ordinary shares, and that of the convertible

● go for the large and easily marketable issues

The biggest issue of all is the Hanson 10 per cent cumulative unsecured loan stock (CULS) 2007/12. 10 per cent is the gross, or before-tax, 'coupon' or dividend paid on the CULS. The actual rate paid to the private investor will be this less 25 per cent tax or 7.5 per cent. If this were a convertible preference stock, and not a CULS, then the interest rate would be quoted net of tax as 7.5 per cent. Whichever the way of quoting, we are always paid net of the tax, and normally in two instalments at six monthly intervals.

Conversion dates run from 1990 to 2007. After this year, and up to 2012, any stock not converted into ordinary shares can be re-deemed – or bought back – by the company at par, or £100 for every £100 of stock, even if we bought it for £124.

Conversion terms are that every £100 nominal stock held can convert into 77.519 ordinary shares. This is sometimes described as a *conversion rate* of 77.519.

So the *conversion price* is CULS price of £124 divided by 77.519 (the number of shares for every nominal £100 of stock) or £1.60. How does that compare with the ordinary shares? They are priced at £1.31 in the market compared to the conversion price of £1.60. This means the CULS are at a *premium* to the ordinary of (£1.60 ÷ £1.31) or 22.1 per cent.

The major brokers track the movement of the 'premium' which, in the case of this Hanson issue, has varied during the year from 2 per cent to 29 per cent. So 22 per cent seems high, but what level of premium is worth paying?

The yield on the ordinary shares before tax is 4.69 per cent; the 'flat' or actual yield on the convertibles – ie ignoring the loss of capital if the bonds are held to maturity and repayment is at par – is 8.33 per cent before tax. This is a yield improvement of two-thirds, and seems worth having.

But a complicated computer calculation based on the premium also indicates that, if investors think the dividend pay-out on the ordinary shares of Hanson will grow by more than 6 per cent a year then they will get a better return by buying the ordinary shares than by paying the premium for the convertible.

This research from the major houses should be available to your stockbroker. A good rule of thumb is only to buy when the premium indicates a dividend growth rate of 10 per cent or more; such a rate of dividend increase is the maximum we can reasonably expect a company to maintain; in more difficult economic conditions 5 to 6 per cent is a more sensible target.

Chapter Eight

The practical investor – risk and reward

It is a quintessence of academic learning and a paragon of fraudulence; it is a touchstone for the intelligent and a tombstone for the audacious, a treasury of usefulness and a source of disaster.

CONFUSION DE CONFUSIONES, *1688*

Mr Len J is in his middle fifties. He and his wife took early retirement three years ago (1985) and now live on index-linked pensions of £16,700 a year. They own their house outright, except for a small secured loan of £2500, and save about £500 a month from their combined pensions and investment income. Both their children are now working.

Len's first investment was bought shortly before the 1974 crash. His next was a poorly performing unit trust but further investments, mainly Japanese and Australian unit trusts, were more successful. All of these had to be sold in 1982–83, and the proceeds used to support the children at university.

Len was reluctant to start investing again, despite increased capital from redundancy money, until he knew he and his wife could manage satisfactorily on their pensions. He was also concerned at the level of the markets and, for this reason, concentrated on income trusts rather than growth opportunities when they re-entered the market in 1986.

Len is a cautious investor, understanding instinctively that money should be invested for yield; he takes pleasure in his dividend cheques, particularly when they have increased over the previous year. Len finds it difficult to commit himself, and prefers to buy several small amounts of the same share – thus giving himself the ability to correct timing mistakes. He finds it easier to sell than to buy, and so went into the crash with more cash than shares.

Len's portfolio in December 1987

Security	Present value	Cost including expenses	Estimated income
Abbey Nat. Sterling Asset a/c	£40,000	£40,000	£4109
Portfolio 30 Gilt 'Bond'	£5000	£5000	£ 428

Cash and Gilts = £4500 or 79% of value of portfolio

Security	Present value	Cost including expenses	Estimated income
Wm Morrison S'kets Convertible preference	£1350	£1498	£ 97
P&O Red Preference*	£ 900	£ 546	£ 45
BG Convertible Trust	£ 689	£ 693	£ 56
Fidelity Global Convertible Trust	£ 419	£ 500	£ 24

Bonds = £3358 or 6% of value of portfolio

Security	Present value	Cost including expenses	Estimated income
British Gas	£1375	£1485	£ 134
British Telecom	£ 820	£ 520	£ 47
Rolls Royce	£ 594	£1165	£ 40
Arkwright Income	£ 830	£1000	£ 55
FS Higher Yield Fund	£ 810	£1000	£ 44
Holborn Equity Income	£ 782	£ 700	£ 36
Sun Life High Yield Income	£ 625	£ 700	£ 40
Sun Life Man Income	£ 583	£ 600	£ 34

British shares and trusts = £6419 or 11% of value of portfolio

Security	Present value	Cost including expenses	Estimated income
Fidelity European Income	£ 782	£1000	£ 38
Royal London International Income	£ 326	£ 500	£ 24
Sun Life Managed Growth	£ 394	£ 600	£ 12
Wardley International Income	£ 726	£1000	£ 67

Foreign trusts = £2228 or 4% of value of portfolio

	Present value	Cost including expenses	Estimated income
Total	£57,005	£58,507	£5330

*   held for discounts on channel ferries

Len avoided market risk by keeping most of his capital in cash. By so doing, he also missed the rewards of the earlier rise in the market – prices are still above their end-1986 levels – and ran the risk of falling interest rates and inflation. Len's investment policy was right for 1987, but it came about by chance rather than design.

A history of investing only as and when funds are available is not a good preparation for thinking through the structuring of what is now a sizeable portfolio. Not surprisingly investment managers commented that: 'The portfolio lacks a theme with eleven separate unit trusts, which include three mainstream UK equity trusts, and no less than five international trusts.'

As it happens, Len can accept such strictures with equanimity: his capital is still intact. The market is now better priced than a year ago, so Len needs to think through how he should invest. He is out to purchase a rising income. He needs a portfolio structure that will protect him from further market falls, and allow him to sleep soundly at nights. Within that policy, which shares should he buy, and why the complaints about the number of unit trusts that he holds? Surely that is sensible diversification?

Is superior performance possible?

The answer to that is no but why it is so requires some understanding of MPT – a portmanteau description of studies and ideas from academics interested in stock market behaviour. Modern portfolio theories stem from the failure of professional managers to do significantly better than the market. If fundamental analysis was doing its job, managers with the right brokers – ie those spending most money on research which they then first offer to client investors with the biggest pockets – ought to do a lot better than the rest of us.

They don't. The majority – about 70 per cent – of all fund managers do worse than the market, as measured by the major indices such as the *FT*–Actuaries All Share index for London, and the Standard and Poor's 500 index for New York. This is neither surprising nor worrying. First, an index is the market average and an average means some have to be below while others are above. Secondly, indices do not include transaction costs which are significant in these days of 'short-termism'. A recent survey reported that pension funds, on average, now hold shares for less than two years.

The statistical average of fund managers – or the mean of their performance – has a deviation, or gap, of about 20 to 25 per cent between the best and the worst. Splendid – except further statistical studies showed there was not much point in identifying those good managers for there is little or no performance consistency between one year and another. In other words, this year's hot-shot performer may well be next year's dunce – and indeed vice-versa – but we have no way of knowing in advance.

Fund managers and portfolio managers

MPT studies were not greeted with overwhelming enthusiasm. They were, of course, produced by other-worldly types such as ivory-tower academics and, even worse, boy-geniuses with PhDs in mathematics and statistics. Neither type could easily appreciate the real problems of fund management, in particular they had trouble with the fact that business and bonuses depend on persuading trustees of pension funds – or even us in our humble role of unit trust buyer – that *we* are so much better at managing money than *they* are.

Certainly neither could accept that managing money involves owners as well as managers, and might require as much art as science, and more instinct and common sense than detailed analysis. Qualities such as owner satisfaction are hard to measure for statistical correlation.

The years of the bull market have encouraged a belief, amongst trustees of pension funds as well as ordinary investors, that investment is a financial race meeting, with the different national stock markets the horses, and the fund managers the jockeys. Each quarter the punters compare performances and, if unhappy with the result of their bets, switch horses, sack jockeys and start again. As all values on the security markets are relative, so all performance has become relative. Horses, jockeys and trainers – the research brokers – all jostle to make it to the top 'quartile' of performance; reality insists that one hundred will not go into twenty-five even though, with the right choice of comparative index, certainly more than 25 per cent of managers claim membership of that top quartile.

Competitive requirements may mean that this is the way fund managers have to sell themselves, whether to us as direct investors or to the trustees of our pension funds. Fortunately, we do not have to accept these terms. We need portfolio managers, not fund managers. A portfolio manager exploits the much-abused fund manager in choosing the constituents of a portfolio. Few of us have the expertise to follow overseas stock markets or technical sections on our own so, if we want to invest in Japan or bio-technology companies, we should find a fund that does this, and check out the long term performance of the investment house.

However, the function of a portfolio manager is to achieve our investment objectives with the least possible risk. Performance requirements for us should be absolute, and not relative. We wish to end 1987 as rich as we started it. Any portfolio manager who expects praise from us because, we are told, our portfolio has only lost x when the market has lost 2x, is 'bad, mad and dangerous to know'.

One of my readers recently joined the Fidelity Personal Portfolio Management Service because her former adviser had actually reduced her fortune by such ill-considered 'performance management'. Yet the five years during which her money declined in value saw an exceptionally strong bull market. The average pension fund, according to the main portfolio performance measurement companies, has had an annual rate of return over the last ten years of 20 per cent on UK equities, 15 per cent on overseas equities, and just over 16 per cent on the total portfolio of shares, property, bonds and cash. The Micropal unit trust index increased over the five years to September 1987 from £1000 to £4214. Management fees, when combined with ignorance or incompetence, can seriously damage our financial health.

There is another difficulty involved in the pursuit of short-term superior performance. American research shows that analysts are not very good at forecasting future profits, and err on average by about a third. This is not surprising, given the problems of analysis, and the increasing pressures on analysts to pinpoint 'out-performing' shares over a timescale which is getting shorter and shorter.

Most analysts admit to using past history, and Professor Little demonstrated in the nineteen-sixties that last year's earnings give no clue to this year's profits. The best analysts, and managers, have always used their intuition as much as financial logic. They may be sure that they know what is good value but they also know it may take time, even years, for the market to realise this, and follow them.

If the analyst is denied the firm foundation of fundamental research, and forced increasingly into very short time views, then current market sentiment is bound to influence conclusions. 'Growth analysis' seems to have largely replaced fundamental analysis and this involves the very thing against which Dodd and Little both warn – projections of future profits based on very recent experience. Much analysis assumes that company profits and share prices will be what they will be, because they are now what they are.

Other studies showed that share prices themselves did not behave in any preordained fashion. As a coin may come down heads ten times in a row, yet statistically the eleventh time is still a 50:50 bet, so also with shares. The fact that they have gone up for the last month does not mean that tomorrow they have a greater chance of rising than falling. This 'random walk' theory of share price movements – that share price movements are unpredictable – then led on to further studies which claim that the market is efficient.

Basic principles: diversification of portfolios

This Efficient Market Hypothesis (EMH) – the one adumbrated by Charles Dow in Chapter Three in simple English – is based on studies which show that investors are not fooled by the 'creative accountancy' of corporate financiers. Whatever is to be known about a company is known, and so is reflected in the share price. Because market prices immediately adjust to new information – political, economic, industrial and corporate – they will always reflect 'true' values.

Since in this efficient market of perfect knowledge, undervalued or overvalued shares cannot exist, managers cannot do better or worse than competitors by superior 'share picking'. Performance depends upon being in the right market at the right time, and getting the right risk profile for the portfolio.

The investment rhythm of the business cycle

There is a rhythm in economic life. Economists call it the business cycle and, in fact, argue that there is not one business cycle, but several, with each taking place over different time scales. It is when cycles coincide that business activity can be very fruitful – or appallingly unprofitable. However, since there is neither agreement amongst economists about these cycles, nor any satisfactory explanation as to what causes them we should, as investors, just concentrate on the obvious.

As economic activity gathers pace, new workers begin to spend their wages on food and necessities, and the basic companies – food manufacturers and retailers, brewers and transport companies – do better. Then, as the boom gathers speed and people begin to feel better off, the companies that depend more on our discretionary spending begin to benefit – the clothing companies, ritzier retailers, advertising and employment agencies, housebuilders, paper and packaging companies and manufacturers of consumer durables, from vacuum cleaners to cars.

At this stage, with economic activity putting pressure on factory capacity, the makers of capital goods begin to see their own order books growing bigger, and profit margins improving. Then, as the rate of expansion puts the whole system under strain, and governments act to keep inflation from getting out of control, tightening monetary conditions puts the process in reverse as marginal businesses go bust, and others lay off workers.

Most industries – and companies within them – are mature. Their sales growth is determined by the growth of the economy, and profits by the competition. In some years they will do exceptionally well; this may be the result of economic expansion but often it is a recovery from periods of economic difficulty, an uncompetitive currency compared to foreign competitors, or restraint on profitability caused by social and political pressures. During such times, profits and dividends will rise at above average rates. All of this has been happening to British companies in the nineteen-eighties. Then things go back to normal.

The balance of company risk

If we could foretell the future, and were very cautious investors, we would buy shares in companies whose business cycles complement each other. As one does badly, another does well. The return on our portfolio, say we had only two such shares called A and B and the same amount of money in each, would look like Figure 22.

Figure 22

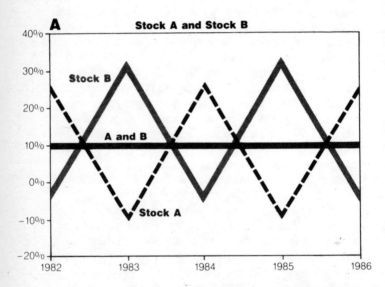

Source: *Registered Representative*

Each company goes through 'boom and bust' over the cycle earning from a maximum of 30 per cent to a loss of 10 per cent on assets, but our 'portfolio' earns us 10 per cent each year. This uncertainty of company performance is known in the trade as 'company' or 'specific' risk – as opposed to market risk which hits all companies alike.

The portfolio not to have is one in which the business cycles of the companies concerned move in perfect step with each other, such as companies B and C in Figure 23.

Figure 23

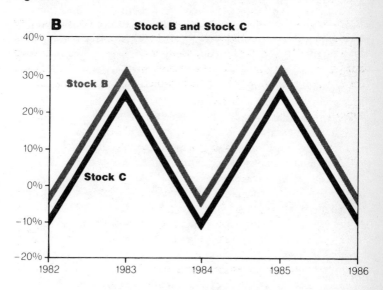

Source: Registered Representative

Yet this is the sort of portfolio many of us end up with, for it is very human to have more of what looks good and is doing well; to hold Laing and Wimpey, say, is to have this type of risk, for both are contractors with big housebuilding activities. Whatever affects one will equally affect the other. Or we might have Next and Ratners and, though one sells clothes and the other jewellery, we have again doubled up our company risk. Both these companies are retailers, with a range of goods that in their prices and fashion appeal to similar age and social groups.

Systematic risk or birds of a feather flock together

If our portfolio, instead, concentrates on 'tip sheet stocks', and gamma- and delta-rated companies – as have those of Andrew S and Kenneth M – this risk becomes greater and gets a different name.

This is called 'systematic' risk. Laing and Wimpey will both do badly in a severe recession, but this will be nothing new to them. They are large and established companies and have lived through such problems in the past. Next and Ratners have both expanded enormously over the last five years, and have yet to be 'seasoned' by really hard economic conditions. Smaller, less successful companies amongst the gamma and delta classifications, which have blossomed in the summer of the bull market may well shrivel when winter comes.

It is this similar though adverse effect of a tightening of monetary and financial conditions on companies in different industries, but at the same stage of development, that is 'systematic' risk. Its measurement is called 'beta' and defines the volatility of share prices against the market average.

The theory goes that companies with higher systematic risk have more volatile share prices – they go up faster and further than those of seasoned companies, or companies in mature industries, but equally come down faster and further when the market goes into reverse. A beta of 1.0 means that a share is no more and no less volatile than the FT index; 2.0 that it is twice as volatile while 0.5 means it bounces around only half as much as the index.

Our objective is control and not elimination of company risk

In putting together our portfolio, we aim to control – but not to eliminate – company risk. The reason is that we wish to do better than the market and the elimination of company risk from a portfolio means that it will perform as well, or as badly, as the market itself. Indeed, several major funds are now run on an index basis as pension fund trustees decided, on the basis of MPT, that if fund managers could not beat the market, why pay them to do what could be done for nothing (not exactly true, as they discovered that it still takes money and brains to set up their funds to track their chosen indices).

Market risk cannot be eliminated; it can only be insured against through our portfolio structure. Company risk can be reduced substantially, though not entirely, by diversified shareholdings. Academic studies assuming market risk at 30 per cent, and graphically presented in Figure 24, show that the company risk of a

Figure 24

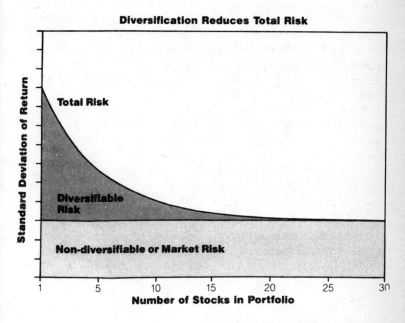

Diversification Reduces Total Risk

Source: Registered Representative

portfolio is reduced substantially with ten or more holdings, and virtually eliminated with twenty shares or more.

Depending on our mentality, we should aim to invest in between five and fifteen companies. Any more than this, and we lose control. If this degree of concentration seems too high a risk for us, then we will be better off investing at one remove in an investment or unit trust.

Diversification: theory into practice

So Len has not really diversified his portfolio. A unit trust has
thirty or more shares, so company risk is as much reduced as it ever
can be. Buying three UK general funds does not eliminate any
remaining risk, but simply adds to Len's administrative burden.
Five international trusts ensure that Len will do no better than the
average of all the world's stock markets, and give no guarantee that
he will not do worse.

Had Len followed the logic of his own income objectives, he
would have developed an investment strategy like this:

Len's current strategy		*What it should have been*	
Mixed income UTs	2	1	UK bond UT
Convertible UT	1	1	UK convertible UT (existing)
UK equity UTs	3	1	UK equity UT (from existing 3)
International UTs	5	1	International bond UT
		1	International convertible UT (existing)
		1	European UT (existing)
		1	Pacific UT (switch from general)
		1	North American UT (also switch)
Total	11	8	

The portfolio would have been better diversified for reward as well
as for risk. It would also have produced a better yield, and given
Len greater control of policy so that he could switch his interests
easily within the three major economic blocs, or between fixed
interest and shares, as his reading of the financial outlook dictated.

Even someone as level-headed as Len got carried away by
promises of better than average returns. Fortunately, because the
Barlow Clowes 30 Portfolio is UK-based, he will probably escape
the misfortune of those now wondering how much of their £138
million will ever be recovered from the Gibraltarian sister company. Following the decision tree on page 131,* Len should have

---

* Len, as a standard-rate taxpayer looking for a high income, with no risk, needs a
short-dated gilt with a medium coupon while, if Len were prepared to forgo some
immediate income, he could have bought an index-linked short-dated gilt.

invested in a short dated gilt with a medium coupon and bought through the post office for £21 for £5000 worth of stock.

What Len should have asked himself, and the managers or salesmen of the Barlow Clowes funds, is how they could offer a better than market rate, after the deduction of annual management charges, initial charges, and commissions to sales agents. A second question is why, when it is so simple and cheap to buy gilts through the post office, use an expensive fund? Anything out of the ordinary all too often turns out to be just that, and Len has had a lucky escape.

If Len had wanted a risk that might produce a reward then he should have bought the price-volatile Treasury 2.5 per cent 2020 index-linked gilt which was then (1986) yielding more than the yield on the FTA but with yield and capital both protected from inflation by government guarantee.

How professional managers reorganised Len's money

Unit trusts are not necessarily the right answer for Len, even though he obviously prefers the more cautious investment approach. Stockbrokers asked to review Len's portfolio both thought he should invest directly. This is cheaper in initial costs than using unit trusts, or 'insurance bonds', and more exciting for those who enjoy the market. Safety comes from diversification within industrial sectors, and the choice of 'blue-chip' shares.

Manchester-based Henry Cooke Lumsden were relaxed about the immediate future in early 1988, and proposed using the present trading range of the market to restructure the holdings to a tighter, better balanced growth portfolio though still one with a better than average market yield and, in deference to Len's caution, with large cash holdings.

Their recommendations were to increase the bond holdings at the expense of the cash – they considered rightly that interest rates were due to fall – and to switch most of the unit trusts into blue chip companies that are all mature, and cover a wide range of business activities. They maintain an international involvement for Len, but with a sharpened theme by increasing the Fidelity European holding, and switching all other trusts into an investment trust concentrating on the Pacific markets. Despite these proposals,

Len's exposure to market risk is up by not much more than 10
per cent of portfolio value – £14,000 compared to his own £8500.

The Henry Cooke Lumsden policy for Len

	Security	*Sector holding*
£ 5000	liquidity reserve	
£20,000	investment reserve	
	Cash (44%)	£25,000
£ 5000	Treasury 2% IL 1996	
£ 5000	Portfolio 30	
	Gilts (17%)	£10,000 cost
£ 1498	Wm Morrison convertible preference	
£ 546	P&O redeemable preference	
£ 693	BG convertible UT	
£ 500	Fidelity Global convertible UT	
£ 2500	Hanson 10% CULS	
£ 2500	Williams Holdings convertible preference	
	Bonds (14%)	£8237 cost
£ 1485	British Gas	
£ 520	British Telecom	
£ 1200	Ladbroke	
£ 1200	Maxwell Communications	
£ 1200	National Westminster Bank	
£ 1200	Pilkingtons	
£ 1200	Prudential	
	UK shares (14%)	£8005 cost
£ 3000	Fidelity European Income UT	
£ 3000	TR Pacific Assets IT	
	International (10%)	£6000 cost
Portfolio total at cost		**£57,242**

The theme is of confidence in the British economy through large
British companies held as shares and convertibles, with the European and Pacific economies playing minor supporting roles.

Henderson Crosthwaite's office in Cheltenham are noticeably
more bearish than Henry Cooke Lumsden. Like the Manchester
firm, they recommended alternatives to the Abbey National
sterling asset account which would give greater flexibility and
better yields, and suggested that £10,000 of this cash should go into
gilts.

They propose an immediate improvement to the portfolio's quality by the sale of the privatisations and some of the unit trusts, and a switch into two good investment trusts. They intend to increase liquidity with further sales in the expected strong rally in the spring and want to keep their options open; depending on how both the political and the market situation were developing, they would either recommend that Len go into convertibles – as a safety-first way into the equity market – or add to his gilts.

Henderson Crosthwaite Cheltenham office review of Len's portfolio at December

Security		*Sector holding*
£30,000	liquidity reserve	
£ 3905	awaiting reinvestment	
	Cash (59%)	£33,905 cost
£10,000	Treasury 6.75% 1995/8	
£ 5000	Portfolio 30	
	Gilts (26%)	£15,000 cost
£ 1498	William Morrison convertible preference	
£ 546	P&O Red preference	
£ 693	BG convertible UT	
£ 500	Fidelity Global convertible UT	
	Bonds (6%)	£ 3237 cost
£ 1000	Arkwright Income UT	
£ 700	Holborn Equity Income UT	
£ 1200	Investors Capital IT	
£ 1200	Merchants IT	
	UK trusts (7%)	£ 4100 cost
£ 1000	Fidelity European Income	
	International (2%)	£ 1000 cost
Portfolio total at cost		**£57,242**

The theme of this first stage of the restructuring is very much one of 'wait and see'. Len's exposure to market risk has been reduced, and the portfolio prepared so that Len can either build up the gilt holdings, if recession develops, or push more heavily into convertible bonds if the 'soft landing' seems more likely. Potential concentration will be on the British economy, but through investment trusts rather than direct.

Len's portfolio and the efficient market hypothesis

The rearrangement of Len's portfolio seems far-removed from MPT and the problems of multi-million pound investment portfolios, yet the issues are the same. These are how best to deploy money to get the best return for the least risk. This means buying good value in the stock market, but how is good value to be identified?

MPT, it seems, does not have all the answers. Beta, for instance, can only be measured retroactively. American academics have been at it again and according to their research, it seems that beta changes over time. Those 'high-beta' portfolios, with their much greater systematic risk, have not actually done better than 'low-beta' ones despite the theory. This conclusion is not shared by some of the measurement companies in Britain, who claim that the significant difference in pension fund performance over the crash depended on their beta or risk characteristics.

So the importance of this is not the figure – for all that some unit trusts are now pushing beta numbers in risk classification of their portfolios – but the principle. Systematic risk is real, and something we need to remember when choosing shares.

The Efficient Market Hypothesis itself, with properly discounted information leading to continuously adjusted true market values, all calculator-driven and not an ounce of unreason around, came unstuck on 17 October 1987. An addition to the theory has now been added to put Humpty Dumpty back together again.

The market has investors. These are rational, sensible folk who buy when shares are cheap, and sell when they are dear, and remain profoundly uninfluenced by fashion. Normally we good guys control the market and ensure that it is efficient, that all information is properly discounted, that everything is truly priced, and that nothing is over- or under-valued.

There are others in the market. These – and of course we have nothing to do with such types – are the short term speculators, impressed by every passing fad, and quite unaware of the important financial function of the market place. No doubt, somewhere between these two groups, can be discerned those professional operators, working the 'bigger fool' market. Every now and again the baddies ride into the market and get the upper hand . . . It's nice to know that share-price academics are devotees of the cinema and its key plot!

Speculator and investor both

But that great English economist John Maynard Keynes – no mean speculator in currencies and shares himself – was complaining sixty years ago that: 'The actual, private object of the most skilled investment today is "to beat the gun" as the Americans so well express it, to outwit the crowd, and to pass the bad, or depreciating half crown to the other fellow.'

The reality is that investment has two parents; though one is the cautious desire to protect and maintain what we have, the other is the wish to win and to make. As none of us has the characteristics of only one of our parents, so equally we must accept this dual influence in our investment life. Our task is to recognise which conditions require which impulse to be in the ascendant.

Our problem remains. The market is superbly effective at ensuring that share prices quickly and efficiently impound a wide range of knowledge and opinions about companies. Few, if any, individuals have the perception to outguess, with any consistent success, the total of human forecasting ability that prices shares, and so makes the market.

The market is good at pricing relative values because that is what it is all about, though it does get carried away by fashion, as history and the Goldman Sachs study show. However, the market does not seem so good at establishing absolute values. Yet those are the ones we want to know. Like merchants throughout the ages, we want to buy cheap and sell dear. It is a proven way of making money.

Charts and the future

Charles Dow thought he knew the solution to this problem. Like today's supporters of the EMH, he believed the market was efficient and share prices reflected all that was known about the economy and the company. Where he, and the many followers and developers of his ideas, part company with the EMH theorists is in the assessment of investors.

Technical analysis, the school to which the Dow Theory and

similar theories belong, knows that investors are not rational. Instead, like Pavlovian-trained sheep, they career one way or the other led by the bellwethers of fear and greed. (It was a technical analyst who remarked that, compared to investment managers, a flock of sheep is a rabble.) So by ignoring completely both economic conditions and company financial health, but closely analysing past and current price movements instead, an investor can identify those turning points which say 'buy' or 'sell'.

This was too appealing an approach for an academic with a computer to ignore, and indeed it was the use of computers to 'prove' these theories that started the academic study of portfolio theory. Sure enough, whichever chartist theory was tested, and however exhaustively it was examined for predictive capacity, commonsense won out. The future cannot be foretold. Worse, share price movements are random – which is why this part of MPT is called 'random walk' – and the patterns that chartists watch for exist in their imagination only. History tells the same tale.

The market guru of the nineteen-seventies was Joseph Granville, whom many would personally credit with the sharp price collapse of 1981 in New York and London. Alas poor Joe – he stayed bearish and failed to see the start of the 1982 bull market. His mantle was soon donned by Robert Prechter, devotee of another chartist theory called, from its originator, the Elliot Wave Theory, and convinced by this that the Dow Jones index would peak at 3700. His explanation, I believe, is that he misread the beginning of the upwave; had he not done so, then he would not have been 1000 points out in his prediction of the top of the market.

Indeed, even if we ignore the facts clearly demonstrated by several academic studies that historical share price movements cannot be used to predict their future course, we might still have a problem. Chartists often find it hard to agree on what the patterns made by prices are and, more importantly, what they mean. Naturally, there is more than one theory. No matter, for the market needs prophets. Money is important to us emotionally and actually, and the uncertainty of investment decisions creates such excitement and anxiety that for many this can only be relieved by believing that the future can be known.

Basic principles: keep investment simple

Successful investment is much more prosaic. It needs time and effort, and above all else judgement. Judgement not in the abstract but very precisely in the sense of: 'Are share markets fairly priced compared to alternative investment markets? Is this share sensibly priced compared to that? Does it make sense for my portfolio, in view of my own financial needs?'

These judgements must be based on knowledge and facts. They are much easier than judgements we make quite frequently but think nothing of such as – Can I trust him? Would I want her as my friend? Are these people I want to work for? Is this the school for my child? Nor are they more difficult, or in a different class from our normal financial decisions – we like this house, but they are asking too much; we need a foreign holiday but it would be unwise to spend the money now; I deserve a raise, and this is a good time to ask for it; those are helpful people, and their goods are fairly priced.

Knowing sufficient to make those investment judgements takes time and work. If stock markets don't interest us then, though we may put in the time, we won't do the work. So if we do not have the time, or can never develop the interest, it is best to find others to do it for us. We have two choices. We can go directly to investment fund managers – investment trust, unit trust or life assurance company – and get them to do it for us. Or we can talk to financial advisers – stockbroker or investment broker – and choose one we trust to act as our manager.

'Big Bang' and the FSA have started a process of change that will take some years to complete. Services seem certain to become more expensive, and investment 'packages' more alluring. Managing our money is perceived to be a very profitable business, particularly when we can be persuaded to deal on a 'discretionary' basis. Good advice at sensible prices can be found, but we must know where to look and then find it ourselves. How to do this, and what it will cost, is the subject of the next two chapters.

If we have the time and inclination then we should act as our own investment manager. We will still need help and advice, and we will need a broker with whom we can develop an advisory relationship. But we must also know where to go for information, what to look for in the financial papers, and how to develop our own investment style so as to beat the market. That is the subject of the last two chapters.

Checkpoints

- Reward in the investment markets is the other side of risk

- There is no way that we can avoid market risk but a portfolio balanced between cash, bonds and shares can protect us from its consequences

- Any 'generalist' unit or investment trust has already eliminated company risk as far as is possible within its portfolio; more than one in our portfolio won't improve our risk factor and may harm our reward. This is the way to invest if we only want to participate in the market, or invest in specialist sectors

- If our objective is to do better than the market, then we must aim to control but not to eliminate company risk; our portfolio should have not less than five nor more than fifteen shares for control and reward

- Private portfolios often unknowingly increase company risk because of systematic risk. This is particularly dangerous when monetary policy is tightened, and economic growth slows. We should check our portfolio for this. Remember that specialist investment or unit trusts – emerging companies, technology, property or other specialist trusts – might increase this risk if we also hold such shares directly

- Have we a portfolio diversified to reduce risk and increase reward, or is it so random a collection of holdings that it eliminates reward and increases risk?

- Financial prophets don't stay the course. Even if we want to believe, we should still ask ourselves why, if they are any good, should they want to tell us their secrets? If they are charlatans, do we need them?

- Recent performance may sell us the manager and the fund, but don't believe that this necessarily means that performance this year will buy us any extra groceries

Chapter Nine

The choice amongst fund managers

Whoever wishes to win in this game must have patience and money, since the values are so little constant and the rumours so little founded on truth. He who knows how to endure blows without being terrified resembles the lion who answers the thunder with a roar, and is unlike the hind who, stunned by the thunder, tries to flee.

CONFUSION DE CONFUSIONES, *1688*

Statisticians may assure us that share prices are random, and that no investment manager shows consistent ability. Common sense tells us that some managers do better than others, and some investors get richer than their fellows. Common sense is right.

The problem lies with the statistical tools that are available. If performance varies by 20 to 25 per cent about a mean, and if good performance is to do consistently 5 per cent better than that mean, a great number of observations are required before it can be stated that the better results are due to skill rather than chance and luck. The several years that these observations take also see individual fund managers changing jobs, being promoted, going to other firms, retiring, losing their touch, getting rich and lazy or even going mad.

The fact that statistical methods cannot prove that superior investment performance exists, does not necessarily mean that it does not. It does, though like everything else good, it is rare. However, there are two quite separate concerns that we, as private investors, should have. One is to put together a portfolio; if we want geographical diversification, or to follow specialist investment sectors, funds are the cheapest and safest way to invest. Once we have made that decision then we need to identify the good fund manager, the investor whose art and skill enables a particular investment fund to outperform all others.

Figure 25: Though difficult, it is worth looking for good managers.

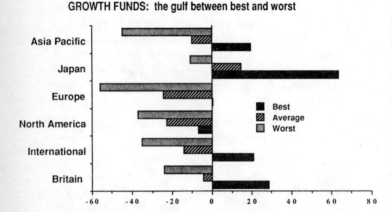

GROWTH FUNDS: the gulf between best and worst

Source: Financial Adviser

Basic principles: overseas investment

It has so long been accepted that overseas investment is right, that the original reason has been forgotten. This was that the relative decline of the British economy, combined with taxation, inflation and the never-ending fall in the value of the pound, made British companies relatively unattractive as investments.

Now, probably for the first time in living memory, the British economy is not in relative decline. Maybe the long-term weaknesses that have destroyed British power in this century are still there, but even if they have not been solved, some of our international competitors seem to have problems of their own. For the next few years, at any rate, the British economy may be no worse a place to invest than alternative economies.

It is hard to get investment decisions right. It is harder still to get such decisions right in overseas markets where the rules of success are subtly different, as in America, or a completely different world, as in Japan. The pension funds, with all the skill that money can buy, have not succeeded as the figures quoted on page 145 show. These decisions are made harder still by the currency factor: not only must we make the right investment choice, but we have to get the currency choice right as well.

No investor should invest for fun alone; we invest for money, and money that means something to us is the money we use in our daily life. International investment is more or less successful depending where we start from. Figure 26 shows that little divided the overall performance of the three major stock markets last year.

Figure 26: International investment needs two correct decisions – the right currency as well as the right market.

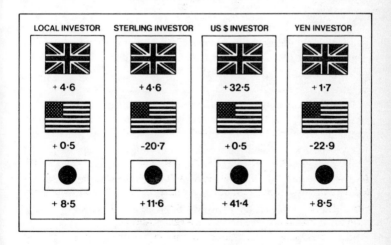

Source: County Natwest Woodmac

British, American and Japanese all had a disappointing time, with the Japanese doing best and the American worst. The second column, though, shows that a British investor did very much better than a Japanese through investing in the Japanese market, but lost 20 per cent of capital through venturing in the American market. On the other hand the American investor, despite the crash, made a stock exchange fortune last year, provided only that no investment was made in America but only in Japan and Britain. This is how currency fluctuations dwarf share price movements.

Once again, we need to look at relative values, and the risk we run for the reward we get. If the pound weakens against the yen, if the authorities' support of the Tokyo market continues to justify valuations two or three times higher than any other market, if capital values increase sufficiently to make up for minuscule dividend yields and high fund management charges, then we might do better in the Tokyo market than in London. To me, there seem to be a lot of 'ifs'.

Theory into practice: choosing funds

Martin Riley demonstrated how a combination of portfolio and fund management skills paid off for the fourth *Sunday Times* investor. The Quicklies inherited £50,000, but as a working couple have no time left over from their demanding jobs to oversee investment affairs. Equally, their high earnings and long-established and valuable endowment policies – used by them for the purchase of their home, and the finance of their children's education – enable them to have simple investment objectives. They want to own shares in international companies for long-term capital growth, and have no need for dividend income.

Stockbrokers Henderson Crosthwaite have always encouraged private clients, helped in this by their four provincial offices.* But investment performance has never been simply a matter of size and resources; it is about personal relationships as well. To be successful a portfolio manager needs to be knowledgeable and shrewd –

---

* Cheltenham, Hereford, Horsham and Worcester

fashion rarely brings success in money matters – but capable of dealing with clients on a basis of complete openness and trust.

The investment strategy of Henderson Crosthwaite is wealth management rather more than portfolio investment. Martin Riley, who runs the private client department from the London office, rightly says that he will get no thanks from clients for losing them money, even if he does lose them less than other managers. Henderson Crosthwaite concentrate on investment trusts, as a way to get clients like the Quicklies international diversification together with full-time professional management of portfolios as cheaply as possible. Holding investment trusts also limits the Quicklies' need to trade their portfolio, and this keeps transaction costs low.

But Riley and his colleagues also look out for 'good values' – strong balance sheets and better than average yields – as well as out of the ordinary opportunities. This policy produced excellent results for the Quicklies' portfolio. In fact, investment trusts are the ideal equity investment for us as private individuals. After many years, the managers of these long-established investment vehicles are making a real effort both to bring themselves up to date, and to make themselves more widely known.

Investment trusts: recent history

Investment trusts, unlike unit trusts, are companies whose shares are quoted on the stock exchange. The term is a misnomer, and stems from the fact that Foreign and Colonial Investment Trust was first established under trust law; shortly thereafter all concerned decided these new entities should really be companies, but the name stuck. For a century they prospered as the investment medium of the moneyed but cautious classes, and the better Scottish managers became greater experts in the US market than American brokers themselves.

1945 brought in a generation during which social attitudes were hostile to private wealth, and the middle classes were forced to sell shares to pay taxes. Draconian foreign currency regulations, and tight profit and dividend control on British business, stimulated the appetite of the emerging institutional equity investor for overseas investments, but this could only be satisfied indirectly. As fast as private individuals sold their investment trust shares, the institutions bought. Today, some 75 per cent of investment trust shares are still held by institutions – but both the investment world, and the investment competence of the institutions have changed since the fifties and sixties.

UK institutions now have the confidence, and the legal right, to invest anywhere in the world. In some ways, holding investment trust shares is degrading to their dignity: they are paying someone else to do the job they themselves are being paid to do. They would sell, except that the shares of investment trusts nearly always sell at a discount – on average between 15 and 25 per cent – to the market value of the securities held as investments. Most managers long since decided that they preferred blows to their egos, than the blow to their pockets which selling £1 for 80 pence would entail.

There is no universally agreed explanation for this discount. It is possibly the 'lumpiness' of the market – we might wish to buy £5000 of an investment trust but an institution is more likely to want to sell £50,000- or even £500,000-worth of shares. It could be that many managers, their companies and their jobs safely cocooned in the arms of the assurance companies and pension funds, simply went to sleep. It might be that the brighter managers decided that there was a lot more profit in managing pension funds, or developing unit trusts to sell us, than resuscitating a comatose section of the investment market.

Generations pass, and attitudes change. Turning 80 pence into £1 does something for short-term investment performance, particularly when no risk is attached to the venture. Investment trusts hold very marketable shares; these can easily be turned into cash if someone else controls the trust. The institutions began to hawk their large share holdings to fast-growing companies looking for a way of buying cash in exchange for their own shares. Slowly, investment trust managers realised that, unless they both improved investment performance and thought of ways of reducing the discount, they would end up losing their funds and their jobs.

The first stage was to improve investment performance. The second was to buy off those formerly complacent but now threatening institutional shareholders. These needed to be persuaded that there was now real pressure on managers to do a really first-rate job in making the most of their assets. So managers and shareholders of some trusts have agreed that, at some specified date in the future, shareholders will have the right to vote on whether the trust continues, will be sold up and the cash distributed, or 'unitised'. In this case the investment trust becomes a unit trust, the shares become units and this way also, investors realise the full value of their asset.

Exploiting net asset values: the Henderson Crosthwaite approach

These are the situations that Henderson Crosthwaite favour. One favourite, which Riley bought for the Quicklies was Ailsa Investment Trust. When Jacob Rothschild and David Montagu took management control of Ailsa in 1981, Montagu was granted options on 2 million Ailsa shares at 59.9 pence a share compared to the then asset value of about 54 pence. The purchase price of 126 pence, when Riley bought in December compared to an asset value of 152 pence. Shareholders must vote for unitisation or break up in 1990 but Riley thought this decision might come sooner.

Energy Resources and Stockholders Far East were Panama-based investment trusts, managed by the Govett investment trust and pension fund management company, and both trusts were subject to unitisation or break-up in 1988–89. Riley liked these for the Quicklies as an entry at a significant discount to two important but tricky markets. These are energy, which was seen as very speculative in December 1986, and Japan and the Far East where prices looked – as they still do – very high to Western eyes. In addition Riley invested in other investment and unit trusts to give the Quicklies a geographically diversified portfolio. At the end of August this policy was showing a 50 per cent rise on the initial investment of £50,000 in December 1986.

Valuation of the Quicklies' Henderson Crosthwaite portfolio at the end of summer 1987

Security	Purchase cost including expenses £	Expenses to date £	Value at 30 Aug 87 £	Estimated income pa £
Save & Prosper HIBA	4670	nil	4668	429
Cash = £4670 or 8% of portfolio at cost				
*Equity Consort IT	7106	299	9200	275
Ailsa IT	5807	137	8055	154
Govett Energy UT	8139	139	12,809	275
*Govett Far East UT	10,709	298	15,607	31
ITs held for reorganisation = £31,761 or 56% at original cost				
Gartmore Am. Securities IT	5899	139	7360	77
Baring Korea Europe IT	665	nil	1950	0
Friars House Capital UT	5083	302	7637	110
Mercury Common Market UT	6188	356	6615	91
ITs held for management = £17,835 or 32% at cost				
PEP Scheme: London Merchant Securities	1998	27	3159	0
Capital Gains Realised	(4264)	427	n.a.	n.a.
Total	52,000	2124	77,060	1442

* = securities sold and bought back

This increase is partly the result of the booming market of early 1987, but it also reflects the success of Riley's policy, as well as active supervision of the portfolio. The key results, however, came from his choice of investment trusts, and his willingness to 'bed and breakfast' some early gains.

Govett Far East and Equity Consort – a Rothschild-controlled investment trust investing in the UK – each doubled in value. This is not clear in the valuation because both were 'bed and break-fasted' in March. The shares were sold, and immediately bought back, to turn book profits into real profits. This selling, and buying back of shares the following day, may seem expensive. The cost of stamp duty, together with one full commission on the two transactions, together with VAT, came to £327 which is a significant proportion of the Quicklies' total costs so far of £2003.

The flexibility gained in the management of a portfolio makes the cost worthwhile. Riley was able to use up the Quicklies' annual capital gains tax exemption of £6600. This is only £5000 now, but from April 1990 it is likely to be £10,000 as separate taxation for husbands and wives comes in. This transaction established a higher 'base' cost for these two shares. This will alleviate the tax burden on the portfolio; if the shares fall then that will create a capital loss to be offset against profits elsewhere while any further rise will only be taxable against the new base cost of the shares.

Govett Far East was the other of the two Panama-based investment trusts which changed their names during 1987 to emphasise the Govett management connection, and then unitised themselves through Guernsey companies. Prices went up sharply, partly as the discount vanished but also as these sectors returned to investment favour. For this reason, Riley held them in the portfolio.

The PEP investment was also much in Riley's style. A famous growth stock of the nineteen-sixties, London Merchant Securities is controlled by Lord Rayne and has a good London West End property portfolio, but it has many other interests today, including 30 per cent of Lord Delfont's quoted First Leisure group. The company's energy interests were recently converted into a 30 per cent stake in the quoted Carless Capel oil independent. For many years the share price has under-performed the market, but the 5 per cent yield was attractive, the price was below asset value, and the major shareholder is in his seventies. The purchase was made at an opportune moment, despite the crash.

The Quicklies were lucky to be allotted one hundred shares in the Baring Korea Europe Fund. This is one of the very few ways in which it is possible to invest in the Korean market – not only an economy well on the way to becoming a 'new Japan' but also benefiting substantially from Japanese direct investment. More importantly, for private investors, investment trusts are the safest way to invest in such 'frontier' markets. Because they are 'closed end' – in other words the investment fund cannot increase and decrease in size as our enthusiasm for out of the way investments waxes and wanes – the managers can concentrate on long-term ir.vestment, rather than worrying that next month they will be forced to sell shares to repay unit holders.

The managers of Ailsa confirmed shortly after the crash that they recommended immediate unitisation. This is now Bishopsgate Special Situations UT and the elimination of the discount meant that the new units were valued at £1.48. This helped the portfolio to recover in 1988 from the fall of the previous October, as did the sale of the Equity Consort shares to clients of Rothschilds. However, short-term performance of this particular portfolio is of rather less importance than the principles espoused by Riley.

The first is always to look for good value in our investments. One well-proven way to do this is to buy companies when the value of their shares is less than their 'break-up' or net asset value (NAV). Riley bought LMS for this reason but, of course, it is simpler and easier to calculate these values for investment trusts than it is for manufacturing companies. Selling off land, factories and offices can take time, and costs money: selling shares can be done immediately and for a very tiny commission. 'Regression to the mean' implies that, sooner or later, these anomalies will be rectified.

During the first part of 1988, Riley once again showed the value of this principle. He was asked to manage a 'speculative' portfolio for the *Sunday Times*, based on the assumption that dealing rather than investment would create better stories after the crash.

In February Riley invested the bulk of this portfolio in 50,000 shares of Edinburgh American Assets IT at 94 pence a share. This trust was one of several managed by the Edinburgh-based Ivory and Sime management group, and was part of a complex and imaginative restructuring designed to reintroduce nineteenth-century investment advantages to twentieth-century trusts.

During March, Riley accepted the restructuring proposals, sold all of the new share 'classes', but kept those of GBC Capital. The value, in cash and shares, was £55,194 compared to the original outlay of £47,603. GBC Capital is an associated Ivory and Sime IT, managed in Canada, and concentrates on emerging growth companies in North America. The managers had announced their intention, subject to tax approval, to unitise.

Later in March, 43,400 more GBC shares were bought at £1.02

each, for a total investment of £44,620. These were added to the 6600 shares from the original reorganisation. The portfolio now has 50,000 GBC shares and the unitisation is going ahead as tax clearance has been given. The asset value of GBC is £1.28 and the price is now £1.12 but will probably be at least £1.25 in 'unitised' form. So far, this portfolio is up by a third and without risk although a huge amount of paperwork is involved in these re-organisations.

Costs as a factor in investment performance

Investment management costs money. Some of this is inescapable, but much is discretionary. We need to realise that we can choose how much we pay for many unit trust and investment trust groups share the same managers. This is particularly relevant in our choice between investment and unit trusts, and insurance bonds.

The difference in costs can be seen practically in the cost of the Fidelity 'Growth' portfolio for the Quicklies, compared to that of Henderson Crosthwaite, and shown in the table. Both portfolios did well in 1987, and both bettered the World Index as measured by the *FT*–Actuaries indices: the value of the Fidelity portfolio was down by 5.54 per cent, and that of Henderson Crosthwaite by 3.68 per cent, compared to a fall in the World Index of 5.91 per cent.

How two managers performed and charged

Portfolio managed by	Purchase costs including expenses	Value at 27 Nov 87	Estimated income pa
Fidelity	£4538	£49,120*	£ 756
Henderson Crosthwaite	£2124	£50,088*	£1442

* includes £2000 invested in Personal Equity Plan in addition to the original £50,000.

Initial costs: investment and unit trusts, and bonds

An investment of £5000 in an investment trust will cost approximately £120.50 of our capital. This is commission of 1.65 per cent on the purchase price, VAT on the commission, stamp duty of 0.5 per cent on the purchase, and the stock exchange levy of 0.60 pence. A similar investment in a unit trust will cost £250 – a front end charge of at least 5 per cent of which 3 per cent goes to intermediaries and 2 per cent is kept for management expenses – and another 1 per cent or 2 per cent to cover stamp duty, commissions and levy. The minimum cost to our capital, which is expressed as the 'spread' between buying and selling prices of units, is 6 per cent or £300 and can be as much as £350 or £400.

It is true that when we come to sell the investment trust shares we will have to pay commission, VAT and levy – no stamp duty on sales – while there is no charge on unit trust sales. But for the minimum period of two to three years that we should expect to hold any equity investment there is, on average, an extra £200 of our capital working for us.

The initial costs on 'insurance bonds' are higher still. Commissions to intermediaries, in the past, have been between 4 per cent and 6 per cent. The life companies also have costs, which must be deducted from our capital, though what these are is not openly disclosed but these extra costs are sometimes described as 'capital units'. However as investors became aware that capital units are not the good thing we might assume from the name, the life companies have come up with more bizarre and complex ways of hiding the reality of their charges.

Commissions: level playing fields and transparency

There was an agreement amongst life assurance companies, as part of the new investor protection regulations, that maximum commissions on insurance bonds would be brought down over time to equivalency with those on unit trusts. This was to ensure a 'level playing field' and so encourage the investment broker to offer the best product to clients, not merely the highest commission paying one.

However, as a result of protests from the Office of Fair Trading, the new rules now insist on 'transparency' of commissions – ie a requirement that investment brokers disclose their commissions to us, as stockbrokers and unit trust management companies have always had to do. This has meant, amongst other things, that the commission agreement amongst life assurance companies is now a dead letter.

Traditionally, new companies have entered this business by offering higher commission rates. At this moment, there seems no reason to believe that this will change but much will depend on the new regulatory authorities. Moreover, it is very unclear how these same authorities will require the life companies to disclose 'sales costs' of investment products, when sold directly by their own sales teams rather than through the networks of commission-earning intermediaries.

Caveat emptor *in a confusing world*

Until these issues are resolved, we need to look closely not only at the investment performance statistics of life assurance companies, but also at the charging structures on their different products. This is not easily done, yet is important because the life assurance industry is far the most important player in the financial services industry, particularly as it affects us in our purchase of houses, protection of our family, investment of regular savings, and planning for retirement. About the only satisfactory way of informing ourselves is through the regular surveys carried out by *Money Management*, a monthly magazine which is part of the *Financial Times* group and specialises in 'packaged' investment services.

Annual management fees: investment and unit trusts, and bonds

The same charging difference exists on annual management fees. These fees are a percentage of the capital value of the funds under management, and are deducted from the income of the fund. Investment trust charges average between 0.25 per cent and 0.5 per cent of the value of funds managed though, with some of the new style management contracts, these charges are being increased to 1 per cent. Unit trust management charges vary between 0.75 per cent and 1.25 per cent but are being increased. The new average will probably be about 1.25 per cent compared to the present 1 per cent.

This is not as big a change as it appears. New pricing rules, and methods of creating and liquidating units in response to investment demand for units, make it much harder for managers to make extra money at the expense of existing unit holders. The change in annual fees is part of the new openness.

Life assurance companies do not disclose their internal costs for 'insurance bonds' but they are unlikely to be less than unit trusts. However broker-managed insurance bonds generally have another 1 per cent management commission on top of everything else; this was traditionally levied by the life company on behalf of the broker but this may not continue. It appears to have fallen foul of the new rules.

Constraints on investment policy: investment and unit trusts and bonds

Neither investment trusts nor unit trusts have to pay capital gains tax; we pay instead when we sell our shares or units. Life assurance companies have to pay capital gains tax on gains taken within their investment funds. Most of us do not have sufficient wealth to use up our annual exemptions, so we are not payers of capital gains tax and this is an added cost to us. It can also be a constraint on investment management flexibility though the taxation of life assurance has been so generous in practice that this has probably not been a problem to managers of life funds.

Life companies have large and skilled property investment departments, and this is an advantage that neither investment nor unit trusts have. Most insurance bonds include both a 'property' and a 'cash' component, and generally switching between the different sectors of an insurance bond is free. Furthermore, no capital gains tax liability is incurred because there is no switch of investment. It can be argued that this privilege is worth paying for in higher initial charges, though few of us make use of it.

Unit trust policy is constrained by Department of Trade & Industry rules and, up to now, unit trusts have been prevented from investing in the derivative markets, so that they could not use options or futures. Nor could they borrow money, invest in unquoted shares, or use the foreign exchange markets to 'hedge' their holdings of foreign shares. Tax regulations stopped them offering 'money-market' type funds. However, most of these things could be done by 'off-shore' funds – that is management groups officially based in the Channel Islands or Luxembourg, and, less frequently, in the Isle of Man, Bermuda and Hong Kong – and 'off-shore' from the regulatory requirements of the investors' government.

In some of these territories the regulatory climate is more relaxed than in Britain, but funds based on these centres and run by the major British groups* are safe enough. Furthermore, the regulatory framework for British-based trusts is being eased, so a greater variety of funds can be expected in coming years.

None of these restrictions has ever applied to investment trusts. Possibly the greatest advantage that these have had, compared to unit trusts, is the 'closed-end' nature of their funds. A manager who knows that the volume of investment funds will remain the same from year to year is in a more relaxed situation than a manager who must worry about short-term performance. These performance figures, now quoted regularly in most newspapers, have a significant effect on the willingness of unit holders to stay invested in particular funds.

Investment performance compared

Doctor Samuel Johnson's comment on the plight of the Reverend Dodd – 'depend upon it, Sir, the knowledge that one is to be hanged in a fortnight's time concentrates the mind wonderfully' – has been appropriate for sleepy investment trust managers. It is not certain that such bracing advice is equally helpful to unit trust managers, already under considerable pressure from their marketing departments for performance figures with which to sell group competence.

The difference of investment performance between investment and unit trusts is small, but between them and bonds it is very significant. Since life assurance companies are extremely competent investment managers, as proved by their unit trust subsidiaries and endowment funds, much of this underperformance

---

* ie the parent companies are quoted on the Stock Exchange, or are part of large banking groups, and all are fully authorised by SIB in this country.

Figure 27: The average growth of £1000 invested in investment trusts over periods of one to seven years, compared with RPI and a similar sum invested in a building society, unit trust or insurance bond.

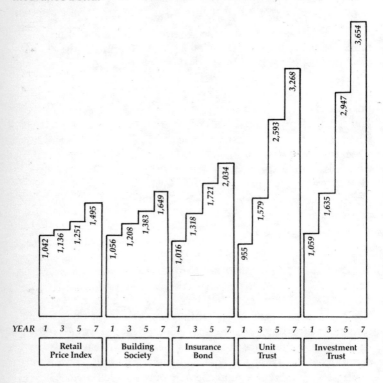

Source: 'Money Management', Micropal and AITC

must reflect the higher costs of the bonds. All these figures again emphasise the importance of equity investment as part of a long-term saving policy.

New developments from investment trusts

One recent and important development within the investment trust world has been splitting the values inherent in an investment trust portfolio into different classes of shares. Five investment trusts reorganised themselves this way during 1987 and 1988. (General Consolidated; River & Mercantile; River Plate; Scottish National; TR Technology.) These now offer a specific date for the end of the trust and, allied to that, a cocktail of shares from which we can choose those which most precisely match our objectives. These include:

Stepped preference shares which pay a reasonable dividend now. The dividend will increase by a set percentage each year and, on redemption, will be repaid at considerably above par. These are good shares for the recently retired, needing more spending income than offered by index-linked gilts.

Zero preference shares are paid no income at all, but have it ploughed back into the assets underlying these shares so that these will be redeemed at significantly more than today's value. These are good choices for investors, still working, but expecting retirement, and a drop in their earnings, within the next ten years. Theoretically, they should go up in price every year, allowing high-rate taxpayers to sell some shares each year and take these proceeds tax free within their annual gains tax allowance. This requires great faith in the short-term price behaviour of the stock market.

Both classes of preference yield about 11 per cent to redemption, and the security of these returns is based on priority over the assets of the trust.

Income shares give an excellent yield of 9 per cent at their current prices, have a very remote possibility of an increase in dividend, and are entitled to some modest part of the growth in the assets of the trust. Basically, these are for those wanting a good yield now, and not too concerned about future capital values except in nominal terms. These are an alternative to a high-yield gilt.

Capital shares get neither income nor guaranteed redemption values. They benefit instead from the growth in the assets of the trust, after the rights of the preference shareholders have been met. The conservative policy of most managers, combined with their objectives of a high-yield portfolio, makes these a highly geared bet 'on the market' for optimistic, and earning, investors who are prepared to forget about them for the next ten years.

Warrants are like a long-lived option, and give the right to buy the capital shares at a predetermined price some time before redemption. These are both a cheaper, and even longer-odds bet on the market than the capital shares. These are fun investments to give young children, which might pay for more than a good 21st birthday party.

Neither calculations nor decisions are easy – see notes to this chapter for an example – but are regularly calculated by research brokers. County Natwest Woodmac is preeminent for investment trust research, and this is available to us through the constituent offices of National Investment Group. The thoughts of James Capel – top-rated research broker overall – come through the offices of Allied Provincial Securities. A third research force is Alexanders Laing and Cruickshank with nine provincial offices concentrating on private-client stockbroking.

However, the three private-client brokers who really specialise in this field are Henderson Crosthwaite, the Edinburgh-based Robert White and London-based Oliff & Partners. Oliff is a newly formed stockbroking firm, concentrating solely on investment trusts and undervalued asset situations for institutional and larger private client (£50,000 upwards) business.

There are still several investment trusts with a share capital simply divided into two; the income shares get all the income and the capital shares all the capital growth. Some of these, like Ambrose and Yeoman, also have limited lives. These shares can sometimes offer equivalent returns, though sometimes with less risk, than the more complex capital structures described above.

An alternative cheap and simple approach

Some fifty investment trusts (but not including any of the split value trusts mentioned above) now encourage us to invest in them through regular savings schemes – minimum £20 a month – through reinvestment of dividends and, most useful of all, the investment of capital sums of, on average, £250 and upwards. All is arranged by the investment trust managers, leading to extremely low commission rates of, again on average, 0.2 per cent and a complete absence of the administrative hassle of investment.

Details of the savings schemes, the investment objectives of the trusts concerned together with their one-, three-, and seven-year performance records, and addresses of managers are available free from the Association of Investment Trust Companies.* But we can also get further information from this source, including details on all investment trusts and their managers, together with a list of stockbrokers prepared to advise on, and deal in, investment trusts for private clients.

The discount between the Net Asset Values (NAVs) of investment trusts, and their quoted share prices average between 15 and 25 per cent depending on market mood. One cardinal rule is never to buy investment trust shares outside this discount range (figures also supplied by AITC) and never, ever to pay a premium. These are seen – on specialist Japanese trusts most recently but before that on European trusts – but they never last.

Generally, it is better to buy trusts managed by specialist groups, who have more to lose if they do badly, than trusts managed by merchant banks. Finally, within the general or specialist sector that we want, look for the best performance record over the longest period. We should not choose poor performers in the expectation of a reorganisation; it happens, but not sufficiently frequently to justify the wait.

Value for money in unit trust portfolio services – an example

Many of us understand that, over time, equities have been the only form of investment consistently to beat inflation. We know we have to identify 'value' in stock markets because that is always rewarded. We believe that the globalisation of security markets has made it even more difficult for us as private investors. We think

---

* AITC, 16 Finsbury Circus, London EC2M 7JJ. 01-588 5347. Also recommended: *More shares for your money*, Christine Stopp, Rosters, 1987.

that we ought to keep up with changing trends. But how do we do all this, particularly if we do not want to use a stockbroker, and have never heard of investment trusts?

One answer is professional help to form and manage a unit trust portfolio. All too many investors and advisers approach unit trusts as if they were on the race course, and the sad thing is that many investors, encouraged to invest like this, failed entirely to improve the value of their portfolios over the five years of the bull market from 1982–87. Of course, those front-end charges and portfolio selection fees made their advisers rich, and were good for the unit trust managers, but enriching our advisers should not be our investment objective.

A unit trust, just like an investment trust or insurance bond is already fully diversified against company risk. Diversification with trusts is for geographical purposes or industrial specialisation. It can make sense to 'deal' in unit trusts, trying to outguess the market as to which industrial or geographical sector will outperform the market. There is simply no statistical evidence to support the belief that new trusts beat old, small do better than big, last year's poor performer will be next year's winner. To try to identify top-performing managers, because of the statistical difficulties, is not feasible on historical evidence; but that is not to say that we can't sometimes get it right using intuition.

Yet the way some investment management groups are organised seems to encourage better than average results from their investment managers. This is as true of pension fund managers as it is of unit or investment trust groups. As investors we have a chance of identifying these companies by looking for consistency. Any search of Opal or Finstat figures for those management groups whose trusts regularly appear in the top quartile – the top 25 per cent of the total – year after year shows that certain names keep on recurring.

These are the groups to whom we should go for portfolio management services. We can achieve discounts on switching trusts within the group. Possibly, by talking directly to the managers, we will also get discounts on the initial charges. It is always worth asking for this even though most groups deny that they offer them: they do not like to upset their intermediaries. When managers have had to buy units back from existing holders, it is more profitable for them to sell them to a new buyer than sell shares from the trust, and liquidate the units. By going direct, waving a cheque under their noses, and starting at a 3 per cent discount – which is the minimum they pay a broker anyway – it is amazing what can be achieved.

The standard of service that we should expect is set by Fidelity since they have deliberately set out – and, from my experience with the *Sunday Times* portfolio, succeeded – to keep their investors aware of what they were doing and why; other unit trust portfolio services should be compared to this both for price and service. Fidelity do not claim to be cheap, but do argue that their service and performance is worth the fees they charge.

Fidelity run four separate portfolios – growth, tactical growth, income and growth, and income – with a minimum investment of £10,000 and the table shows the performance of two of them. The columns show capital values, the amount and increase in dividend income, and total returns, and none of us should be surprised that there is little difference between the end result of the two portfolios.

Fidelity portfolio performance: 5 years to 1.1.88

	1984 £	1985 £	1986 £	1987 £	1988 £
Growth and income portfolio					
Value	12,900	15,519	16,962	18,539	18,219
Income	457	451	583	558	685
Total return	13,357	16,692	17,545	19,097	18,904
Income portfolio					
Value	12,740	14,689	15,306	18,245	17,898
Income	560	603	810	825	937
Total return	13,300	15,292	16,116	19,070	18,835

Peter Hargreaves, the former stockbroker who now runs this Personal Portfolio Management Service for Fidelity, claims that their skill as investors is in identifying trends, picking shares that are relatively cheap compared to the market as a whole, identifying the right market and currency to be in, and taking action even when this involves realising losses in the portfolio. Fidelity regularly monitor world markets, and change the portfolio 'mix' as different markets wax and wane in their underlying value.

Fidelity manage 18 unit trusts authorised in Britain, and another 22 'offshore' trusts run from the Channel Islands and Luxembourg. So choosing the right trust for the separate portfolios is as important as getting the right market. The manager of this service can choose which of Fidelity's fund managers to back – each portfolio consists of seven or eight trusts only – or can go outside the group if Fidelity cannot offer what is needed.

Changes in the portfolio are always gradual; selling out of a market is a decision with a 50:50 chance of being right, and choosing a new market gives the same odds. Fidelity prefers a salami-slice approach which enables them to change direction without significant loss if they have misjudged either a trend or a market. This gradualist approach can still significantly alter the balance of a managed portfolio over time, but without taking the risks of black or white decisions.

Fidelity do have one principle: they are always in the market. Their experience of investment management is that no one can be consistently successful at going into cash at the correct moment – and then reinvesting in the market at the right moment. To do one is rare; to get both right is a miracle. Fidelity believe it is cheaper and safer to stay invested, for equities have consistently shown the best returns of any investment medium. As Hargreaves says: 'The big unknown is not the return, but how long we will have to wait for it.'

Regular letters explain Fidelity's investment views and reasons for action, while further information is always available from a freephone number, so subscribers to this service are kept fully informed. Hargreaves arranges seminars around the country three or four times a year, and valuations come quarterly, while every April sees full tax information supplied to investors.

Cost is an initial 5.25 per cent on the initial investment. After that, all other switches within the portfolio are charged at 1.25 per cent. This includes stamp duty. Quite apart from investment skill, this is one of the advantages of going direct to a fund manager; otherwise switching from one trust to another is very expensive with the full 5 per cent up front charge levied on each purchase. The annual management fee is 1.25 per cent, already charged on the income of the fund, and a further 0.5 per cent a year on the value of the portfolio up to £50,000, and a 0.25 per cent on sums above that.

Future for insurance bonds

Insurance bonds initially allowed life companies to sell investment advice through their network of brokers without infringing the Prevention of Frauds Act. Moreover the heavy marketing costs were partly compensated by Life Assurance Premium Relief. Now, under the new laws, there is no legal need to wrap up investment advice as life assurance. The tax advantage (LAPR) was abolished in 1984. Most life companies have formed unit trust subsidiaries and these, supported with the full weight of the considerable investment skills of the life companies, are making life uncomfortable for the independent management companies.

Nor is the famous '5 per cent tax-free income' quite what the salesmen would have us believe it is. This is the claim that we can withdraw up to 5 per cent a year tax-free from a bond; however, at the earlier of twenty years, or encashment of the bond, and assuming that we are 40 per cent tax payers we will then have to pay tax due. With a unit or investment trust portfolio, we can equally withdraw 5 per cent a year tax-free subject to that figure being less than our capital gains tax exemption.

These insurance bonds were useful for tax planning, but now with the new personal tax system, they have outlived their usefulness except as higher than average commission paying schemes for salesmen. The life companies have recognised this with the 'broker-managed insurance bond' for they have stopped paying the extra management commissions on these funds.

Broker bonds always had a deliberate obscurity of structure. Investment brokers, as our agents, were advising us on the best investment proposals from life company third parties. But at the same time, they put themselves forward as the investment manager of those life funds. This was with the connivance of those third parties since the life companies then paid additional but undisclosed commissions out of our income to those same 'independent' agents of ours.

According to *Money Management* figures, a sample of broker bonds lost 26.5 per cent of our capital over the six months ended 1.4.1988 while insurance bonds lost only 20.1 per cent. Over longer periods bonds have shown themselves to be significantly worse investment packages than either investment or unit trusts. If we want the considerable investment expertise of the best life companies, we are better off investing either traditionally through their endowment policies, or in their new unit trusts.

Checkpoints

• A trust portfolio is already diversified fully against company risk. We only need more than one if we wish to diversify geographically or by specialist sector.

• Look for long run and consistent performance over many years, certainly five but preferably ten years or longer. Check the record of the management group as a whole as well as the specific trust we are interested in. Most records are too short to identify above average performance as management skill rather than chance.

• Be careful to check all costs, and remember the importance of compounded interest. The more capital we have, after management fees, the more income, and the more income we get, the better that compounding will work for us.

• This works even better with investment trusts since we can buy £1 worth of investments for 80 pence.

Notes – warrants

A warrant is the right to buy the ordinary share of a company at a fixed price some time in the future, very often a matter of years. Eurotunnel has outstanding warrants; so has National Westminster Bank though these are Euro-warrants and quoted in Swiss Francs. The most common warrants are those of investment trusts. A warrant can be considered as a very long term option.

The value of a warrant lies in this characteristic. For a small outlay now, the investor can take a view on the long term performance of a share. If the choice of share is right, then the investor makes proportionately more than by buying the shares directly. The cost of the warrant reflects this increased profitability factor, known as gearing, as well as the value of the 'time'.

There is a calculation which shows the price level of the share, above which we will make more money buying the warrants. This is called the fulcrum price. The formula for this is:

$$\frac{\text{Current price of shares} \times \text{Exercise price of warrants}}{\text{Current price of shares} - \text{Price of warrant for one share}} = FP$$

How this works can be seen with another Riley favourite. Overseas Investment Trust has just under 2 million warrants in issue. The price of the warrants is 31 pence, and each gives the right to buy one share of OIT at 202 pence up to 31.12.1998. The present price of OIT is 180 pence, and the net asset value is 236.

The fulcrum price on OIT is:

$$\frac{180 \times 202}{180 - 31} = \frac{36,360}{149} = 244$$

The secret is to know whether 244 pence is a likely price for OIT in the future. At this time of doom and gloom, it may seem not – but before we make that decision, we should remember historical probabilities. Since 1920 equity prices, excluding dividends, have grown by 6 per cent a year. The rule of 72 says that 6 per cent compound growth will double OIT's net assets in twelve years, to about 472 pence. Let's say we are in for a recession in 1989–92, and the stock exchange won't do well – but what about the next six or seven years? And inflation will speed up this process.

Nor need we rely on the UK market. OIT has about a third of its assets in North America, another third in Japan, some ten per cent in the rest of the Pacific and the remainder in Europe. So this is a choice for those who want to hedge that British 'economic miracle' in case it turns out to be less well founded than currently believed.

An important point in the OIT warrant price is that it is 'out of the money'. The exercise price of 202 pence is above the ordinary share price of 180, though below the asset value of 236. This can be dangerous if corporate activity leads to an early liquidation, particularly as warrant holders normally have no vote and must rely on the goodwill – never in great supply – of either the defending management, or the bidders for the trust. The rights of warrant holders in such circumstances is another factor to consider.

Investment is all about offsetting risk, so Riley recommends an investment trust 'cocktail' to offset the risk of OIT with the surer returns of the zero preference shares of TR Technology. This is 60 per cent in the UK, 32 per cent in USA, and 9 per cent in Japan, and concentrates on technology stocks – from seedcorn ventures to massive quoted companies such as Matsushita Electrical and Cable & Wireless. This is one of those 'separated' value or split level trusts, and the zero preference shareholders take precedence over all other shareholders. These shares will be redeemed in 1998 at 313.2 pence.

A generous present for a favourite godson might be, ignoring costs and rounding present prices:

| 760 | TR Technology 0% Preference Shares at 92 | = £700 |
| 1000 | Overseas IT warrants at 30 | = £300 |

Value in 1998	*No change OIT*	*OIT* $\times$ *2*	*OIT* $\times$ *3*
760 TR $\times$ 313.2 =	£2380	£2380	£2380
1000 OIT Warrants	nothing	£1580	£3380
Value of cocktail	£2380	£3960	£5760

Chapter Ten

Selecting an investment adviser

Ours is a non-profit organisation. We didn't plan it that way – that's just the way it worked out.

ANON

It is amazing the number of businesses that now consider themselves capable of selling us investment advice – banks, obviously, but also building societies, accountants, solicitors, insurance brokers, life assurance salesmen, financial planners and even stockbrokers. With the exception of the stockbrokers, all others have the great advantage of being able to tell us how to invest without benefit of training or experience, or any need to prove that they know what they are talking about.

While this is partly the result of deregulation, it is also the product of long-term changes in the savings industry. The effective withdrawal of the banks a generation ago from this market, and the switch of building society strategy in the nineteen-seventies to lump-sum investment rather than regular savings left this field open to the life assurance companies.

These companies, as they became increasingly 'investment'-rather than 'protection'-minded, built up sales networks of commission agents and commission-only salesforces. The tax advantages of life assurance, the complexity and long-term nature of their contracts, the profitability of the business, and the fight for market share led inexorably to a high commission structure.

The effectiveness of this strategy is seen in the figures; some three hundred and fifty stockbroking firms, but over eight thousand Fimbra-registered investment brokers (or investment advisers, financial planners, investment consultants or whatever sounds best) and uncounted numbers of company-controlled salesmen. Not all concentrate on investment advice as such; there is even more commission setting up pension schemes, arranging endowment policies for mortgages, or planning the disposal of our financial assets. These also have an investment management component, even if it is packaged so well that we never see it.

Now that we have become rich again, and looking after our investment needs is seen as a potential business bonanza, banks and life assurance companies are locked in battle for control of this market. The management fees on investment packages are attractive: the initial fees are worth having too. What we pay can vary significantly depending upon whom we approach.

Theory into practice: the cost of advice

Eamonn and Shelagh K are in their fifties and have no children. Their house is worth considerably more than their mortgage of £22,000. Shelagh must retire next year (1989) when she will be 55, and her husband has the opportunity of taking early retirement. If they exercise this option, they will have joint pensions totalling £12,000 a year after tax and capital of £27,000.

Their pensions are index-linked, but this does not start until three years after the date of their retirement, and Eamonn and Shelagh's net take-home pay – if they do not find other employment – will drop by some £10,000 a year as a result of retirement. They hope to get other jobs, do want to invest, but need income now.

Eamonn and Shelagh are the type of clients most at risk from incompetent advisers since they have no experience of investing, and are not sure what they want from their capital. They know they want it invested for safety and yield, with some prospect of an increased income in future years, but are not sure what they can reasonably expect. They would like 10 per cent on their money and cannot accept less than an income of £1700 before tax, or a yield of slightly over 6 per cent.

The managers' proposals

This was the brief given to four investment managers at the end of 1987. All four are competent, well established, and sensible and have come up with four different plans. One is a traditional stockbroking proposal, from National Investment Group (NIG), while another is more of a unit trust service, from Natwest Stockbrokers (NS). The remaining two managers are both influenced by financial planning attitudes, even though one of them is a long-established stockbroker. Both of these offer plans which are two to three times more expensive in initial cost than the stockbroking solution.

Two of the managers were very bearish in their proposals – NS and Fleming Montagu Stanley (FMS) – while NIG and Save & Invest are more optimistic. All meet the key needs of income and safety, and MS and Save & Invest have arranged for monthly payments of income.

The financial adviser's solution

Save & Invest is a Fimbra member running 'share shops' in Glasgow, Edinburgh and Manchester, and specialises in income packages. They have created a portfolio with an after-tax income of £2025. The portfolio, despite this high level of income, includes £7000 of UK equity unit trusts. This income level has been achieved by putting £15,000 into two insurance bonds invested, to confuse the issue, in gilts, bonds and possibly property.

Eamonn and Shelagh's income will depend not only on the interest earned by the bonds but the manager's success in running a portfolio of fixed-interest securities to produce capital gains. So far, Aetna and Scottish Mutual have been successful at doing this. Should they fail to do so, then the yearly income payments promised can only be maintained by distributing part of the initial capital invested.

When market circumstances improve, the £12,500 invested in the Scottish Mutual Safety Fund can be switched, at no further cost, into Scottish Mutual's Growth Fund. This switch, from a fund predominantly in fixed interest securities, property and cash to one invested more heavily in shares, will mean a reduction in income. The switch gives the flexibility to go into the share market when it looks safe, and the money then has a chance to beat inflation.

The Save & Invest portfolio

Security	Amount invested £	Net income £	Investment manager	Cost* £
Cash:	5000	300	Building Society	None
Insurance bonds:				
Aetna gilt bond	2500	250†	Aetna Life	150*
Scottish Mutual Safety Fund	12,500	1200†	Scottish Mutual Life	900*
Cash and fixed interest = £20,000 or 74% of total				
Shares:				
Income Unit Trusts	7000	275	6 different managers	420*
Shares = £7000 or 26% of total				
Total	27,000	2025	8 managers	1470

* assumes bid offer spread of 6% which is at the lower end of the likely scale of charges.
† includes capital gains or, if none, use of initial capital.

The investment manager's answer

FMS is an old-established City stockbroker, now owned by the Save & Prosper unit trust management company, but still independent in its investment advice. However, this connection is encouraging the development of investment packages to make direct share investment easier for the investor and more profitable for the adviser. Their planned return of between 8.7 per cent and 10 per cent before tax will depend on their final choice of insurance bonds with £13,000 to be invested in a high-income scheme. This is a five year plan, with no switching possibilities, so the only equity exposure will be in the £10,000 invested in unit trusts.

The Fleming Montagu Stanley portfolio

Security	Amount invested £	Net income £	Investment manager	Cost* £
Cash	4000	280	Building Society	None
Insurance bond – 5 Year High Income	13,000	1040/1300†	not yet chosen	780*
Cash and fixed interest = £17,000 or 63% of total				
Shares UT Portfolio	10,000	400	selected trusts	600*
Shares = £10,000 or 37% of total				
Total	27,000	1720/1980	2 managers	1380

* assumes bid offer spread of 6% which is at the lower end of the likely scale of charges.
† includes capital gains or, if none, use of initial capital; actual income will depend on bond finally chosen.

In addition to the initial costs, the management of this unit trust portfolio by FMS will cost Eamonn and Shelagh 1 per cent a year plus the annual management charges incorporated in the unit trusts, probably a total 2 per cent a year. For this fee they get their own account executive, and all end of year tax computations. More significantly, after the initial 5 per cent charge, which comes out of the bid offer spread, MLS rebate 3 per cent further initial commissions, and any volume discounts negotiated, to their account.

The banker's approach

NS were more bearish, and have recommended only £5000 in an equity investment. This is the EBC Amro UK Income and Growth trust, which itself is 60 per cent invested in bonds. The remaining £22,000 is in cash – with an imaginative use of the National Savings Bank rather than a building society – and bonds. The choice of the new Fidelity bond fund suggests that NS are not too happy with the inflationary prospects of the UK; bonds are good to hold in a recessionary world, but only if inflation is kept under tight control. Other countries are still better at that than we are.

Natwest Stockbrokers portfolio

Security	Amount invested £	Net income £	Investment manager	Cost* £
Cash	7000	537	National Savings	None
Bonds				
Treasury 9% 1992	10,000	657	Quoted security	100†
Int. Bond UT	5000	255	Fidelity	300*
Cash and fixed interest = £22,000 or 81% of total				
Shares				
EBC Amro Growth	5000	277	EBC-Amro	300*
Shares = £10,000 or 19% of total				
Total	27,000	1726	3 managers	750

* assumes 6% bid offer spread.
† assumes 1% purchase commission.

NS have put together some clever electronic dealing systems – tried out on some of the privatisation issues – and, with the lower volumes of a bear market, are making progress introducing new and easier stockbroking services through the branches of the National Westminster Bank.

The stockbroker's advice

NIG is a national firm created under the impetus of Big Bang out of provincial stockbroking firms, and this portfolio comes from the Doncaster office. With its national structure, NIG is combining the best of provincial broking – accessibility, low costs, convenience – with the administrative and systems muscle given by 125,000 clients. Though it offers the lowest return, it has the most potential with a selection of major British companies. The portfolio is tilted towards safety – over £19,000 in cash and bonds – but the selection of convertibles gives it added interest and growth prospects.

The National Investment Group portfolio

Security	Amount invested £	Net income £	Investment manager	Cost £
Cash	6227	467	Lancastrian BS	None
Bonds				
Treasury 9% 1994	5023	329	Quoted security	50.00
Dixons 5% convertible preference	2585	158	Quoted security	62.83
Hanson 5.75% convertible preference	2788	155	Quoted security	67.71
P&O 6.75% convertible preference	2709	169	Quoted security	65.81

Cash and fixed interest = £19,332 or 72% of total

Security	Amount invested £	Net income £	Investment manager	Cost £
Shares*				
Barclays Bank	1479	68	Quoted security	36.50
British Aerospace	1580	85	Quoted security	36.50
British Petroleum (fp)	1515	74	Quoted security	36.50
Commercial Union	1605	64	Quoted security	36.50
Maxwell Communications	1489	98	Quoted security	36.50

Shares = £7668 or 28% of total

	Amount invested £	Net income £	Investment manager	Cost £
Total	27,000	1667	1 manager	428.85

* costs rounded to £36.50 but calculated on NIG's minimum commission of £25 + VAT + stamp duty at 0.5% and stock exchange levy of 60 pence.

Each of us must make a decision on which financial manager to choose on the basis of personal chemistry, convenience and trust. Mental comfort should take precedence over cost. Nevertheless, my preference would go to the stockbroker. There are several reasons, practical and psychological. More of Eamonn and Shelagh's money is working for them; over £1000 of costs out of £27,000 seems a lot to me and NIG's charges of £428 much more reasonable.

The portfolio is well diversified, but the equity income of £389 will certainly increase by a good 10 per cent this year. This income is genuine; sometimes with insurance bond income we consume our own capital without knowing it. The heavy emphasis on gilts and convertibles will protect against a further market crash, yet those convertibles will benefit if a 'soft landing' keeps economies and markets happy.

Stockbrokers have rarely had a good press, and their unpopularity makes them shy and hidden types once out of their natural habitat within the City of London. As the *Investor's Chronicle* commented: 'When a prominent broker told us once that stockbrokers rank somewhere between badger gassers and bookies in public opinion, he was probably being a little unkind to the badger gassers.'

Good brokers are not easy to find, yet their training and skill makes the effort worthwhile. The country broker almost certainly has more time, sympathy and understanding of his – yes, women have made it to the City but not yet to provincial stockbroking – private clients and their needs.

The security markets today

Until Big Bang there was a separation between owners/dealers in securities, and advisers/brokers. This was the single capacity function which worked on the assumption that preventing temptation was a good way of avoiding dishonesty. Now the markets work on dual capacity, and the assumption is that competition drives out sharp practice.

Security markets today involve several different functions with close though not necessarily essential links. Understanding these relationships helps us decide the commercial interests of the type of adviser we choose.

Dealing Since dealing in money markets and foreign exchange has been exceptionally profitable for banks nearly all felt that 'jobbing' or dealing in securities was equally essential to their future. The level of capital required now means that few, other than the banks, can afford to be dealers or, in the Big Bang parlance, market makers.

Traditionally a service function to assist clients in executing transactions, dealing in currencies, foreign exchange and 'negotiable paper' became a profit centre for the banks during the nineteen-seventies. Jobbing in shares rounds out the banks' dealing functions.

Trading in bonds and shares, supported by distribution to meet real investment demand, creates the liquidity of markets. A good dealer should be indifferent to the value of what he deals in as his concern, in buying, should only be his certainty that he can sell on at a better price.

As a result of Big Bang the number of dealers in bonds and shares has increased tenfold though the amount of profitable business has not increased by nearly that much. It seems likely that many banks will pull out of some or all of their market-making activities as losses become insupportable.

Research Unimportant to the dealers since dealing has a very short timescale while investment – which is supported by research – should have a timescale of some years. Research likely to change prices is important to the dealers, and is usually told them beforehand. Known as 'front running' this is of little importance to the investor, though more so to competitive dealers.

Research is the 'value-added' ingredient that helps the sales team distribute securities to the institutional investment markets. The top research houses are all owned by large financial companies, and there is considerable competition to be 'ranked' as a leading research house by institutional investors. The best known rating is that organised by Extel (the suppliers of company financial record cards):

Research brokers 1988

	Ranking	*Rating*	*Owners*
James Capel	1	Very good	Hongkong & Shanghai Bank
BZW	2	Good	Barclays Bank
Warburg Securities	3	Good	Mercury Securities
Phillips & Drew	4	Good	Union Bank of Switzerland
County Natwest Woodmac	5	Fair	National Westminster Bank
Kleinwort Grieveson	6	Fair	Kleinwort Benson

Research brokers 1988 – cont.

	Ranking	Rating	Owners
Hoare Govett Citicorp	7	Good	Security Pacific Bank
Scrimgeour Vickers CL-Alexanders	8	Good	Citicorp
Laing & Cruickshank	9	Fair	Credit Lyonnais
Kitcat & Aitken	10	Fair	Royal Bank of Canada

Distribution Buying and selling securities on behalf of investors to earn commissions is what traditional stockbroking was all about. Post-Big Bang firms are equally concerned to sell the securities that have been created by the activities of colleagues in the corporate finance departments.

Traditionally, institutional investors generated their own research, but are becoming increasingly dependent on the major research houses for advice both on market sentiment and individual investments. As the institutions can now go direct to security dealers, and buy and sell without paying brokerage, the sales teams must rely on the standing of their researchers to earn commissions from these investors.

It is the institutions, and particularly their fund managers, who decide which research houses to back. Their tendency at the moment, possibly the result of a low level of investment activity, is to patronise fewer brokers. The 'also rans' in the research stakes face the difficult choice of investing heavily to win back business, or to pull out and concentrate on retail distribution or fund management.

Fund management Since it is the institutions which set the level of commissions – and indeed who is 'in' and 'out' amongst the research teams with their voting for the Extel survey, and market gossip – it is only wise that security firms protect their dealing and research profit margins by developing in-house business. Nearly all now actively chase after pension fund management and promote investment services to us – unit trusts, off shore funds, investment management services.

Retail distribution Selling securities to us is a very different business from dealing with the investment manager of a life company both in attitude, and administrative systems. Some stockbrokers always had this ability. These used to be known as 'private-client' houses and many have remained 'agency brokers'. Most no longer do basic research but buy it in from the major brokers, concentrate on getting timing right, help their clients to decide on the right investment policy, and follow local companies.

However this type of agency broker always considered themselves perfectly capable of running portfolios for private individuals. Despite a nearly doubled commission, they could not easily be persuaded to sell us unit trusts rather than shares. Fund managers had to turn instead to the life assurance networks. While these lacked the portfolio management skills of the stockbroker, they more than made up for this in sales enthusiasm. If a few of their clients ended up losing money with a Barlow Clowes or Macdonald Wheeler, it was really no different from the nineteenth century – a few investors lose but rather more gain.

Now, while the SIB still does not require these investment brokers to know anything about investment, it does require them to run their businesses in a more formal way. This increase in regulation is seen as an opportunity by the life assurance companies, the banks and the building societies to gain market share from these independents, and to improve the profitability of their own widespread – but underused – branches. It is also seen as an opportunity by lawyers and accountants to develop their services to us.

Most importantly successful development of this retail market is seen by the banks as a help to their very costly market making functions. We should expect many more offers of investment help from our bank. We also need to decide whether we want 'advice' or 'product'.

The choice of adviser

This decision depends less on the amount of capital that we have, than on our attitudes. Lawyers and accountants can be helpful in clarifying these and helping us define our investment objectives. They can also be useful as a source of introductions, as these firms will have one or two long established relationships with stock-brokers. Using them as an investment adviser only adds a middle-man, and further time and administration costs, but using their stockbroker can benefit everyone. They share commissions with the stockbroker, which costs us nothing since we still pay the same brokerage, and we have someone else to complain to if the relation-ship goes wrong.

The banks will undoubtedly develop – though they have not yet done so – an impersonal, efficient and mechanical service for investors. It will be reasonably priced, probably rather boring but safe and secure. The Fimbra investment broker will be the oppo-site of this – very friendly and approachable, more expensive than the average, and likely to push unit trusts and insurance bonds. The better ones will certainly be expert on the use of assurance products for tax planning, may be imaginative in the development of unit trust portfolios, and should be safe provided that they are fully authorised by Fimbra.

How to find a discretionary stockbroker

Those of us who intend to be serious about our investment must either go direct to investment trusts, or use a stockbroker. Pro-vided we are serious investors with about £10,000 or prepared to save £2–3000 a year, we can find a stockbroker. Our choice will then be between a discretionary service, where they handle the administration and take all decisions, or an advisory relationship where they still handle the administration, but discuss proposed actions with us.

Success depends crucially on personal chemistry: private-client stockbroking relationships are anything but mechanical, and in-vestment skill is at least as much an art as it is a science. This is not a relationship that we discover just by walking into an office that appeals to us. We have to work at it, as Philippa B discovered. When we last heard of her she was just about to write to eight stockbroking firms.

B to Taylor – February 1988: the briefing letter to the initial list of advisers.

This letter went to the eight firms we agreed on, and I am now sending you their replies together with my reactions. Do you agree with me?

Briefing letter

I am writing to ask whether you think you can help me. My husband died last year, leaving me with two children aged 9 and 12. I am 40. My house is now paid for, and is worth about £150,000. I have £68,000 on deposit with building societies and am being paid for my husband's share of his business. This is another £43,648. I am getting eleven quarterly payments of £3722.53 and the first one was paid last month (December); there are three final payments of £900 to be made in September and December 1990, and March 1991.

I am very worried about how to invest this money. It is all I have, apart from a widow's pension of £55.82 a week, with which to support myself and my children. I earn another £38.00 a week, and this may increase when I have finished my training to be a secretary. There is an NPI annuity which pays a further £10.29 a month.

I met a financial adviser from my bank, but was very confused by their scale of charges and the risks they talked about. Also, the crash last October has frightened me. I want to invest this capital properly, so I have a good income, but I cannot afford to lose it.

What I need is at least £7500 before tax from my money, and some confidence that this will increase over time so that my income will keep pace with inflation. This seems reasonable to expect when I have got the extra money from my husband's business, but more difficult now that I only have £68,000, plus the quarterly payments.

If you think you can help me, please write to me with your suggestions and charges so that I can study them. Once I have done that I would like to meet you. If you need more information, I am on this number in the afternoons.

Taylor to B – March 1988: the first sift using common sense.

As you have now seen, common sense goes a long way in sifting out the people you want to deal with. Stockbrokers, bankers and the like are

*in business like anyone else, and the same rules apply to them as we
apply to all our other decisions. It is a privilege for them to have your
business, not the other way around.*

*Let me now give you my reasons for suggesting the firms in question,
what I think of their suggestions, and your initial reactions.*

Bell Lawrie I admire this Edinburgh-based stockbroker, particularly for their good communications with clients. Their suggested
policy for you makes a great deal of sense. This is to invest your
present capital of £68,000:

Building Society	£10,000 to produce income of	£1000 pa
Government bonds	£20,000	£2000 pa
Convertibles/Shares	£48,000	£2500 pa
Total	£78,000	£5500 pa

As they say: 'The target income of £2500 from the £48,000 is, if
anything conservative . . . this is also the source for the main
growth in capital and revenue [which I expect] to develop on an
annual compound rate of at least 5 per cent.'

This is £2000 a year less than you need. So, they suggest you use
the £15,000 a year capital payments, which you are getting over the
next three years from the sale of your husband's business, to invest
in short term low-coupon gilts which offer the prospect of low-risk
capital growth. If you had it all now, which you don't, you could
expect another £4–4500 a year. So instead they suggest you use
both capital, and income from it, for the following:

● Pay premiums of £3000 a year into a Clerical Medical 10-year
Maximum Income Plan to give you in 1998 about £48,000 capital,
subject to a continuation of present bonus rates. These are based on
the success of Clerical Medical in investing your money. However,
under tax laws which are about to be changed, you can choose to
take an income from the policy, while still leaving your capital
intact. If they continue to invest successfully, this income could be
£4500 a year or so, tax paid!

• Spend some capital to make up your income shortfall, which is at the maximum of £2000 a year now but will reduce as the portfolio income increases.

Over ten years your portfolio income should increase to cover this income shortfall completely, and you will still have the benefit of the MIP. The time pressure on agreeing to the MIP is because the tax benefits of these plans are about to be cancelled, and if you accept this you have no time to consider other proposals. I agree with you that the letter is difficult to understand, so go along with you in striking this firm out.

Parrish This is a grouping of small private client firms, and is itself quoted on the stock exchange. In principle, because stockbroking is such a 'feast or famine' business, I would be against going to a quoted company, which is only a stockbroker: the need to satisfy shareholders with profits may conflict with the need, sometimes, to do no dealing for clients. Stockbrokers only earn commissions when they buy, or sell, shares or unit trusts for clients. The Swiss bank owners of institutional brokers Savory Milne thought highly enough of them to hand over their whole 'private client' side to them, so they were worth a try. I agree with you – a very nice letter, which doesn't answer any of your questions. Another no.

Robert White Another Scottish firm, this was the private-client arm of Wood Mackenzie. Robert White is now part of the TSB, and intends to open offices throughout the country. The advice given is sensible, for I believe that investment trusts are one of the best methods of investment for private individuals:

Building societies	£22,000 to produce income of	£2200 pa
Government bonds	£45,000	£4100 pa
Investment trusts	£17,500	£1600 pa
Total	£85,000	£7900 pa

Investment of additional funds as they become available

Investment trusts	£40,000	£2000 pa

I don't think the firm should have included the £10,000 that you keep in the building society as a 'disaster' fund in their calculations. None of the others did. Also, their letter which concludes '[if] . . . some of the points raised in this letter may be a little confusing to you . . . then I suggest you telephone me . . . I am only very occasionally in London, and am not planning a visit in the next month or two' does suggest a somewhat off-hand attitude towards whether you become their customer or not. Once again I agree with your 'no'.

Henderson Crosthwaite Though London based, with some country offices, this firm has always specialised in private client business. My experience of them has been that they are excellent stockbrokers, because they understand that their prime duty is to safeguard their clients' capital. Indeed, I was sure that they would end up as one of your short-list. But there can be no excuse for not answering your letter, particularly after a telephoned reminder, so yet another 'no'. (HC were upset to hear of this. Internal research suggests that Philippa's letter was sent to their old office, and not forwarded on to them.)

Parsons (Allied Provincial Securities) I cannot agree with your reaction here. It is certainly a very friendly and sympathetic letter but, as for everything else, I am amazed. Parsons were the driving force behind the creation of Allied Provincial Securities. This is a nationwide grouping of provincial stockbrokers supported by the research of James Capel, generally regarded as the best research broker.

So why not 1. introduce you to an office closer to you than Glasgow? 2. offer you a stockbroking service, which is what you asked for, rather than 'financial services' with their significantly higher (and undisclosed) commissions?

And what advice! As most of the other letters have shown, you can achieve your income in a reasonably straightforward way: there is no need to have a range of inflexible life assurance policies. The suggestion that you put £18,000 of your capital into annuities astounds me.

The life assurance company will only invest that £18,000 in a way similar to that proposed by your other stockbrokers. Should you die during the five- and nine-year terms of these annuities, all this money is lost to your children.

If you really want to spend this £18,000 of your capital over the next few years, which is what this recommendation amounts to, you can do this yourself easily enough without paying fees to a life assurance company, or commissions to Parsons.

The three other firms all answered promptly with details of their services and charges, and these are the ones you should now see as stage two in your plan to get a financial adviser. You must get detailed investment suggestions from both Penney Easton and Godfray Darby when you see them – on the lines of the proposed investment policy from Gerrard Vivian Gray. Then we can compare their proposals.

B to Taylor – March 1988

Now that I have appointments to see the last three, what should I ask them and how good are they technically?

I have arranged to see Mr Bell of the new Guildford office of Godfray Darby, but I am rather confused by a letter from them that I should not invest at all, but keep everything in National Investment Bonds and a building society. Mr Bruxner-Randall of Penney Easton, and Mr Roddy Macleod of Gerrard Vivian Gray have both suggested that they come and see me at home.

Is there anything in particular that I should ask them, and in the end how will I choose amongst them? [yes, see questions of administration].

Taylor to B – May 1988: technical competence but also personal chemistry

It has been quite an experience – as much for me as for you – but now that you have chosen your adviser, you can see the need for a little technical knowledge as well as keeping your common sense well to the fore! The three firms that made it to your shortlist all responded promptly and efficiently to your query, described clearly who and what they were, showed by their attitudes that they were keen to have you as a customer, and you liked all of them when you met them.

Godfray Darby This is a constituent of National Investment Group, the other national chain of provincial stockbrokers established in competition with Allied Provincial Securities. NIG buy in good research and the new Guildford branch is very convenient for you.

You were impressed by Mr Bell, and very taken aback by being told that you should not invest in current conditions. When we spoke on the telephone, I told you I can think of good reasons why Mr Bell might take this attitude, but I do agree that he should have given his reasons. His recommendation that you protect your income from inflation by working was, even if apt, not relevant to your discussion.

By approaching advisers in the way you have, and going through their proposals, you have gained confidence about handling your own financial affairs. You need better reasons than an implied 'don't bother your pretty head with such matters'. Money is too important – and too emotional a matter – for it not to be something that we must all understand. Stockbrokers need to learn that the world has changed since Queen Victoria died.

You were quite right to take up the suggestion of Penney Easton and Gerrard Vivian Gray that they see you at your home. This is a very proper response, for you are an important customer, and you are contemplating a long-term commitment.

Penney Easton Is – or was, because in May they merged with Parsons and became part of APS under the name Parsons Penney & Co – a Scottish-based broker with branches throughout Scotland and Northern England with one in Wales and another in London. The investment policy of gilts, convertibles and blue chips that Mr Bruxner-Randall described is very sensible. Penney Easton took research from Barclays de Zoete Wedd and, as a firm, concentrated on identifying not only good companies, but also when the shares of such companies were sensibly valued.

Gerrard Vivian Gray Has three offices in London and Southern England, and is now owned by Gerrard & National. This is a discount house – that means a banker's bank.

Of all seven replies to your original letter, that of Roddy Macleod was both the fastest, most imaginative and precise. You liked the fact that he took most interest in you yourself, your background, and your concerns. This is not silly emotionalism but is important because a good financial adviser, like the old-fashioned GP or family solicitor, needs to know you to advise you properly. Equally, such a relationship must be based at least as much on respect and friendship as it is on mutual financial benefit. So personal chemistry is important. And though this was one of the two firms that I would have chosen, I don't think that I ever let my prejudices show. Good luck, and best wishes.

The Macleod/Gerrard Vivian Gray portfolio

Security	Amount	Yield	Income	Dates paid
Bonds				
Treasury 13% 2003	£20,000	10.60	£2121	January & July
Treasury 9% 1994	£29,000	9.04	£2623	May & November
Hanson 10% convertible 2012	£ 5000	8.30	£ 415	September & March
Equities				
BP New	£10,000	10.50	£1050	February & August
Scottish National Investment Trust	£10,000	9.10	£ 910	April & October
United Biscuits	£ 5000	5.70	£ 285	January & July
Total	£79,000		£7404	

Macleod to B – April 1988

With regard to the amount available for investment, I have now upgraded this to £79,000. I set out a revised list of potential investments . . . all dividends are paid net of the basic rate of tax . . . and we will register all stocks in your own name so that dividends are automatically mandated to you at your home address. You will notice that the dividend dates do appear to give you a reasonably constant flow of income . . . we are getting the income more or less to the £7500 that you require and this . . . will only increase . . . as more contributions come in from your husband's business and also . . . an increasing dividend from some of the equity investments.

. . . Interest rates can move either way and, at present, there is a

sharp diversion of view as to the outlook over the next year. Commentators are forecasting a heavy balance of payments deficit this year, which I think is over-gloomy, and also a sterling payments crisis as this unfolds. Obviously, we cannot afford to take too many chances and this is why I have put in a relatively short dated gilt in the Treasury 9 per cent 1994 where the capital value will really not depreciate as the redemption date is only five years ahead. The longer-dated gilt has more volatility but it does afford a high-running interest rate which I think is useful for our purposes.

The Hanson convertible is one of the best ways of giving a high income with an equity appreciation possibility. It is exercisable from 1990 onwards and, in the meantime, gives a yield well above that of the ordinary shares . . . Scottish National Investment Trust income shares again give you a very high yield and . . . receive all the dividend income for the trust and . . . should the income of the investment trust rise . . . then you will find yourself on an increasing dividend payout. United Biscuits is a very large company, and, as a food manufacturer, has a very basic business so should be alright whatever befalls the economy. It gives a good yield as well.

With regard to the BP, this looks fairly large at the present moment but we can decide in August whether to sell some of the shares to pay the second call or whether to use another tranch of the capital payments to take up the full amount of the shares. More likely we will sell some of the shares we have bought to provide cash to pay the call on the balance.

Checkpoints

● Establish a list of possible advisers from the AITC and Stock Exchange lists, recommendations from friends or professional firms you know, from the yellow pages or even names you see in the financial papers.

● Write down your investment objectives, and then write a briefing letter for your adviser which should include both your investment objective and your financial circumstances.

● Write to at least six of the firms on your list with this letter, analyse their keenness and competence, and come up with a shortlist. Use common sense and intuition at this stage rather than getting involved in their investment proposals.

• Interview at least two of the firms from the shortlist. Ask them to justify their investment proposals and explain what their fees and commissions are, and how they earn them. Judge them on the way they answer, and their personality as well as that of their firm. A good adviser can make up for weaknesses of a firm; a commission-hungry firm will not keep good private-client brokers.

• Take time and if the first attempt fails, try again with a different list. Investment is a never-ending horse race; success depends not on *when* the bet is placed but *how*.

Notes: questions and answers on administration

It is very important to have these clear at the outset. Most stockbrokers failed to invest in their administration office systems during the nineteen sixties and seventies. The tremendous volumes of business from the bull market, and the privatisations, showed the weaknesses of 'back offices'. The backlog of business is now mostly cleared up while the introduction of new systems for registering our ownership of shares, and automatic execution of small deals will help reduce costs from next year. In the meantime these are the questions to be answered by our adviser before we start dealing.

How do I pay for my purchases?

Traditionally stockbrokers ran client accounts to handle the movements of cash involved in buying and selling securities, and receiving dividends. The more farsighted encouraged clients to open high interest current accounts, on which they had signing rights for the purchase of shares. This is simple and easy, but only to be used with advisers of undoubted standing and covered by a compensation fund. If dealing with anyone else, we open our own HICA and make cheques payable to the fund manager, not to our adviser.

Our adviser should instruct all companies or trusts in which we have invested either to pay all dividends directly to our own bank account, or to reinvest these dividends in further units or shares (an increasing number of industrial companies now offer this option in addition to all unit trusts and most investment trusts).

Who will hold my shares/trust documents for me?

The new Taurus system due to be introduced in autumn 1988 will do away with the dreadful confusion of the present stock-exchange paper chase. Our ownership of shares will be registered on a central computer databank through the nominee company of our stock-broker. The same principles apply here as they do with cash: when dealing with anyone other than a stockbroker, have documents of title in our own name. The advantage of the stockbroker's nominee system is that it can avoid confusion during takeovers or rights issues, when a lot of paperwork is generated: we can use our bank to hold these documents, but this will incur charges, and possibly time and confusion between bank, broker, and us.

How often will I get a valuation?

This should be every six months, there should be no charge, and the valuation should show a detailed breakdown of what was bought, when and for how much.

What about my tax records?

Most advisers leave this up to us, which is why the bank account, the dividend record, the valuations and contract notes are so important and must be kept safely and together. However, this may be one of the fee-earning services that advisers will try to develop.

How often will I hear from you, and what will you tell me?

Any competent adviser should inform us every time they buy and sell something on our behalf, even when we have given them authority to act freely on their discretion – hence 'discretionary' as opposed to 'advisory' accounts – and tell us the reasons why they have acted. We should certainly have heard from them at the time of the crash – if only to say 'don't worry – we will tell you if you should do something' – and they should always be available to us at the end of a telephone if something worries us, or we need money suddenly.

We should expect to meet our advisers regularly – certainly once a year – to review our financial position, and also to check that our investment objectives have not changed.

Everyone will say the right things; having met our potential advisers, do we believe them and what evidence can they produce that they will live up to their words? Ask to see their regular reports to clients, copies of the valuations they send out, and the names and telephone numbers of four or five referees. Firms not prepared to do this are also firms not worth doing business with.

What other services do investment firms offer?

Some have colleagues who specialise in insurance and tax planning, and if we talk to them, what will this cost us? Do they keep commission they earn on things they sell us, or are these disclosed and counted against fees we might be charged? This is another area of rapid change and firms all have different attitudes to charging.

What is this going to cost me?

Commissions are pretty well standard on buying bonds and shares BUT ask:

- Any commissions on buying or selling unit trusts? (No should be the answer.)

- Any charge for valuations? (The answer should be no.)

- Any charge for use of nominee company? (This is changing, and small fees are coming in.)

- Any charge for records for tax purposes? (Yes, if they offer this service. Most don't.)

- Any charge for meetings, telephone calls etc? (No, never.)

- Any other charge, other than commissions? (In most cases no, but some firms are thinking of introducing investment management charges for discretionary clients.)

It is now a requirement of the new rules that our investment objectives and risk preferences, together with all charges, are set down in a letter to us, and this must be signed and exchanged before the firm can deal with us.

Chapter Eleven

Appointing and using a stockbroker

Never give anyone the advice to buy or sell shares, because, where perspicacity is weakened, the most benevolent piece of advice can turn out badly.

CONFUSION DE CONFUSIONES, 1688

Private clients are much more important to stockbrokers than we think. Just over half their commission earnings came from us last year – £555 million – and we generated a further £65 million of commissions with our forays into the gilts, foreign equities and traded options markets. According to a Stock Exchange survey only 11 per cent of us choose, like Mrs Philippa B, to have a discretionary account. 56 per cent of us prefer a traditional advisory relationship. The remaining third of us are sufficiently sure that we know what we are doing to have 'execution' or 'dealing only' accounts.

Doing without an adviser: the IC high yield portfolio

Some of us who do without advice follow investment systems. Not surprisingly, investors have searched quite as long and hard as alchemists ever did, for a way of choosing investments that will make money for us on the stock exchange with certainty. Though many of these systems are based on discovering the secrets of the patterns made by share price movements, there are other approaches. One, at least, has a long and proven record of success.

Since 1955, the *Investor's Chronicle* has published a high yield portfolio every six months. This was originally an idea of a London stockbroker, is entirely mechanical and needs no investment judgement. The latest portfolio, published in the issue of 10 June 1988, includes valuations of recent portfolios. All have done better than the market, and the valuations do not include reinvested income. The table shows when these £3000 'mechanical' portfolios were invested, how much they were worth in June 1988, and how well they have done in comparison with the FTA index. Few investment or unit trusts have done as well.

Performance of a mechanical investment system

IC high yield portfolios	Date invested	Value June '88	Overall change
59 Series	June '85	£4786	59.5%
FTA 500	703.90	995.03	41.1%
60 Series	Dec '85	£5074	61.1%
FTA 500	755.82	995.03	31.6%
61 Series	May '86	£4634	54.5%
FTA 500	877.37	995.03	13.4%
62 Series	Nov '86	£4580	52.7%
FTA 500	863.61	995.03	15.2%
63 Series	Apr '87	£3653	21.8%
FTA 500	1138.56	995.03	(−12.6%)
64 Series £10m cap	Dec '87	£3307	10.2%
FTA 500	904.20	995.03	10.1%

The system is simple. £3000 is invested in 30 shares (though in these days of minimum commissions we would find it cheaper to invest larger amounts) and all are of companies quoted on the main market. The rules for inclusion are that a share must yield more than the FTA index, have a market capitalisation greater than £10 million (increased from £3 million for the 64 series), and be quoted at a price above, or at least equal to that of twelve months earlier.

Mining and finance companies are excluded, as are quoted subsidiaries of other companies, and any company that has cut the interim dividend. The thirty highest-yielding shares are then picked for the portfolio, and equal amounts of money are invested in each. If there is a rights issue, sufficient of the rights are sold to take up the remainder of the entitlement.

When there is a takeover, the cash is held for reinvestment in the highest yielding share, not already held, from the next portfolio. Sales only take place when a company fails to pay a dividend, or cuts it so much that the yield then falls below the FTA index, and provided also that the share price is below the level of a year earlier. This price rule is designed to prevent unnecessary trading in shares when a company may only be facing a temporary setback.

Margaret Allen has produced some fifty of the sixty-five port-folios and says: 'Valuation is too time-consuming [to do for longer than the first three years] but that does not mean that the portfolios have then exhausted their potential . . . the first one . . . had Great Universal Stores and when I last valued it in the mid-seventies, the initial £3000 investment had risen to around £65,000. Not bad for something which requires no investment analysis.'

An American alternative: the low-PER system

American investors claim similar results for 'low-PER' portfolios. A recent report in the *Financial Times* talked of the Brandywine Asset Management company, founded in 1986, which did twice as well as the Standard and Poors 500 Index by concentrating on low-PER investment policies. Had they been able to persuade their clients to follow their computer models their performance over the crash, it seems, would have been even better than it was.

But why should such apparently perverse policies as those entailed in high-dividend or low-PER share selection pay off? Conventional wisdom has it that a high PER and low dividend yield signifies a growth company that will increase profits and dividend payments faster than the average; the lack of such distinguishing marks identifies 'boring' companies with little prospect of im-proving profits or dividends, while low PERs combined with high dividend yields are the mark of Cain. These are the shares of very risky enterprises, or of companies expected to reduce their dividends or, indeed, go out of business altogether.

David Dreman* quotes Graham Dodd (of *Security Analysis* and *The Intelligent Investor*) on this subject as saying: 'The truth of our corporate venture is quite otherwise [than investors think]. Extremely few companies have been able to show a high rate of uninterrupted growth for long periods of time. Remarkably few also of the large companies suffer ultimate extinction. For most, this history is one of vicissitudes, of ups and downs, with changes in their relative standing.'

Dreman argues that the difficulties of analysis, when combined with market fashion, inevitably leads to over- and under-valuation of individual shares. As Dreman's financial writing developed from his work as a New York stockbroker, his views are grounded in practical experience. He believes that picking low-PER shares mechanically, and using rules quite similar to those of the IC, will produce above-average returns. As with the IC system, there are risks, for sometimes those market ratings are right. The companies do end up bankrupt or, more likely, with a capital reconstruction at the expense of shareholders.

Rules for low-PER investing

Dreman's rules for low-PER investing are:

- Invest equal amounts of money in at least fifteen, and preferably twenty shares, but spread amongst several different sectors of the stock market.

- Only buy large or medium-sized companies. This means, for us, choosing amongst the 600 or so alpha and beta stocks. The reason for this rule is that such companies are more in the public eye, less able to over-indulge in creative accountancy, and will attract institutional investment when fashion changes. The shares chosen should have PERs 20 per cent lower than the average of the FTA index but this is only a rule of thumb. Bigger or smaller percentages can be chosen. Best of all is to use your broker to use either Finstat or Datastream, as does the IC for the high yield portfolio. These data banks list the major companies by deciles (10

---

* *The New Contrarian Investment Strategy*, David Dreman, Random House 1982.

per cent of the total) or quartiles (25 per cent of the total). Then, like Brandywine, we can concentrate on the bottom quartile or, like Dreman, look amongst the bottom twenty per cent or, with less risk and less reward, amongst the bottom forty per cent.

• The other advantage of Finstat and Datastream is that they can be programmed with several requests, which helps with another of Dreman's rules. This is to choose low-PER companies that also have better than average performance characteristics. For instance, we can not only search for those low PERs, but ally them to a history of earnings and dividend increases over the last three years, and a strong financial position – twenty per cent earnings growth with at least five per cent dividend growth annually, and net borrowings of less than 20 per cent of shareholder funds could be an example.

• Sales should take place when the PER of a share moves to, or above, the market average regardless of how good the company's prospects might appear. If this improvement of the PER comes about because of a drop in earnings, then the shares should be held for recovery in profits. However, after holding any share for two to two and a half years and if the ranking has deteriorated – ie the PER has gone from a 20 per cent to a 30 per cent discount to the market average – this should then be considered for sale. Shares sold must be replaced so that the number of shares – and as far as possible their relative values – remain fixed.

Facts and fallacies: the importance of human nature

If these 'contrarian' investment policies, as they are sometimes called, work so well, why do not more investors follow them, and so invalidate them? The reason according to both Dreman and Brandywine, is human nature. As one of Brandywine's directors put it: 'People don't have enough conviction to concentrate on things which are out of favour, and take the time to wait for them to mature.' That image of instant wealth is too strong for us and it is very human to state: 'I have made up my mind – don't confuse me with the facts.'

Dreman, in fact, prefers to use low PER policies to identify possible investments, and then choose actual investments through fundamental analysis. This enables him to find those companies with strong balance sheets and good earnings prospects which are, for one reason or another, in the market doghouse. To do this, we will need an advisory account with a broker.

Stockbrokers and what we think of them

The *Investor's Chronicle* 'Good Broker Guide' was compiled from a survey of 1287 readers, and published between 5 June 1988 and 17 June 1988 inclusive. The IC cautions against taking the results too seriously; the sample was small, and conditions exceptional. Top marks went to Henry Cooke Lumsden of Manchester; Henderson Crosthwaite came second; Allied Provincial Brokers and A J Bekhor tied for third place; National Investment Group were fourth; and Redmayne Bentley fifth.

Many stockbrokers allowed their administrative systems to decay during those years when the private individual, as a direct participant in the market, appeared to be a dying species. The trading changes following Big Bang and the regulatory requirements of the SIB, required most of these financial control and administration systems to be redesigned anyway. Then the privatisation programme brought in 7 million new investors over five years. This combination of events, allied to the final run of the bull market, created great confusion. Few of us were entirely happy with our stockbrokers last year.

According to one reader, and not disproved by the survey: 'London brokers are like double cream – rich and thick.' Though our complaints about brokers are damning, brokers themselves are equally damning about our ignorance of what to expect from our broker. The IC lists our most frequent complaints as:

- My broker fails to alert me to imminent new issues, or get me in on placings

- He fails to tell me when to sell shares I already hold

- He fails to volunteer advice when companies in which I hold shares receive a bid

- He fails to provide me with adequate research circulars or newsletters

- Sometimes his tips aren't too good, either

- And, though he can execute orders efficiently enough, he is often much less efficient at dealing with the consequent paper-work, and sometimes slow to pay up

Changes in stockbroking practice

The introduction, late in 1988, of a screen-operated system for execution of small bargains – the computer will place our order automatically with the market maker offering the best dealing price and create all the necessary documentation – followed by auto-mated settlement procedures in 1989 will make a considerable difference to private-client brokers. Increasingly, many of them are also 'contracting out' the remaining administration to specialist firms, leaving themselves free to concentrate on advice and man-agement.

The dramatic increase in the costs of City firms have also forced stockbrokers to reconsider their role. Many of the best known have chosen to become simply dealing and research houses, and have sold or closed their private-client departments. Others, while still welcoming private clients, make it clear that it must be on a discretionary basis and, unless we have funds in excess of £100,000, probably in unit trusts.

Some brokers are choosing to research and service 'niche' markets for institutions and individuals alike. New firms are being created as partners in businesses now absorbed by the banks and financial conglomerates decide they prefer freedom to security. Some of the bigger investment brokers have chosen to join TSA rather than Fimbra, and this infusion of new blood will also affect the way stockbroking will work in the future.

Most stockbrokers have decided to concentrate on private-client business, and have spurned market-making functions. Basic re-search can now easily be brought in, and good brokers realise that research is only part of the answer to private portfolio manage-ment. Judging how to use it is both the greater and more difficult part. These brokers have been more than happy to take on the disgruntled clients of those firms who have lost the skill or desire to manage private clients.

FSA monitoring requirements have done us all a service by forcing stockbrokers to bring their internal management systems up to date. The development of specialist 'back office' contractors, as well as the Stock Exchange computerisation of many clerical procedures will make it easier – and less costly – for new stock-broking firms to establish themselves. The SIB also makes stock-brokers acknowledge that, in addition to advising on, and then executing, our buying and selling orders, they must consider our investment objectives within the overall disposition of our financial assets.

And all private-client firms must decide whether to continue in the traditional way, and get paid by commissions on transactions carried out, or to charge fees as investment or 'asset' managers. Discount broking services* have already come for those who want a dealing only service and these can only improve with the new exchange systems.

Advisory and discretionary stockbroking services will, under the pressure of this bear market, develop the sense of purpose neces-sary to satisfy our needs – or go out of business and be replaced by the stockbroking subsidiaries of the clearing banks. Although it may take some effort because stockbroking is changing so fast, the firm – and the individual in that firm – that is right both for us and the sort of business that we want to do, does exist. They just take effort and patience to find.

---

* *Sharelink* from British Telecom and Albert E Sharp of Birmingham, *Stocktrade* from Robert White, *Brokerline* from Waters Lunniss, and those from the clearing banks all seem to go for a minimum of about £15–20 and £100 maximum.
Discount Brokers International have a higher minimum of £25 but are cheaper for larger deals. However, events move so quickly that we need to check regularly on how this new service is developing. The IC is good for this.

Theory into practice: use and abuse of an advisory relationship

We need a stockbroker to deal for us. Many investors consider that is all they are good for, if the figures on 'dealing only' clients are to be believed. They have two other, and equally important, functions and the small savings on discounted execution services can be a false economy. To get the best out of our stockbroker, we need to know what they can and cannot do. This I explained to Mr Andrew S whom we left, financially embarrassed, earlier in the book.

S to Taylor March 1988

I have decided to sell all the unit trusts, and insurance bonds. This money, placed on deposit, will solve my income problem for the time being. I don't intend to do anything about the shares until I find a new adviser . . . having made an involuntary investment of £90,000 in learning how not to invest, I don't want to waste either the money or the lessons. Obviously, in future I shall commit only those funds that I can afford to lock away for an indefinite period. Neither Hoare Govett nor Quilters seem at all interested in my business, and I would like someone close at hand that I can talk to.

Taylor to S March 1988

As a client, you would probably do better with an advisory relationship, than a fully discretionary one. You obviously enjoy the market, and appreciate that success requires more art than science. Living outside the big cities is an advantage. Even with your capital, and as an active dealer, you have already found that you are not an interesting account for large London brokers.

You would certainly appeal to a London private-client specialist, but a country broker will have much more time for you and, with the new dealing systems, is in as good a position to deal as someone in Throgmorton Avenue. Moreover, being out of the London hurly burly, they don't necessarily get carried away by emotions as much as people in the middle of it all.

What you are looking for is someone:

● who is not necessarily clever, but is shrewd, aware of market stories and a steadying influence on your more speculative and optimistic attitudes

● who knows that nothing is certain in investment, that it is all about offsetting different types of risk, and that patience and following where the clever money is going works out better than frenetic dealing

● who is with a firm that follows a group of companies in detail and is knowledgeable about their activities, and possibly buys in research from one of the major research houses. But there are several thousand quoted companies and unit trusts. Not even the very largest brokers can follow more than a few hundred of these. Everyone has to specialise. So you must follow your own interests, while your broker will supply information and act as informed critic

There are branches of four private-client* brokers close to you. I suggest you write to them explaining what has happened, and that you are worried about continuity of management because of your earlier experience. This should not be a problem with a country-town-based broker, but stress your concern anyway.

Include details of all portfolios with the letter. Tell them how much you need for your new business, and what you will have left for investment. Indicate the level of income you need from your cash, both before and after you have invested in the new business. Tell them that you are looking for one firm, on an advisory basis, to take over your various accounts, realise the cash you need for business, and restructure the rest to face a bear market.

On the basis of the replies, see or talk to them, and decide who you feel most comfortable with. Stockbroking is a business like any other – it is all about who seems keenest to do business, whose competence impresses you most, and with whom the personal chemistry works best.

S to Taylor May 1988

I have now seen all four firms. The managers are all very different in their approach. I particularly liked HC because they forced me to go through my family, business and financial situation before they would

---

* Laing & Cruickshank, Henderson Crosthwaite, Heseltine Moss, Robert White.

express any opinion at all, and L&C seem very enthusiastic to get my business. But the advice from all four is the same. I find this discouraging.

● *They are all very gloomy about the market, and none will tell me what to buy, nor advise me on what I should trade in, nor how much I can expect to make.*

● *They all say I should be liquid, though they are either reluctant to say what I should sell, or recommend that I should sell everything and be very careful for the next twelve to eighteen months.*

Taylor to S May 1988

These brokers are all thinking of your investment objectives, which is to have sufficient income to live, and enough cash to buy your business. The bull market is over, and we are back to a normal humdrum world.

● *Dealing is a very particular skill. A few have it, most don't. Dealing is hard to do at a distance from the market, nor is it a stockbroker's function. You should run a mile from anyone who promises to make you dealing profits. Anyone who can do that, does not need us. Either they can earn enough not to need to work or, if they enjoy working, then they are chief dealer for a bank*

● *In the market of the last decade, it was hard not to make money through increased share prices. In normal markets, making money this way takes time – but nobody knows in advance how much time – and only dividends can be relied upon for spending money*

● *You can expect your broker to manage money for you and, as a discretionary client, this management will make money for you over time. You can expect your broker, in an advisory relationship, to help you manage your own money; this way you should also, in time, make money for yourself*

● *What none of us can expect is that our broker will make dealing profits for us. Brokers are managers or advisers, but not traders. It was not easy to make such profits even in the nineteen-fifties when insider trading was the norm. Today, it is very hard as the multi-million pound losses of the major security houses show. If we wish to make dealing profits, then we have to make the decisions ourselves, and we will do better talking to an options broker*

This is the message that you are getting. As an advisory client, you must decide what to buy and sell. They will give advice on what they think the market will do, suggest the investment strategy that you should be following, propose shares that they follow as constituents for your portfolio, and get information for you on the companies you like. But the decisions are yours, not theirs.

S to Taylor June 1988

I will concentrate on those companies of which I have some experience, such as hotels, leisure, drinks and services. So I have given myself a list to follow, and am selling those shares which I don't understand such as oil, property and a lot of the 'penny stocks' I was dabbling in. I have also allocated the remainder of my shares to 'sell now', 'wait', 'hold' and 'bottom drawer' – those are the ones that have dropped so far in price it is pointless to sell them. The brokers seem to agree with this – but it is always me doing the talking. Surely I expect more from them than agreement?

Taylor to S July 1988

The FT last week had a story that should answer your question about brokers.

> *It seems that shortly after Albert Einstein gained admittance to Heaven, he began organising his social life. His first acquaintance told him his IQ was 210, so they agreed to meet daily to discuss Einstein's new theory of cosmology. The second was also very intelligent, and with an IQ of 160 both agreed that they should meet weekly to discuss and listen to music. The third, though well turned out as befits a stockbroker, unfortunately only had an IQ of 80. 'No matter,' said Einstein, 'let's meet monthly, and discuss the stock market.'*

Doubtless the mortal Einstein appreciated that we have more ideas for investment, than we ever have funds to invest. And it is all a matter of relativity. Our function, and that of any investor, is to be a critic of alternative choices. Deciding on values is only part of the job. We need to identify the mood of the market, and think through the way fellow investors will react to news and developments. After all, part of investment success is outguessing fellow investors. This requires less an outstanding intellect than shrewdness, the empathy to understand other people's dreams, and practical commonsense.

A few of us make successful assessments alone and at a distance. Others prefer to discuss and compare their ideas. The stockbroker, as a market professional, often sees matters differently, though not necessarily more correctly. Therein lies the value of discussion between our broker and ourselves; if our broker is too busy to discuss our investment ideas with us, we have chosen wrongly.

Another stockbroking function is to supply us with information which, though published, is simply too expensive for us to buy as private investors. Our broker should let us have copies of this, assuming that we have an advisory relationship with them, and particularly if we are an interested and serious investor.

Extel company record cards are summaries of the capital history of a company, balance sheets and profit and loss accounts over several years, earnings and dividend records, and key points from the most recent Chairman's statement. A useful ancillary to these are Macarthy cards which cover recent press stories and comments about the company.

Virtually all stockbrokers have computer access to Finstat and Datastream, detailed and comprehensive data banks of market information on a company. These enable us to 'sift' the market for those shares with the characteristics we want, such as PERs or dividend yields better than the average, or companies with plenty of cash in their balance sheets.

Somewhere in the background brokers have voluminous research reports, on the economy, industries and companies. These are not normally sent to clients because postage is expensive, clients take no notice of them, and stockbroking overheads are too high anyway. But if we ask, we should certainly get them and, if they don't have them, we have again chosen the wrong firm.

Stockbrokers: a final word

We cannot expect our stockbroker to take as much interest in our money as we do, nor be any better than anyone else at forecasting October crashes. It is harsh to blame our brokers for not telling us when to sell. Experience has taught brokers that getting a sale recommendation wrong for advisory clients is rarely forgotten; conversely, correct advice is never remembered. Moreover, each and every one of us has different purchase costs for those shares, and different tax problems.

What is unforgivable is that advisers should go to ground because things have gone wrong. Internal administration might have cracked up, they could be as confused as the rest of us, the crisis may well make them busy, but advisers have a duty to find the time to talk to us when disasters happen. That is when we really need someone with whom to decide the best of several unfavourable courses of action.

Advisers who 'disappeared' during the autumn and winter of 1987–88 are simply not worth employing. Experience and maturity make good stockbrokers, and they know that 'there is nothing new in Wall Street . . . Whatever happens in the stock market today has happened before and will happen again.'*

Checkpoints

● Decide what sort of investor we shall be, and then the sort of relationship we require from our broker. Are we 'systems' followers, or do we do our own thinking? Are we active investors, following the tip sheets, or slow and cautious planners? Do we want only information, or 'tips', or discussions?

● Check beforehand that the broker can, and will, work with us in the way we want. Ask to see the research that the firm has, and not just the monthly newsletter. Find out what companies and industries the firm follow as their own speciality.

---

* *Reminiscences of a Stock Operator*, Edwin Lefevre 1923.

- Ask the firm to describe its 'identity' – what do they see as their main function, what particular skills do they consider themselves to have, and how do they differentiate themselves from their competitors?

- Ensure that the firm has Finstat or Datastream and find out the terms on which they will use this for us. The same goes for Extel and Macarthy.

- Find out who our 'account executive' is to be, and ensure that the personal chemistry is right. Otherwise, ask for another. The firm is important, but the person we work with is at least as important.

Notes: changing structure of stockbroking

We should use a stockbroker to buy shares for us, and help us do better than the market. Frankly, if we are content to follow the market, then the main unit trust groups will give us a cheaper, and probably better unit trust portfolio management service than any broker.

Stockbroking is evolving so fast that predictions are impossible. The best country brokers are turning into businesses that can certainly challenge the big London brokers on private-client service, and give at least as efficient administration as the clearing banks. Some of the brokers from the big financial conglomerates are leaving to set up new broking firms. Any comment on brokers is bound to be unfair to those left out and, in many ways, small firms can give us a better and more personal service.

Greene & Company is a small private-client London firm that has always specialised in asset-value situations; Discretionary Unit Trust is their in-house fund and ended 1987 top of all UK unit trusts with a total return of just under 37 per cent compared to 8 per cent for the market. The record so far this year is equally good.

Simon Knott, the senior partner of Greene & Company, argues that, in looking for a good stockbroker, we should look for someone young from a well disciplined house. That way we get the energy and dedication of someone building up his business, combined with the stock selection and market discipline of a good firm. As he says: 'If you are a new client, and the broker is experienced and good, he won't have time for you; if he does have the time and is experienced, then he can't be any good.'

This comment, pertinent as it is, presents a Catch 22 situation. It is difficult to know, and needs careful questioning on the way the firm works, as to whether or not a firm can discipline either itself, or its young brokers. The 'busyness' is easier, and is the reason that Mr Andrew S finally chose Laing & Cruickshank, which was a new branch looking for business rather than the well established and large Henderson Crosthwaite branch.

A significant internal difference within stockbroking firms is that between the 'attache' and the salaried employee. These attache client executives find and manage their own business for part of the commission while the firm organises premises, administration and information. Such 'half-commission men' can be good stock-brokers for those committed to active dealing, and wanting regular contact with their broker. They can also be terrible commission-hunters, destroying our fortunes with unnecessary and excessive 'churning' of our portfolio.

This may become a danger with the large banking groups, as the accountants get to work demanding 'a return on the assets' expended in the purchase of the business. However, the IC survey commented that: 'One of the complaint options least frequently tipped was "rings me too often" . . . compare this with the 40 per cent who expressed . . . dissatisfaction because their broker was too slow off the mark . . . Clearly the aggressive share salesman has not yet replaced the dozy English gentleman of popular imagination.'

There are now the two national stockbroking branch networks of Allied Provincial Securities and National Investment Group, created out of rather more than a dozen country firms. Their intention is to maintain the best of the small 'country practice' service with the administrative and research capacity of the biggest firms. Each has over 100,000 clients, are backed by substantial minority shareholders, and all are keen to expand by taking over other small firms.

Most of the major cities has a 'lead' stockbroker, and these are thriving on the well publicised difficulties of their London rivals.

The most important of these for private clients seem to be Bell Lawrie and Neilson Milnes in Edinburgh, Campbell Neill and Greig Middleton in Glasgow, Wise Speke in Newcastle, Rensburg in Liverpool (these two, about to merge firms, alone have 80,000 clients between them), Henry Cooke Lumsden in Manchester, Redmayne Bentley in Leeds, Albert E Sharp in Birmingham, and Stock Beech in Bristol.

Several firms, including some of those mentioned, have regional branch networks. This may be a pattern that will develop further, possibly in alliance with building societies. Laing & Cruickshank, Henderson Crosthwaite, Heseltine Moss, Charles Stanley and Buckmaster Moore all have such networks. Robert White wants to develop one. However, Gerrard Vivian Gray has sold off some of its branches. The problem with branch networks is not premises but finding the right people. We have the same problem.

Chapter Twelve

Managing a portfolio

Take every gain without showing remorse about missed profits, because an eel may escape sooner than you think. It is wise to enjoy that which is possible without hoping for a continuance of a favourable conjuncture and the persistence of good luck.

CONFUSION DE CONFUSIONES, 1688

Risk, reward and relativity are the heart of successful investment. We should invest when the rewards we expect to achieve justify the risk we take relative to alternative investments. But these decisions are a matter of judgement, and judgement is suspect when it comes to investment.

However, we have erected some defences against market madness. First we have established an income target for our portfolio. Whether we need this for living on or not, it is an important element of our overall investment policy. As we have seen this annual income, compounded over the years, is by far the greatest part of 'capital growth'.

Secondly, we have set a policy matrix of cash, bonds and shares. This is partly determined by the income target we have set ourselves, and should be flexible within the rigid parameters of our minimum cash holdings, and our maximum share exposure. These rigid parameters, together with the income target, are our investment policy.

Exactly where we position ourselves within that matrix will depend on our view of the market, and the reward we expect for the risk we must take. This is our investment strategy.

To help determine that strategy we need a third figure. This is our target for 'total return'. Total return is the combination of real money, or dividend income, and 'maybe' money, or the capital appreciation (and sometimes depreciation) of our portfolio. Meeting that target tells us how good we have been at investing. It also identifies the risks we need to run to get that reward.

The risk level we are prepared to accept will partly determine the total return target we set ourselves. Practicality must also play a part. The total return on equities since 1920, after inflation, has been 7.5 per cent. The government will guarantee us, depending upon the index-linked gilt we choose, a total return of between 3.5 and 3.8 per cent. Inflation seems likely to average between 3 and 5 per cent a year. There seems no good evidence that the government either can, or will, reduce it to less than this; most economists believe that an external 'shock' to the system would be needed to push it above this level.

So in monetary terms, we need to aim for more than 7.5 per cent a year – 3.5 per cent on index-linked gilts plus, say, 4 per cent inflation – otherwise there is little point in taking the risk of holding shares rather than the gilts. The returns achieved for this decade have averaged 20 per cent or so; to prove our cleverness, we could target more than the long term average of 7.5 per cent plus inflation. But we need to remember regression to the mean. If recent figures have been so much better than average, can they continue at this level? Indeed, might they not fall in the next few years to below the long-term average?

Basic principles: the economy and the stock market

One reason why the London share market is influenced by the behaviour of Wall Street and the American economy, is because what happens there will sooner or later affect us here, and the outlook for British company profits is the real concern of investors. They determine dividends.

Phillips & Drew have put together a dividend series covering the last fifty years which shows that the dividend yield of the market has averaged 5.3 per cent over the full period, and 4.3 per cent over the last five years. So, with a forecast increase of 10 per cent to 15 per cent in dividend payments on 1988 profits and the market yielding 4.1 per cent on historical dividends, the market does not look too expensive. But that 4.3 per cent is based on annual 'real' dividend increases during the nineteen-eighties of 10 per cent a year.

This is nearly seven times higher than the long-term growth rate of 1.5 per cent. The cover for these dividends, or level of profits backing them, is now about three times. Companies can pay out higher dividends, even if they do not make more profits. In the end, though, dividends cannot continue to increase unless company earnings also rise. Can profits continue to rise at the cracking pace of the last few years? As companies have rebuilt their profitability so shares have risen in price. The P&D chart shows the rise of the FTA index compared to the turn around in companies' rate of return on assets, with both figures adjusted for inflation.

Figure 28: How better profitability of business has been reflected in improved share prices.

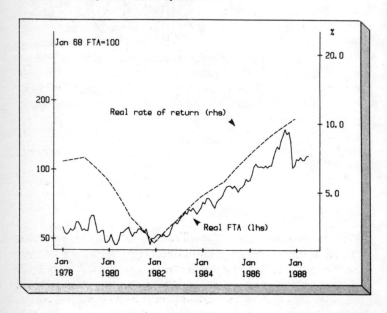

Source: Phillips & Drew .

P&D also argue that, compared to the nineteen-sixties, share prices and profits now show much closer linkages. They have calculated year on year price changes of the FTA index with the quarterly series of year on year changes of total company profits. As they say: 'The best percentage change in the FTA index has preceded the best percentage change in profits by some 6–12 months . . . the correlation of market swings and profit changes has been reasonably close, an arguable exception being . . . the 1980 profit down-swing.'

Figure 29: Share prices are based on the profits of companies.

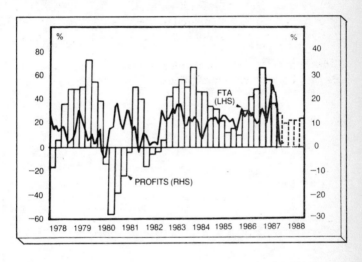

Source: Phillips & Drew

1980 was also the year of the Thatcher government's first tax-cutting budget, as well as the introduction of union legislation. The market could be forgiven for being optimistic, despite the poor profit outlook. Nine years on, and the market doubts whether this rate of profit increase can be maintained, let alone improved. The argument now is more about whether profits can keep rising, rather than by how much they can be expected to improve.

Rethinking total return targets

A slowdown in profit growth from 1989 and beyond has implications for dividend payments, quite apart from whatever problems the world economic situation will bring to Britain. If the increase in dividend payments begins to slow, will the market once more expect dividend yields of over 5 per cent? What will this do to total returns?

The stepped preference shares of the 'separated value' investment trusts were created during 1987 and 1988. They presently yield 6 per cent. Annual increases in this yield of 5 per cent for the next ten years, and their repayment values, mean these shares have redemption yields, or total returns over the period, of a little more than 11 per cent. These are the conservative expectations of professional investors, who will be helped in achieving these returns by the structure of their trusts.

On reflection, between 11 and 12 per cent seems a tough target to set ourselves, and one more likely to be achieved as an average, than an actual figure every year. We might choose higher returns than these, but this will require us to take much greater risks. As it is, these suggested targets, if achieved, will double our capital over the next six to seven years. It is better to start with a hard though achievable target; we can always change it as we gain experience and confidence.

Theory into practice: managing portfolios

The market has no difficulties at all in impounding all currently recognised knowledge in short term share price levels. It is this that makes dealing so hard, and justifies the adage that 'the market is always right'. The efficiency of the market mechanism makes forecasting sharp price breaks, whether upwards or downwards, almost impossible. So while, in theory, buying at the low and selling at the high is the answer for investors, few succeed in putting this into practice.

Managing portfolios: timing

Investors attempting to outguess the market direction all too often end up predicting 'all eight of the last three share price crashes' as the market saying has it. Moreover, despite claims made with hindsight, none of the major 'chartist' prophets got their clients out of the market before the October crash. To call the top or bottom of the market correctly is hard; to do both is impossible.

Being out of the market has as many risks as being too heavily in. October 1987 was a bad experience, and new investors during 1987 lost money: everyone else who invested in shares is still better off. An effort can be made to time the purchase or sale of individual shares.

Whether or not the statisticians are right that patterns made by share prices are a meaningless jumble, many investors think the opposite. It is investors' actions that make the market so, in the short term at least, what is actually happening to prices may well tell us something that statistical tools cannot yet evaluate.

Technical analysis lays great store on trend lines. The theory is simple. Technical analysts, like the followers of EMH, believe markets to be efficient, though driven by crowd behaviour rather than company analysis. If a share price is moving on a different trend line from the market, then that is significant.

When the trend is that the share price is rising faster than the market, that is a sign to buy. Even more important is a change in relative momentum; if the trend line shows signs of becoming steeper relative to the market, then it is 'pile in, lads, boots and all!' The converse is equally true, but it has to be said that identifying trend lines is sometimes easier done later with hindsight, than at the time we need to make decisions.

There are several ways of following these movements. One of the most respected teams of technical analysts is that headed by Robin Griffiths at James Capel. Since he is also the editor of a fortnightly subscription service called *Amateur Chartist*,* private investors can follow his ideas in this; they are also presented within a longer time

---

* *Amateur Chartist*, 3a Fleet Street, London EC4Y 1AU. 01-625 8656. £60 pa (£20 discount for first year): J R & S Purdue, 1 Port Hill, Hertford SG14 1PJ. 0992 587392 for individual charts.

frame, compared to his advice for the professionals, and this is more useful for us. Many of the charts used are supplied by a charting service, from which we can also order individual charts.

Alternatively, if we have either an Amstrad PCW or IBM PC compatible, we can be our own chartist. The manuals of *Share-track** and *Sharemaster* give a good grounding in the major chartist theories such as Dow, Elliot, and Coppock. These are incorporated in the programme, which puts them on the screen, and allows us to develop our own timing theories from the input of market indices as well as the prices of our own shares.

These programmes also develop trend lines, and compare these with the market indices. Bernard Jones of Kleinwort Grieveson started as a dealer, became a fundamental analyst, but now concentrates his energies on technical analysis. Interestingly, he has found technical analysis most useful for making money as a private investor. My own belief is that it is a valuable thermometer. It may not tell us what to buy, but it can indicate the feverishness of the market as a whole, and the level of enthusiasm for the shares we like.

Managing portfolios: choosing value

The market is always 'right' in short-term pricing but, because of the power of the emotions involved, it has real trouble in deciding on 'absolute' values. Hence market panics are occupational hazards for investors. The market also has some, though fewer, difficulties in deciding on relative values, other than in the short term, as between one share and another. Here again hope and fear play their part so it can take some months, and occasionally years, for these relationships to be adjusted.

This is our opportunity. We have established an investment policy that requires us to aim for a reasonable yield both to meet annual income targets, and to achieve our total return. Such yields

---

* *Sharetrack*. Micro Investor Software (page 125) £65–£245 depending on machine: both *Sharemaster* and *S Plus* incorporate portfolio management programmes as well as the charts. Synergy Software, 7 Hillside Road, Harpenden, Herts AL5 4BS. 05827 2977. £100–£245 depending on machine.

frequently come with shares on low PERs. Investing in large companies with these characteristics is a key step in following Graham Dodd to successful investment, for to quote Dodd:

> Some enterprises that are long established, well financed, important in their industries, and presumably destined to stay in business and make profits indefinitely in the future, but lacking in growth appeal, will tend to be discriminated against by the stock market. This is especially true in years of subnormal profits; they will sell for considerably less than they would be worth to private owners. This last criterion – a price substantially less than value – constitutes the touchstone for the discovery of true investment opportunities in common stocks.

Evaluating risk and reward within the portfolio

Security	Yield	PER
Wellcome	0.70	44.80
Health & Household	2.62	17.32
Beecham	4.10	14.70
Glaxo	2.60	13.70
FTA 500	4.08	12.85
ICI	5.00	9.80

The profitability and importance of the health industry argues in favour of at least one company being held as a 'core' share of any portfolio. Though ICI is classed as a chemical company, it has substantial pharmaceutical interests; approximately 10 per cent of the company's sales last year were of such products, though these accounted for some 25 per cent of profits. Some brokers consider ICI's pharmaceutical portfolio to be one of the more exciting within the industry.

Institutional investors can afford to buy Wellcome. But the likelihood of Wellcome following the Glaxo pattern makes it a very risky way for us to aim for our 12 per cent return since all of it must come from an improvement in the share price and, if the price goes into reverse, it will have a severe impact on the total return of the entire portfolio. Wellcome's yield will not take us very far. The advisability of 'locking in' a significant part of our target return from certain dividend income will push us towards Beecham or ICI.

The yields on these shares offer us more than a third of our target return. We can be fairly confident that this will be higher. Analysts expect an improvement in profits from both companies, and a higher dividend. Though such forecasts are often wrong in the detail of profits growth, they are generally right in the trend of profits. We can rely on analysts for these general trends, particularly on unfashionable companies. We need to be wary of their justifications for fashionable growth companies, and detailed profit estimates for years ahead.

Our broker will tell us that Beecham is now very trendy, and on several buy lists in expectation of great results from the new management. The PER is above the market average, which suggests that there is considerable 'hope' in the price; though it is below the sector average, the level of this is distorted by the Wellcome price. The yield is good, and that will help to defend the price if the new management does not turn out to be quite the wonder-makers currently imagined.

On the other hand, our broker will tell us that ICI is a cyclical chemical company, with profits likely to be held back by the strong pound. The price, well below the market PER, shows that it is certainly not fashionable. This year the price has fluctuated between £9.50 and £12.00 and is now about £10.75. First quarter profits were up a little, and the company keeps on saying that it is no longer a bulk chemical company with profits vulnerable to minor shifts in currencies and raw material prices.

Maybe the market will begin to listen, and the company's rating will improve. If not a prospective yield of 6 per cent covers half our target, and is above the long-term market average. When, sooner or later, sentiment changes – it always does – we will probably get the rest of our return in a rush. This is one reason why our target return has to be an average, and not something we aim to achieve in full every year.

However knowledgeable, and whatever the sources of information available to us, that final decision to buy or sell is based as much on our intuitive feel for what is right, as fact. This is true of professional and private investor alike. The future simply cannot be foretold, only guessed. But our portfolio targets set yard-sticks against which we must measure these ultimately emotional decisions. Going through this process may not make us money: it will stop us losing it.

Managing portfolios: the 80:20 rule

Transaction costs are a charge on our capital. The combination of commissions, VAT and stamp duty is 2.4 per cent, and the spread between buying and selling prices is likely to make that up to not less than 4 per cent, so we should trade our portfolio as little as possible. But human nature is against us. However rigid our rules, the urge to 'make money' will overtake us sometime, and usually at exactly the wrong time. So, partly because of this and also because they need to make money too, most brokers operate an informal 80:20 rule.

In practice this means that 80 per cent of the equity money is invested in 'core' holdings. These are the major companies with good prospects; these can, to a considerable extent, be allowed to get on by themselves to make money for us. The other 20 per cent goes into more speculative shares. This 20 per cent requires much more active management and, with a little luck and the right market conditions, will produce very good returns. Active buying and selling in this category of our portfolio keeps our broker profitable, and us happy.

This is a good rule to apply to our own portfolio management. We can invest with this section of the portfolio in 'hot shares' and other fast moving speculative companies and so inoculate ourselves against doing anything silly with the 80 per cent. But, if we work at it, some of those risky shares will turn out winners that can in time be upgraded, and become part of our core holdings.

This 80:20 rule can be followed as suggested here; alternatively, and cheaper both in transaction costs and (possibly) capital gains, the 80 per cent could go into investment and unit trusts so that we can concentrate entirely on the 20 per cent. Or we can develop a different risk profile with more of our funds on deposit, a matching amount in unit or investment trusts, and the remainder used to follow fashionable shares.

Managing portfolios: keeping control

Whatever the risk profile that best suits our mentality – and the mood of the market – it must be constantly monitored. Some of our share choices will be good, others bad. Some will not change much in price, but some may have rights issues. Others we will partly sell because we need money for another investment, or want to take a profit. A few will turn out to be big mistakes, and we will watch them sink in price, never gathering sufficient will-power to face the mistake and take the loss.

This happens to everyone, and the only way to avoid this confusion is to control the make-up of our portfolio with regular good housekeeping procedures. Otherwise, we soon end up with so many holdings, bought for so many different reasons, that the portfolio loses cohesion and we lose control.

A practical way of doing this is to set an investment unit of 5 per cent of portfolio value so that a £50,000 portfolio will have a unit of £2500, or a maximum of twenty holdings. Certainly at least one, and possibly two of these blocks will be our cash, or liquidity reserve: others will be cash held as an investment reserve, to take advantage of timing or new issue opportunities, or taking up rights on existing holdings. Bonds will absorb other units. The use of the units will reflect our investment policy matrix, together with the particular strategy we are following at any particular time.

The units left free for shares can be subdivided further. Core holdings might well be a 5 per cent unit, though this could be bought in two parts if we feel uncertain about the price level of the market. If we buy a 2.5 per cent stake, and the market goes up against us in the following months, at least we have bought the first stake cheaply: if the opposite happens, but we still think we are right, then the second purchase averages down the price of the total holding.

We might consider a half holding the right size for the speculative shares that go into the 20 per cent 'fun' part of the portfolio. It reduces the risk, gives more purchase opportunities, and can still be considered a 'first' purchase to be 'averaged-up' if we hit a market favourite. We need to be careful of this subdivision. Twenty shares is probably the maximum that we can hope to follow with any degree of knowledge.

The unit cannot be too rigid, because the market is not. The purpose of the unit approach is to help us control and monitor our risk exposure. However exact the 'purchase' units, their values will soon be very different. So, when we review our portfolio, we need to give ourselves leeway. Otherwise, to maintain these weightings, we will make silly decisions, and sell shares we should not, or end up with two or three shares representing the bulk of our capital, with the rest counting for nothing.

Managing portfolios: comparing performance

The system needs to accommodate real star performers, reasonable successes, moderate performers, also-rans and disasters. Establishing margins around the units is a way of doing this: in other words at valuation that basic unit of £2500 can become as big as £5000 or as small as £2000. The function of these limits is to force us to re-evaluate all our holdings regularly in the light of current market conditions. The unit must always be a percentage of portfolio value. The unit, as a fixed amount, is only so as it reflects 5 per cent of portfolio value at any one time.

If a shareholding is above our unit limit, the shares have gone up in price. But are they now overpriced? Would we be better off selling all of them, or only sufficient to bring the unit back to size (and use up some of our annual gains tax exemption)? Equally, when the opposite happens, were we wrong in our original evaluation? If yes, that means we should sell, painful though this is to pocket and ego alike. At least, we are building up realised losses to set against future gains.

The market is wrong, and our original evaluation of the company is right? If we believe this, then we should have the strength of character to buy more shares, so as to rebuild the unit size, and average down the purchase price of the holding. However, if we find ourselves doing this frequently, we should consider that either our analysis or obstinacy is at fault, and not the market's evaluation of the company.

In principle, the market saying is 'run profits, cut losses' but we know that prices exaggerate reality. The real object of the unit system is to force us to look at all our holdings in the portfolio regularly and systematically. Shares are neither 'good' nor 'bad' only expensive or cheap, and that only in comparison with each other and the market at the time. The stock market is about relative and not absolute values. Reviewing portfolios against unit values ensures we never forget this.

The decision to buy requires a decision to sell, for maintaining portfolio control requires a limit to the number of shares held. Evaluating a potential purchase in isolation is the first part of the process. But if it is good, is it better than an existing holding? If so, why? – is the yield better, the PER lower, NAV greater as a percentage of the share price, current profit prospects more favourable? These are the questions we should always ask before making a change. We are making two decisions, and it is easy to get both wrong.

Managing portfolios: the decision to sell

Selling for professional and amateur alike is a difficult decision. Hope is the strongest of emotions, and it is easy to convince ourselves that a share is bound to recover in price sometime. In the meantime, other opportunities are missed, and we might be wrong anyway. Even today, some companies do go to the wall. Nor need any of us be reminded of last summer: no doubt we all recognised that prices were high – but how foolish to miss that next 10 per cent. Instead, we all got a 30 per cent fall.

Dreman recommends an automatic trip-wire to overcome this problem. Shares should be sold as soon as they are selling at the market PER, however brilliant their prospects. High-yield managers use the same approach, but based on the predetermined level of yield needed for the portfolio. A third alternative is the 'stop-loss'. Though useful for core holdings, this discipline is particularly appropriate for speculative holdings.

The technique is based on the observable fact that share prices behave in very volatile ways even in markets showing definite up or down trends. Share prices go up, fall back a bit, go up a bit more, hang around a lot doing nothing in particular, then fall, maybe recover some of the fall, then hang around a bit more.

We set a 'stop-loss' on our shares by fixing a percentage figure –

say 10 per cent for alpha and 15 per cent for all other stocks – below a set price for a share. Initially, this could be the purchase price, so if we bought for 100, then the stop-loss is 90. But let's assume we timed our purchase right, and the shares zoomed up to 140. The stop-loss percentage of 10 per cent remains, so the stop-loss price is now 126. When the price breaks the stop-loss, we sell, so following the market adage that 'first loss is least loss'.

Using trend lines can help these stop-loss strategies, if we have the machines and the patience to run our own charts, or the *Amateur Chartist* covers our company. Failing that, the stop-loss is a simple kind of trip-wire. It allows us to ride the market up with the share, but warns us to get out if the trend goes into reverse. Trip-wires only advise us that we should act; we must still take that decision.

Managing portfolios: traded options

Professional investors now use option and futures markets regularly. Options give investors the right, but not the obligation, to do something in the future at today's price. Futures are actual contracts to buy or sell something, entered into now, but to take effect sometime in the future and at the prices prevailing then. The difference can be described as between having a bet on a horse, and owning it. The latter is always much more expensive.

Though futures are much too dangerous for any but the most sophisticated private investor, options can be used in a conservative manner to manage our portfolio. Buying 'put' options on the index allows us to 'hedge' our portfolio.

Rather than selling some or all of our shares when we fear a market downturn, the option allows us to bet on the market level. If we are right, and the market falls, the value of our portfolio will decline. But the profits we make on the put option will make up some, or all, of that. Similar procedures can be used with put options on individual shares we own.

Mostly, we can only hedge in this way for a few months ahead, but that is generally sufficient; if we remain bearish, but our fears have not been realised, we can take out further puts. This costs money, of course, but we can regard them as insurance premiums and, while paying these, we do not have to pay the costs – and possible gains tax – of liquidating our portfolio.

If we have shares, which we expect to trade in a lacklustre way and are indifferent as to whether we sell or hold, we can act as 'writers' of call options. This means we take money from someone else who pays us for the right to buy those shares from us at today's price sometime in the future. If the market goes up, we have sold and forgone that profit, but since we had little expectation of a price improvement anyway, we have lost nothing that we really had: if the market drifts sideways as we expect, or goes down, then we keep both option money and shares as the option will not be exercised. This way we have improved our return on the portfolio.

If we have cash, and know that there is a share we would like to buy, but only within a certain price range, we can be 'writers' of put options. We take money from other investors in return for selling them the right to make us buy their shares at today's price sometime in the future. If prices fall sharply, we end up with shares bought badly at above the then market price. Otherwise, we will either be required to buy at about today's level, but less the option premium that we have received or the option is not exercised – because the price has risen too much so that the option is not worth exercising – and we keep the money but buy no shares.

Following these strategies can be a sensible way of improving portfolio returns provided we are always 'covered'. This means we have the cash and desire to buy shares or own the shares and are prepared to sell them. Operating in an 'uncovered' fashion can make us big speculative profits; just as easily, particularly when we don't know what we are doing, it can wipe us out. It has happened to enough investors – innocents and veterans alike – that we should regard this as a real possibility. Luck as well as skill is needed.

Managing portfolios: sectors and diversification

We must avoid systematic risk, as this is the most dangerous to our portfolio when economic conditions turn wintry. It is wise to try to diversify our core holdings between several key industries so as to reduce company risk. We will never guess right all of the time, and the spread of companies and industries improves our chances of making some good choices.

Market sectors can be important to us as a way of outperforming the market, not only to spread the risk of our portfolio. The size of the funds managed, and the method of evaluating management performance, force professional managers to copy the 'weighting' of the market sectors within the index. Unlike us, both practically and in terms of dealing expense, these cannot be 'out' of the major companies and sectors, so they need to approach strategy changes in a different way.

Professionals make marginal adjustments to their main holdings by deciding to go 'overweight' – or have more money invested in a sector or share than index weights warrant – or 'underweight'. Alternatively, by using the option or futures markets, they can change the weightings of their portfolio more cheaply and significantly than by trading in the underlying securities.

These decisions often follow a revaluation of a cyclical sector, such as engineering or building materials, or a change in fashion towards a previously ignored sector. As private individuals, we have the freedom to invest whenever and wherever we want. Successfully moving in before the institutions is difficult, but very rewarding.

Managing portfolios: using particular knowledge

Particular interests or specific business knowledge can help with this. We should invest in those areas where we think we know more than the average either because we work in related industries, and hear the gossip, because with a high spending spouse, we need to take more than a passing interest in the fashion trade, or we have a hobby that is related to some particular industry. For Andrew S the hotel, leisure and drinks industries are naturals while Kenneth M should certainly maintain his medical connections and keep his industry gossip fresh.

This interest is only the start if we are serious. We have to read and to look. The *Financial Times* is a source of advance information when properly read, for its industrial correspondents seem to have a sixth sense in identifying trends – amongst consumers, businesses or industries – that sooner or later become investment themes. In addition both it and the *Investor's Chronicle* cover in detail research brokers' reports, company results and news, and general economic and investment news.

The Sunday papers are used regularly by PR businesses to place a story about new products or services, or profile a client managing director, while they and the dailies are a regular source of market gossip and tips. All newspapers, as well as *The Economist*, run regular features on the economy, and what is happening to industry. This is part of the market, for many agency brokers discover the views of research brokers through their morning papers, and all of us are influenced in our political and economic views by the headlines.

Company secretaries will send a copy of the report and accounts of a company, if asked, and sometimes copies of earlier years if they are still available. Even ignoring the figures themselves, it is surprising what can be picked up from what is said – and, more interestingly sometimes, not said – in the chairman's statement, report of the directors, and notes on the accounts.

'By their fruits ye shall know them' and the way boards of directors handle their shareholders can give some idea of how they regard their customers and workforce. As individual shareholders we may not be that important, but consciousness of markets and good labour relations determine profits in the long run. Pomposity, timidity and conformity are attitudes that sooner rather than later destroy the ability to make the profits that pay our dividends.

The last decade has shown that size and tradition alone are not sufficient for business success. We need to know those to whom we entrust our savings, and reading their report and accounts, and attending shareholder meetings, are about the only ways we have of doing this.

Investment requires time and effort; share-buying decisions are our judgements, however implicit, on the future course of the economy, the outlook of this particular company, and how our fellow investors will react to the same information that is available to us. These decisions can be made blind; we should then only blame ourselves for our lack of success.

Managing portfolios: opportunities

Companies make profits because they can sell things or services. Increased sales require either a generally growing economy – for the bulk of companies – or a new and relatively unexploited market. Those that benefit from these are the growth companies because only they can push sales and profits ahead even if the general economy is going into reverse.

There are other growth companies. Some are solid and substantial businesses that have been allowed to run down by sleepy management, and are then invigorated by new management blood. ICI, Turner & Newall and P&O have been such cases in the nineteen-eighties. Associated British Ports was regenerated, not because of new management but because it escaped government ownership and became a quoted company.

Some companies degenerate so far that 'company doctors' need to be called in to save the company from past excesses. Sometimes these are specialists who treat the one patient – those who regularly followed Ian Morrow over the last thirty years have made fortunes – but today the pattern is more for such surgeons to operate through the 'industrial conglomerate'. Hanson and BTR have been the outstanding examples during the nineteen-eighties while Williams Holdings and F H Tomkins are would-be emulators of such success.

Growth can also come from looking at an old industry, or company, in a new way. There is nothing new in cheap jewellery, but Ratners' approach to pricing and selling has revolutionised this business. Nor is fashionable clothing exactly high technology, but the transformation of Hepworths into Next certainly was. And Tesco, Sainsbury's and Marks & Spencer have changed the pattern of food shopping equally dramatically.

All these companies have made sizeable sums of money for investors. None required PhDs in physics to understand, nor any particular skill in analysis and understanding of balance sheets. They all required awareness of changing patterns, a willingness to remember and follow successful managers, and the patience to live with a changing and developing company. Reading and looking will give us the feel for which companies may prove successful and which not. Investment is the exercise of critical choice, based on knowledge and intuition.

The key beneath all investment success is not profits but earnings per share, and earnings per share that are available for the shareholder, and not earmarked to maintain the company's competitiveness. Ideally, we want to find those companies whose earnings per share grow faster than the average, and whose dividends also increase faster than inflation.

These are the company shares that all investors search for; they are not only found in the high-tech industries, their numbers are small, their above-average growth does not go on for ever but is limited in time, and the rare occurrence of such an investment in our portfolio brings to it that touch of magic which makes the effort and the disappointments of personal investment worthwhile.

Managing portfolios: changing investment strategy

Choosing some of the right individual shares, controlling the make-up of our portfolio, and taking trouble to get purchase timing right, will give us a profitable and successful portfolio. It will not protect us from market risk. Nothing can do that. We can ameliorate this situation by our investment strategy.

Our investment policy needs to be written in stone. Our strategy, or moving within the policy matrix to different percentages of cash, bonds and shares, should attempt to reflect the state of the market. To decide on a more or less cautious strategy means being aware of market sentiment. When we feel that this is feverish, we should move our policy stance towards caution while, if things look particularly gloomy, we can shift to a more bullish outlook. History, as well as Nathan Rothschild, is on our side in stating that we should 'always buy when blood is running in the streets.'

A key warning-light is the relationship between bond yields and equity yields. The long-term rate of growth of the economy, adjusted for inflation, is about 2 to 3 per cent so index-linked gilts with their guaranteed real yields of 3.5 per cent-plus offer us all we want. In practice, of course, we want more. We don't only want to maintain our standards, we want to improve them. Index-linked gilts do have another weakness. They are priced for investors prepared to take returns in capital appreciation; some of us need spending income each year.

Shares and bonds as alternative investments

Nevertheless, gilts are an alternative investment to shares, and index-linked gilts particularly so as they guarantee us protection against inflation while shares can only promise to try. Both in America and continental Europe, professional investors regard the bond and share markets as alternatives. This was the case in Britain until the late nineteen-sixties, and may become so again now that neither inflation nor the taxation rate discriminates so harshly against fixed income.

A popular investment approach in America is Tactical Asset Allocation. This is the use of computer models to assess the relative risk and reward returns of shares compared to bonds. As share prices go up and yields fall, money is switched out of the share market and invested in bonds instead. As share prices fall, and provided dividends are not reduced so that yields rise, the converse happens. These yield relationships are an indicator of the optimism or pessimism of the market.

According to *The Economist*, the yield on the FTA has remained close to 45 per cent of the return on undated gilts since 1969. In America, a similar relationship holds between the S&P 500 and the long-dated US Treasury Bond. And the Datastream chart produced for *The Economist* suggests that markets do get spooked when these relationships get too far out of line, as was happening for much of 1986 and 1987.

All research brokers calculate for their clients what they think these relationships should be. However, the Goldman Sachs gilt/ equity study highlighted the difficulty of this for there is little sign of stability in these relationships. Sentiment affects the speed with which we believe dividends will increase, and the more enthusiastic we get about that, the less the risk premium that we ask to invest in shares rather than bonds. Moreover, much of this research is for institutions, and is hard for us to get.

Figure 30: Values are relative and 1987 showed what happens when bond yields and equity yields get too far apart.

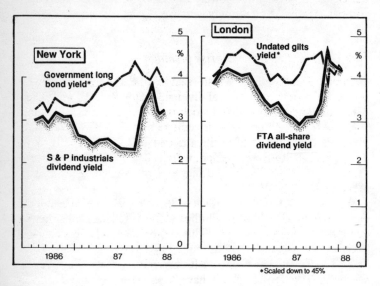

*Scaled down to 45%

Source: The Economist

Inflation and confusion in the equity market

The Goldman Sachs study also suggests that the market is confused, in the short term at least, by inflation. When fears of inflation increase, bond yields rise to protect income from the effect of higher prices. Because bond prices fall, this is interpreted bearishly by investors, so equity prices fall, thus increasing dividend yields. In other words, inflation causes investors to demand a higher risk premium for holding equities.

Dividend yields rise anyway in an inflationary environment as higher prices work through to larger profits and bigger dividends. Real – adjusted for inflation – dividends probably do not go up but nominal – here and now money – dividends certainly do. 'Stagflation' was the curse of nineteen-seventies investment for high inflation combined with no real economic growth meant that dividend increases were apparent, and not real, and none of us was better off in purchasing power. But we were not worse off with equities, as we most definitely were with gilts.

Index-linked gilts and their risk premium

Goldman Sachs suggest investors should take more notice of the relationship between nominal dividend yields and real gilt yields. The long-dated index-linked stock promises a return to redemption of 3.75 per cent. There is some risk in this. The retail price index may get out of line with the real cost of living and, if we decide to sell before redemption, we may not get the price we really should – either because of difficulties of calculation or market mood on the day we sell.

This is a real risk, as is the lack of spending income on an annual basis, so Kenneth Inglis of Phillips & Drew recommends that we deduct 0.5 per cent for this. This means that the adjusted yield becomes 3.25 per cent. This is the best and most certain return that we can hope to buy today. Alternatively, we can buy shares. Historically, share dividends have been even better than index-linked government bonds as an inflation beater. But they are not as certain: dividends from individual companies may not increase, indeed they could decrease or the company could go bankrupt. So a risk premium is needed for this too.

At present, the FTA All Share index yields 4.10 per cent and the Treasury IL 2.5 per cent 2024 yields 3.75 per cent to redemption. The real yield gap is $(4.10 - 3.75) = +0.35$ per cent. This calculation can be done not only for the market, but for each individual share we think of buying. Theoretically, the risk premium should then be much higher, as an individual share is more 'risky' than the market because of company risk, but we can ignore that. All we are trying to do is assess the temperature.

The equity risk premium and the yield gap

To know whether this 'gap' of $+0.35$ per cent makes the equity market cheap or dear needs two guesses – the ones that Goldman Sachs describe as being what investment is all about. What do we believe will be the rate of inflation-adjusted dividend growth, and what risk premium do we need to buy shares and not bonds?

Since 1920, dividends have grown by 1.5 per cent a year. The recent growth of 10 per cent cannot last but, with good cover for dividends and the threat of takeovers as companies prepare themselves for 1992 and the 'One European Market', Inglis thinks 2 per cent is a good bet. Over this same period, the risk premium has fluctuated from nothing to over 12 per cent though it has averaged 6 per cent. But in practical terms, and when not in the grip of either fear or greed, Inglis believes most professional British investors reckon this should range between 1 and 3 per cent.

Mathematically, the real yield gap between shares and index-linked gilts is the equity risk premium (which we will accept as being 1 to 3) minus dividend growth (historically and practically 2 seems very reasonable) minus the index linked risk premium (which is reckoned as 0.5). This calculation gives a range of -1.5 per cent to $+0.5$ per cent for the real yield gap (it is 'real' because both equities and index-linked bonds are inflation-proofed, though in different ways, and with different levels of risk). On P&D's assumptions equities are dear when they yield less than index-linked bonds and the yield gap is a minus figure.

Goldman Sachs do warn: 'The risk premium . . . varies dramatically over time . . . nor on any . . . formulation we have been able to derive, is there any stability in the relative valuation of gilts and equities. The two markets exhibit very different expected returns at different times so there is plenty of scope for sentiment, or other economic factors, to drive the markets a long way from "fair value".'

So we should always cross-check market sentiment as defined by the yield gap with the market yield. This is real, unlike a PER, because it measures the purpose of investment. It is what we get to spend. The yield gap based on the higher risk premium indicates that the market is reasonably priced, and so does the dividend yield. This is 4.1 per cent and expected to increase this year to between 4.5 and 4.7 per cent. At this level it is above the recent five-year average of 4.3 per cent but below the fifty-year average of 5.3 per cent.

Playing the investment game

Does this mean that it is safe to invest? There are no clear-cut answers to when, or how, to invest. The market is not expensive, but nor is it cheap. If we expect a hard landing for the dollar, it ought to be cheap, and the odds are that October 1987 was the first drop of a bear market which has further to fall. But if the new American President, and other world leaders, bring about the hoped for soft landing, then present levels are fair value.

Each of us must make our own decisions on whether the return we can now achieve from shares compared to gilts – or cash – is worth the risk that we foresee; whether, if we choose shares, the yield on our particular choice entitles it a place in our portfolio is another decision; and whether we can reasonably expect increased earnings and dividends from the company we choose which will justify – or even improve – its present price is yet a third.

This thinking can be done alone, and many investors do it; a good stockbroker can make the process more enjoyable, and possibly help our thinking, but the decisions have to be ours. In the end, there are perhaps only two important considerations.

Investment is a game of financial snakes and ladders, in which we try to outwit our fellow investors by reading the mood of the markets and controlling our own emotions. Few of us do it well – why otherwise did De la Vega lose all of his five fortunes? – but we certainly enjoy it the more, the more light-heartedly we approach the game. Being then relaxed, and open to other people's dreams and hopes, we may even make better decisions.

This light-heartedness can only exist if we have first established our financial objectives and investment policy. Then as financial markets crash, and cries and lamentations are heard from television screens throughout the land, we can sit back, smile smugly at the assembled crowd, and say with John Maynard Keynes:

> I feel no shame at being found owning a share when the bottom of the market comes. I do not think it the business, far less the duty of an institutional or any other serious investor to be constantly considering whether he should cut and run on a falling market, or to feel the blame if shares depreciate in his hands.

Further reading and sources of information

Gordon Cummings, *Investor's Guide to the Stock Market*, 4th ed., FTBI,* London 1986.

This is the best general introduction to the technicalities of the Stock Exchange and the way it operates. As is appropriate for an author who is also an accountant, it has precise and useful descriptions of all the major types of securities, together with the key investment calculations. The book shows its age in some ways – the advice on the amount of natural resource shares to hold reflects, we must hope, a vanished world of uncontrollable inflation – but it is an essential book for the serious private investor.

Daniel O'Shea, *Investing for Beginners*, 3rd ed., FTBI, London 1987.

The first, and probably the best, of the general introductions to stock-exchange investment was *Beginners Please*, published in 1955 and developed from the series in the *Investor's Chronicle*. In the early nineteen-eighties the IC began a new and updated series called *Beginners Guide*. This was developed by Daniel O'Shea, who since his work as a journalist on a later edition of *Beginners Please* had gone on to become research director with M&G, the longest established unit trust group in Britain. This book, rewritten from those articles, is an excellent combination of journalism and practice.

Roger Hardman, *Stocks and Shares*, Daily Telegraph, London 1986.

This is useful for the sections on market sectors, where it complements the O'Shea book, as well as an easy guide to fun-

---

* FTBI (Financial Times Business Information Ltd) books are available through mail order from FTBI, Greystoke Place, Fetter Lane, London EC3A 1ND.

damental and technical analysis of shares. A former City editor, Roger Hardman is now working with James Capel, top ranked City research brokers.

Simon Rose, *Fair Shares*, Mercury Books, London 1987.

This is an easy-to-read and simple summation of most of the subjects covered more comprehensively in the three books listed above. It is a good beginning for those not yet sure whether they wish to spend the time, and the money, becoming more deeply involved in the stock market.

Alan Kelly, *Financial Planning for the Individual*, FTBI/Institute of Chartered Accountants.

Though this is really for practitioners, it certainly will help us clarify our own minds on our financial objectives, and the steps we need to follow to attain them. Clearly laid out, it covers simply but in depth all the detail of financial planning.

Investor's Chronicle, published weekly by FTBI, is the indispensable investment magazine for the active private investor. There is comprehensive coverage of the results of all quoted companies, as well as surveys of unit and investment trusts, reports of brokers' research papers on industries and companies, news, recommendations and tips. Back numbers, kept for a year, become a valuable research tool. It is cheaper to buy it by direct subscription.

An alternative, and slightly easier read to the *IC*, is the *Financial Weekly*. Both these magazines concentrate on investment. *The Economist* is more concerned with the political and economic background to the investment scene, as well as business conditions affecting participants in the banking and securities industry. There are also some good monthly magazines for the investor – such as *Money Observer*, *Money & Family Wealth*, and *What Investment* – which cover investment and family finances.

Stock Exchange 'Principles of Investment' courses cost about £20 and consist of eight to ten evening lectures of about two hours each. They are taken by market practitioners, and held in various colleges in Greater London. Well worth the time and money for private investors, they offer opportunities of meeting other investors and asking questions.

Stock Exchange Investor's Club costs £15 a year and has a regular newsletter, together with frequent meetings throughout the country. As membership increases from the present 3000 plus, regional groups are being encouraged to set up local programmes.

Both are organised by Wider Share Ownership, Stock Exchange, London EC2N 1HP. 01-588 2355.

Fortunately, cheap computing power has rendered the tyranny of statisticians no longer so absolute. Our local stockbroker or investment broker should have computer access to all company price and performance statistics as well as financial records and economic statistics. The source of the information is either Extel or Finstat, which is the computerised data bank of the *Financial Times*. Then there are two major systems that analyse and present this information: Datastream and Micropal. These give performance records of all investment and unit trusts, as well as life assurance unit-trust-linked endowment policies, pension funds, and insurance bonds.

Most brokers subscribe to Micropal and Datastream. This computerised data base of company information gives key statistics on quoted companies, and can search the market for companies with specific investment characteristics.

With a BBC micro, an Amstrad PCW or IBM PC compatible, we can have even greater control over our portfolios. There are several cheap and simple software programmes which enable us to plan investment objectives, assess and monitor portfolios, and use share price analysis to develop timing strategies. Through modems these can be connected to price services such as Finstat or Citiservice which can feed into our computer up-to-date prices, value portfolios, and maintain chartist records.

Home computers are not essential, just fun and a slight easing of the administrative chores of investment. Using them for investment, even with pretend money, is a better game than any that the computer suppliers have yet developed.

Information is essential. If our broker does not have Extel and Finstat, subscribe to Datastream and Micropal, and use Extel and Macarthy cards, or won't show them to us, then we should consider switching our business to one who does. Knowledge is essential to any serious investor.